RICHIE

BOOKS BY THOMAS THOMPSON

Hearts

Richie

RICHIE

The Ultimate Tragedy Between

One Decent Man

and the Son He Loved

THOMAS THOMPSON

Saturday Review Press

NEW YORK

Published simultaneously in Canada by
Doubleday Canada Ltd., Toronto.

Library of Congress Catalog Card Number: 72-88667

ISBN 0-8415-0249-8

Saturday Review Press
380 Madison Avenue
New York, New York 10017

PRINTED IN THE UNITED STATES OF AMERICA

Design by Tere LoPrete

Once again, for Kirk and Scott,
And for *Life* magazine

Many people contributed to the making of this book. Among those who gave support, cooperation, and information are Charles Sopkin, Steve Gelman, Janine Coyle, Ralph Graves, Stephen Sheppard, Robert Lantz, Bill Wise, several doctors who asked to remain anonymous, and numerous parents and young people of East Meadow, New York. And special thanks to various members of the Diener family.

"For rarely are sons similar to their fathers. Most are worse. But a few are better."

—HOMER, *The Odyssey.*

Epilogue as Prologue

On a cold bleak day at the beginning of March, 1972, the burial, or at least the service of burial, was quickly done. The minister in attendance had not known the deceased, only what he had learned from the surviving family, and what he had read in the newspapers. Thus his prayers were brief and impersonal and almost lost in the winds that whipped the mourners huddled in the enormous government cemetery on Long Island.

It is perhaps the largest graveyard in the world. According to a spokesman, "certainly it is the most active as far as interment is concerned." More than 180,000 people, all servicemen and their families, rest here beneath the small and precise white tombstones. So regimented are the rows of the dead that the fantasy of a military parade comes immediately to mind, legions of dead stretching to the horizon.

Because there are forty-five services each weekday, rites

are scheduled on an efficient printed worksheet twenty-five minutes apart. To accommodate the great number waiting to be buried, the cemetery conducts what it calls "curbside burials," which are a fast and convenient ceremony, one both efficient and considerate to the bereaved. A striped tent on wheels is set up in advance near a curb and parking area. The cortege is directed to the tent as it enters the main gate. Upon reaching the curb, the hearse is parked a few feet from the tent. Pallbearers and mortuary attendants have but a step or two to guide the coffin inside the tent, where it rests on a small platform. If there are few flowers for this man, then there are always some left over from the man before. The striped tent is almost festive.

This is not the actual gravesite. Not until hours after the mourners have left do the busy gravediggers come around to the deserted bier, and, as the cemetery spokesman puts it, "transport the remains to the actual hole in the ground."

Under the striped tent, Carol Diener bore up well, her eyes reddened from five days of weeping but hidden behind large, shell-rimmed dark glasses. Those about her, however, were openly crying. A decided clash of generations mourned with her. Nearest stood her husband George's allies—solid, middle-class, clad in somber cloth coats. The men were clean-shaven, the women dabbing at their eyes with good linen handkerchiefs or moving a hand to stop the wind from blowing their hair, which had been in curlers all night to look well for this—or any—occasion.

A few feet behind the older people, as if an invisible fence held them in check, were the young—the friends of Richie—their tinted glasses more for decor than as an aid to vision, their colors bright, for they were not yet old enough, or even inclined, to wear mourning garments. They drew back, not looking at the coffin, moving their eyes instead to the skies, watching the gray clouds move in from the sea.

As the Methodist minister finished his last prayer, his black gown flapping in the wind, the sun vanished and grayness settled over the cemetery. The mourners hurried into their cars. The older people moved carefully for the exit in serious and functional vehicles. The young piled into brightly painted automobiles, one with a psychedelic sunburst on its trunk, cars that seemed impatient to burst from this place of death and be on the road where rock music could erase the coldness around them.

That afternoon, the gravediggers carried the casket to its actual site. It was lowered into a thirty-foot-long trench and placed end to end with the other dead of the day. When the earth was put back and smoothed, it began to snow. The carillon broadcast an electronic taps. Whiteness covered the rawness of the long trench, wrapping the forty-four other caskets put into the ground that day with a blanket of order. All was clean, all was conformity. The older people would have liked it.

PART ONE

George and Carol

Chapter One

Forty-three years before the snow fell to end the day at the Long Island cemetery, George Diener was born, in Brooklyn, in a nation about to slip into the Depression. He was a beautiful baby, with fair hair from the German ancestors on his father's side, and the spirit and good humor of the Irish from his mother. There is an early photograph, taken when George was three or four, showing him in a neatly laundered sunsuit, sitting on an outcropped rock in the middle of a swift stream in upstate New York. His face is a canvas of wonder and happiness, yet possessed of a curious mask of privacy, of introspection alien to a boy that young. It seemed to say, leave me alone.

On the day that photograph was taken, his mother had to cry out several times, "George! Get out of there! You'd sit on that rock all day long if I'd let you!" George tested her discipline a few more minutes, watching the small trout flash by, feeling the icy water splash his legs, before he reluctantly waded out, got into the borrowed car, and endured the long drive back to Brooklyn.

There were few such outings in George's young life because his was a city family struggling to pay rent and keep food on the table. His territory had definite limits. Its borders were the Catholic Church and the towering nuns who both fascinated and frightened him; his sister, older by three years, who said everything she did was right and everything he did was wrong; and the crowded apartment in the back of the malt and hops store that his father owned on Seneca Avenue. For one dollar the elder Diener would sell a small can of malt and usually throw in free hops for the customer to make five gallons of legal home-brewed beer during Prohibition.

Early in George's life, his father lost the store and, like millions of other Americans, embarked on a desperate search for any work at all. For a time he conducted a trolley car, then he repaired Model T Fords, finally he found work with security—an important word, that one, the father hammered home to his son—as a mail clerk with Texaco. George's world expanded. With German parsimony and management, the Dieners arranged to buy a two-family house for $8,500 on Autumn Avenue in the melting-pot Cypress Hills section of Brooklyn. The street was tree-lined, the neighbors—a dentist, a fireman, a shoe salesman, a dress cutter—sat on their front porches at night and gossiped across to one another, children ran everywhere with freedom. "And the children are clean!" rejoiced Mrs. Diener. "Look how nice everybody keeps their children."

A black wrought-iron fence marked the fourteen-foot-wide Diener homestead, with black-enameled twin gargoyles carved at the front gate. Here George took to

climbing and sitting. But, like his rock in the stream, like
the trees he would climb in nearby Forest Park, it was
more a place to observe without commitment, more a place
to see than be seen.

Years later, George would say, "The one thing about
my growing up in Brooklyn was how ordinary it was.
It must have been hard eating chopped meat five nights
a week, but when you're in the middle of a Depression
and so is everybody else, then you don't know any better.
I had a father who worked hard, and, even though I cannot remember him ever taking me in his arms and saying,
'I love you, son,' I guess I was secure in his love. And I
had a mother who never seemed to get the mortgage
quite clear. Just when she was near the final payment, she
would have to renew. She never made any money off the
other apartment, because there was always some needy
relative turning up, and Mama would move us up and
down from one apartment to the other to make room.
Sometimes they would bring the dead aunts and uncles
to our house and lay them out in the parlor next to my
bedroom, but that didn't bother me. This was what was
done, this I accepted. I didn't question my parents' authority. I took what was dished out to me."

Despite his acceptance of the rules, there were early
signs that George would not necessarily play the game.
"He's an unusual child," said his mother one night as she
and her husband washed dishes. "He always comes and
confesses when he breaks a neighbor's window playing
ball, when he's done something bad . . . yet when I go to
school to pick him up, he hides and sees me coming and
ducks out the back door to run home by himself!"

Moreover, Mrs. Diener worried that her son seemed
to find more enduring relationships with his animals than
with the friends he seldom made. Is it natural, she would
ask, for a boy to spend *hours* playing with frogs in the

bathtub, or a dog he pulls around by the tail, or a white rat that scampers all over the house? The day the dog ate the white rat, George wept for hours. But these pinpricks of worry would be put aside when the little boy would deliberately do something to make her laugh, when he pointed happily at her ample stomach dancing from the joke, when he cried, "Mama's belly shakes like jelly!"

The Church of his mother dominated George's young years. The family album has a photograph of his confirmation—white suit, red carnation at the lapel, carefully oiled and combed hair, his face a mixture of relief and uneasiness. Shortly thereafter he served his first mass as an altar boy. The instructions were specific: to break in, he would work the side altar, not the main one. On the less important side altar, bells were not used. All went well until George went to change the book. He somehow stumbled into the bells, kicking them down the marble steps. With panic on his face, George heard the clatter echoing for what seemed like eternity. He looked in fear at Father Campbell, who was trying to keep back a laugh.

Whether this event persuaded George he could claim attention by unorthodox behavior, or whether it was simply time for an adolescent boy to break out, the changes now came quickly. Reports came from school that the Diener boy was turning into a prankster. He squirted some youngsters in the hall with a fire extinguisher, and when one of the nuns caught him and told him to follow her to the mother superior's office, he stepped on the sister's hem going down the stairs and almost choked her.

He suddenly found a pack of boys to run with, becoming their premier daredevil. "I wasn't the ringleader," George would tell his own son in later years, "but I was always the one to do dangerous things that would impress the other kids. Nobody could ever dare me to do anything that I wouldn't at least try. I'd take anybody up on anything."

George was first in his crowd to ride on *top* of the elevated train. On the streetcar, he dazzled his companions by daring to pull the emergency handle, and as the train lurched to a stop with lights blacked out, George slipped laughing into the night. His most astonishing feat was leaping onto the outside platform of the last subway car, crouching and hiding, abruptly appearing with his face pressed hideously at the window to startle passengers inside as the train roared through subterranean Brooklyn.

Though only five feet seven and hardly more than lightweight size, George became known as a scrapper who would sail into any fight. The street was his. He so pounded one young adversary that the boy's grades dropped and the mother complained to school authorities that George had damaged her son's brain. One of the nuns investigated and announced, to George's relief, that the boy's work had begun to deteriorate long before his fight with George. What had happened to the quiet child who hid on rocks and tree branches? "Teen-age years for some people are happy," George told his wife years later, "and for others they are sheer hell. For me, they were traumatic. I was so shy and insecure deep inside. Insecure about everything. Everything! I was quite aware of the fact that I wasn't as smart as other people— I hated school, I wasn't as good-looking, I couldn't dance as well, I couldn't get the best-looking girl to go out with me. I had to do *something* to make people notice me, and I damn well did it."

When he was sixteen, George had a friend named Monaghan who disappeared from the public high school that they now attended. The dean of men, a severe disciplinarian, called George to the office. "Where's Monaghan?" asked the dean.

"I don't know," answered George.

"Yes you do. You're his best friend. Where did he run away to?"

"I didn't know he had run away." It was true. This was the first news George had had of his friend's absence.

The dean questioned George sharply for several more minutes, dismissing him with an angry wave of his hand.

Later that day, the loudspeaker from the principal's office ordered George Diener to come to a certain room immediately. Obeying, George found himself in a girls' steno class taught by the dean of men. The bewildered and embarrassed student was told to stand against the blackboard while the dean circled him with a pointer. "This is a liar," announced the dean. "I want you all to see and know one." Some of the girls giggled. George turned red and began to squirm. "This is Mr. Diener, whose friend, Mr. Monaghan, has skipped," said the dean in the voice of a prosecuting attorney. "Mr. Diener thinks he can cover for his friend, but we will find out the truth. I assure you we will learn the truth."

George could take it no longer. He burst from the class and out of the school building. On the way home, he made a decision that had been coming for months. He would quit school. It was 1944, and the heroic war he saw on the screens of Loew's Theater was infinitely more desirable than being humiliated in front of a girls' stenography class, or being forced to read aloud in class when one stumbled over most of the words. He was not sure his parents would sign the document necessary for him to gain entry to a branch of the service, but no matter. If necessary, he would lie. Others he knew had done it. For almost three years now, Autumn Avenue had been at war. Gold-fringed stars hung in front windows, military uniforms transformed neighborhood boys into automatic heroes when they strolled down the block. George had little or no intellectual grasp of what the war was about. But he reasoned it was a good war against a bad enemy. He knew there were rewards for heroics, badges of acceptance and acclaim. If he could win friends by risking death dangling outside a speeding subway train, surely there would be more mature gains in bombing Japan or wading ashore at Guadalcanal.

George told his parents, saying only that he had decided to quit school and try to get into the service (he did not tell his parents of the Monaghan incident until he was past forty years old). There was no family uproar; both parents took the news quietly. The way had been paved for George by other boys in the neighborhood who had dropped out and enlisted before him. Mr. Diener, in fact, shook his sixteen-year-old son's hand solemnly and said, "We've never been butt-in parents. We've let our children lead their own lives and develop their own thoughts. You do what you have to do."

Several months passed before George could get into the merchant marines, for he had decided he wanted to sail and the navy was too difficult for entry at that time. He took odd jobs waiting for his papers to be approved. First he was a handyman at a nearby cemetery. He found the work depressing and switched to a tool company, assembling screwdrivers.

Beside him on the bench was a short, muscular black. The man would work furiously for an hour, then fall asleep right where he sat. One afternoon while pounding handles onto blades, the black flared at George and an argument erupted. Quickly the other workmen cleared away from the two. There had been minor fights between blacks and whites in the factory—one in which both sides squared off with ice picks—but this promised to be a duel between two noted scrappers. Both men seized ball peen hammers in their right hands and circled one another. George watched his opponent closely, waiting for him to swing the weapon. Then he noticed his eyes. The black man's eyes suddenly seemed to die, lose focus, and roll wildly in their sockets. He trembled, his body jerking in quick spasms. Finally he sat down at his work-bench and dropped the hammer to the floor. The fight was over before it began.

In the washroom after work, one of George's friends observed, "You're lucky. I wouldn't take him on again."

"Why?" asked George. "He gave up."

"He's a dope addict. Don't you know what the symptoms are? That's why he keeps falling asleep at his bench."

"I don't guess I've ever seen one before," said George. "Is that the way they act?"

When the merchant marines accepted George in late 1944, he was sixteen years old, with twenty dollars to his name and ten grades of education. He had no church, no girl, few close friends. The relationship with his parents was not a totally warm one, for they were not demonstrative people; but then neither was George. Going to sea in a noble war seemed the best thing he could possibly do with his life.

But there would be no deeds of valor, no medals. George was ordered aboard an army transport and he worked as a waiter in the crew's mess. He never saw the war, never heard a bomb fall, never carried a rifle. Two years later, in disappointment he transferred to the army. "My idea of the military had always been the infantry —the Queen of Battle," George recalled years later. "But the peacetime infantry in 1946 was the worst place in the world a fellow would ever want to be. They had tens of thousands of men to keep busy and nothing to do. I was stationed in Japan and every day our orders would be 'Police This Area,' and off a thousand of us would go with bags and picks, and there wasn't a single piece of paper to be found anywhere on the whole damn post."

When his army commitment was done, George returned to the merchant marine and served another three and one-half years, a total of seven since he left Brooklyn as a teen-ager. The years abroad lodged a few indelible moments in George's memory—the morning sun on the cliffs of Dover, Eskimos in Greenland holding out huge wriggling lobsters and bartering for cigarettes—but mainly his tour of the seas of the world was his initiation in the fraternity of manliness. He would regret the missed opportunities.

"We were tied up in Naples for fifteen days," he reminisced. "I didn't see Capri. I didn't see Pompeii. I *did* see the American bar and the local equivalent of Sophia Loren. I thought at the time I had to be one of the boys, that was the most important thing in the world. I remember we were once in Germany, in Bremerhaven, and a couple of young fellows from the ship rented horses and spent their leave riding all over the countryside visiting castles and monuments. I sneered at them: what a pair of creeps! I went off arm in arm with the boys to the bars and bright lights. But standing there with the beer in my hand, I kept thinking to myself, 'I'd *really* rather be with those guys on their horses.' Of course I didn't say it out loud. How often I've cussed myself for not going with them. I only had one chance in life to see a castle . . . and I blew it."

Home on leave in 1948, George brought gifts to his parents, ate with relish the welcoming feast, and excused himself to walk about the old neighborhood in uniform. A block or so away, he noticed a slender red-haired girl talking to a familiar street figure, a cripple named Murphy who sat outside the delicatessen and sunned himself, keeping track of all the comings and goings on the block.

When the girl moved on, George greeted Murphy and asked her name.

Later that day, Murphy introduced George to the girl. Her name was Carol Ring. She was fifteen and lived four doors down from the Dieners. By nightfall George had decided that he would marry her.

Chapter Two

When Carol Ring was five years old, she was a chubby, impish child with dazzling red curls that tumbled to her shoulders. One day she fell ill with a cold, which hung on for weeks. Her mother telephoned a doctor, insisting that he come in person to the apartment house in a lower-class section of Queens, New York, where they lived. The doctor made a cursory examination and ordered Carol out of bed.

"Make her get up," he said. "A kid gets well by running around."

A few days later, Carol's heart began to pound with loud, frightening beats. The younger cousin who was playing with her cried out in amusement, "Listen to Carol's heart!"

Alarmed, Mrs. Ring rushed to the telephone and summoned another physician. "I'm not calling that shoemaker of a doctor again, that's for sure," she said with maternal wrath. The second doctor came and correctly diagnosed rheumatic fever. Carol was ordered to bed for an indefinite period and prescribed digitalis. The medication caused stomach pains and she cried for hours each night. Her parents took turns sitting beside her bed murmuring comfort. If the mattress was so much as touched, the child would scream in pain. Even when her father carried her in his arms to the bathroom, she shrieked. For a full year Carol stayed mainly in bed, the routine broken only by the times when her mother would carry her to the fire escape in summer and prepare a stack of pillows and insist that she sit outside to let the sun color her pallid face.

When the doctor released her from bed rest after the year, Carol ventured into the street one afternoon and was knocked down by a speeding car. Only a few bruises marked the child, but a curious phenomenon occurred. During an examination to check for internal injuries, the doctor discovered that he could no longer hear through his stethoscope the sounds of malfunctioning in Carol's heart. He assumed that the shock of the car accident had somehow repaired a leaky heart valve. While this is medically dubious, the fact remains that Carol's heart no longer troubled her.

The year of sickness, however, had wrought changes in the child. She was now thin instead of chubby, shy instead of mischievous, insecure with other children instead of outgoing. As the years passed, Carol learned to fall back on her long illness, to use her "heart" when she needed to. It got her out of girls' gym class in school, which she did not like, and it softened instantly her father's stern glare when she summoned up a wan look or put her hand to her heart in the midst of a dressing down. When Carol and her sister, June, older by six years, lay in bed and gossiped after lights out, Mr. Ring stormed in and scolded June for keeping Carol awake. "You get away with murder because of your heart," June would say. Carol tried to look shocked at such an accusation, but she knew it was true. June further complained that her sister got better clothes, more favors, and more attention, especially from their father.

The father, Richard Ring, was an interesting man. During the Depression he first worked for WPA, then as a blotter clerk for a Wall Street firm, finally joining Westinghouse in a minor job. He moonlighted seven hours a night as cashier in a nightclub, pushing himself relentlessly to lift his family from poverty. Thirty years later, he would retire from Westinghouse as a valued executive and a moderately wealthy man. His goals were realized. Yet he would be forced to interrupt his retirement in a house near a golf course in North Carolina to journey in 1972 to the cemetery on Long Island. There he would stand behind his daughter and grip her shoulders to keep from breaking down. The night of the burial he would ask her over and over again, "But, honey, why didn't you come to Daddy for help? You knew I would have tried to help."

Brusque, purposeful, speaking each sentence with authority, Mr. Ring lived by his own rules. When a spoon was missing from his dinner service, he would say, "I have no spoon." And his wife, or Carol, or June, or all three would jump to get him one. It would not occur to him to fetch his own utensil.

He was a man who expected the sun to hide behind a cloud if he pronounced the weather to be gloomy, and he would take no criticism from his wife. The only "arguments" Mr. and Mrs. Ring ever had were over his strictness with their two daughters. But even these could scarcely be called arguments since Ring responded to attacks on his will by even more stern regulations.

When his hard work brought money enough for a down payment on a house on Autumn Avenue in Brooklyn, and when his daughters began evidencing interest in the young men of the neighborhood, Ring announced curfew rules. "If you go out on a Saturday night," he said, "then I want you to tell me before you leave precisely when you will be home. If you say eleven o'clock, then I expect you home at the stroke of eleven. If you arrive at 11:15, then I will deduct fifteen minutes from your next night out as a penalty."

By the time she reached fifteen in 1948, Carol's heart had ceased to be a valuable defense mechanism at home, and her father extended to her the same discipline that June had always received. A spark of rebellion had surfaced in Carol, however, and she decided she was old enough to test her father's commandments, even if her sister had never dared.

On a Friday night, Carol dressed in a skirt and sweater, in bobby socks and saddle loafers, and appeared in the living room ready to go out. Her father was also dressed, preparing to attend a Masonic meeting.

"Where are you going?" he asked in the voice that June always considered to be equal to that of the Lord.

"To a dance," Carol replied. "In the park."

Coming in from the kitchen, Mrs. Ring overheard and repeated what she had said over and over again in recent months. "Dancing! Dancing! You'd dance your life away." She was not sure a girl with a once damaged heart should be doing such things.

Even though Carol remained extremely shy with boys and would cross Autumn Avenue to avoid meeting a group of them walking down the sidewalk, she went with girl friends to every summer dance held on the weekends in the neighborhood parks of Brooklyn.

Ring looked at his watch. "What time will you be in?" he asked.

"Eleven thirty?" Carol's voice was a plea.

He nodded. "Eleven thirty it is."

At 4 A.M. Carol returned, four and one-half hours past

her deadline. Her father was sitting on the front porch, the glow of his cigarette a beacon in the night.

Before Carol could offer her excuse, Ring spoke. "To begin with," he said, "you may not leave this house for the rest of the weekend. You will stay inside and help your mother with whatever chores she has. I will let you know when, if ever, you may leave again."

The next afternoon, shortly before supper, Carol bathed, fixed her hair, and dressed once more to go out.

As she entered the living room, Ring glanced up from his book. "You will recall that you are forbidden to leave," he said.

Carol clenched her fist and stormed into her bedroom. Behind the slammed door, Mrs. Ring could hear her daughter packing a suitcase. She hurried into the living room. "Do something!" she hissed to her husband. "Carol's fixing to leave!"

Ring went to his daughter's room, opened the door, and watched her stuff the suitcase. Carol did not look up. "How much money will you be needing for your trip?" asked her father in a business voice.

"One hundred dollars," snapped Carol, summoning an impossible price.

From a roll of bills in his pocket, Ring peeled off one hundred dollars and tossed it on the bed. "Buy ninety-nine dollars' worth of bus tickets," he said, "and don't come back."

Startled, Carol looked up, but her father was leaving the room.

She had gone too far. She had to leave. But a few hours later, following the silent, trembling exit that proclaimed her new independence, Carol weakened. Even the fantasy of how long and how far she could travel on one hundred dollars had collapsed. She telephoned home.

Her father answered.

"May I speak with Mother, please?" asked Carol.

"You may speak with your mother only in person in her home," said Ring.

Carol sagged. She hung up the telephone and went home. Her mother embraced her, her father tried to keep back his smile, and Carol resigned her rebellious ways. "That was the first and last time I broke the rules," she said later. "I decided then and there it was best to do what people told me."

Carol had seen George before on Autumn Avenue, promenading in his uniform, but she did not know his name until Murphy, the cripple at the delicatessen, introduced them. Immediately she was interested. George was not tall enough—Carol had always dreamed of a man six feet at least—nor was he rich, nor was he a neighborhood hero in athletics. But he was funny, he made her laugh right away with a story from Japan, where he had only just been. He looked a little like Jimmy Cagney and he talked like Eddie Bracken and he had thick dark curly hair and, barely seen, on his upper left arm was a new tattoo of the American flag, the work of a drunken tattooist in the Bowery. Most of all, he was interested in her, which not many boys around had been. Carol had remained thin and shy, and her more successful competition all seemed to be voluptuous and carefree.

Thus began a sporadic three-year courtship in which George would go off to sea in the merchant marine and Carol would weep. When the letters were few and the months between were many, she would declare that she had renounced and forgotten him. But then he would reappear in uniform, drenched in foreign flavors, bringing the teen-age Brooklyn girl tribute from the ports of the world—a stuffed koala bear from Australia, an antique brooch from Italy, a star sapphire from India. How, Carol told her girl friend, how could she not forgive and take back a man who, upon giving her a sapphire, said, matter-of-factly, "We played marbles with these on board ship"?

They dated quietly: an occasional movie, dinner at an Italian restaurant, a favorite bar in Jamaica, Queens, with Carol piling her hair in an Ann Sheridan-inspired pompadour and covering her lips with dark color to look older. One night at the restaurant, George apologized for not taking her to more glamorous places. "I was never much of a Lothario," he said haltingly. Carol suspected more was on his mind. Later, on her front porch as she fidgeted to go inside because she was past her deadline, perhaps her father was timing her and watching her from behind the lace curtains, George proposed marriage.

Carol had a ready answer. No! Not until! "I won't even consider it unless you quit sailing and get a job that keeps you at home," she said. "Do you have any idea what I go through? Every time you leave, usually at midnight when I can't even come down to the dock and see you off, it's a terrible scene. Tears, sobbing into my pillow, worrying that the ship will sink."

George shook his head. That was a decision he would have to think over. Not until this moment had he considered grounding himself for the rest of his life.

While George went back to sea to deliberate, Carol graduated from high school. For a time she had thought of a career as a dietitian, supervising meals in a hospital or university. But she had never liked school and made below-average grades, and now that her diploma was gratefully in hand she took a secretarial course and went to work as a receptionist on Wall Street.

Even though she dated other men and enjoyed flirting and receiving attention from the visitors who passed by her desk, Carol never seriously entertained another man in her life except George. Nor was there another woman in his. Sometimes he would write a letter and tease, "I'd better hurry home because the girls in Japan are certainly tempting." But on leave in March, 1951, on the very first evening of spring, George stood once more on Carol's porch and announced that he was ready to stay home permanently. "There's no direction in my life," he confessed. "I have no idea what I'm trying to make of myself. The only thing I know for sure is that I love you and I need you."

Their engagement was received with favor and enthusiasm by George's parents, who knew Carol to be a "nice, lovely, sweet neighborhood girl." Carol's family, however, disapproved. "George is a little fresh-mouthed if you ask me," said Mrs. Ring. "He called just the other day and asked for you, and when I asked, 'Who is this?' he said, 'Charley Fink!' and hung up in my ear."

Carol giggled.

Ring had a more practical reason for disapproval. "I've never been very impressed by your George," he said. "He seems to have a lot of wild ideas. He's spent too many years running around the world. He doesn't seem to be the kind of boy who will settle down and raise children and provide for them. He doesn't even have a high school diploma."

Wait, Carol said. George has been taking a night course to get his high school equivalency diploma. And besides, seven years at sea is an incomparable education. Moreover, none of this matters anyway because we love one another.

Romantically, Carol wanted the wedding to be on March 21, 1952, the first day of spring, exactly one year from the day George proposed. But the Masonic Hall where the reception was to be held was booked on that occasion, so the wedding was set for April 5, the next available date. The couple had agreed that whoever was more religious could have the service in their church. Because George was a lapsed Catholic, and since Carol was slightly more faithful to her Evangelical faith, she won. The bridal gown was floor-length white lace, from Buckner's Bridal Shop in Jamaica. The wedding party arrived in a dreary spring rain and hurried under umbrellas into the Church of Peace Evangelical of Brooklyn. But after the brief service was over, after everyone had exclaimed over the beauty of the bride's red hair and glowing face, and as the couple left the church, the rain suddenly stopped and the newlyweds were flooded with brilliant sunshine. Carol considered it an omen of good fortune, but so, probably, did the other men and women involved in the 472 other marriages held in the City of New York that day, ordinary people setting out on ordinary lives.

Mr. and Mrs. George Diener spent their honeymoon night in the Barbizon-Plaza Hotel, with Carol slightly annoying her husband by staying up and writing thank-you notes. The next day they left for Niagara Falls.

"Nobody honeymoons in Niagara Falls," said George in later years. "But we did."

Chapter Three

They began with a $500 nest egg, mostly a wedding gift from Carol's parents. "The thing about me you're going to find out," said George, "is that I don't know about money. What I make today I spent yesterday." Carol immediately assumed responsibility for budgeting and handling their small income.

She planned to continue working as a receptionist while George looked for a job. Their first home was a dismal apartment with gray walls in the Richmond Hills section of Queens, which was advertised as a "two-and-one-half-room" suite, but which was in reality a studio—one room that had been carved into a living-sleeping area, a kitchen, and a bathroom. Their first purchases were an inexpensive hide-a-bed on which to sleep and sit, and a secondhand chrome dinette set at which to eat.

Through his father-in-law, who was now an executive in the industrial projects department of Westinghouse,

George obtained a job with that company, assembling electrical control panels. The pay was $30 a week and the work, though tedious and boring, was at least different from the merchant marine. But in less than a year it came to an abrupt end. The electrical union was building a housing development, and the shop steward asked George to buy a $100 construction bond.

The steward made it clear that all union members were expected to buy at least one bond. "I'll be glad to," said George, "when I have the money."

"Well," said the steward, "there's no rush, but you won't be getting any raises or promotions or overtime until you buy one."

George checked his anger. The word "extortion" came to mind, but he chose not to use it. He also felt like hitting the man, but he had long ago told himself that fighting was an immature business. Not since he left Brooklyn to go to sea had he been in a brawl. "In that case," he finally said, "I'm giving you and your union notice. As of now."

In the out-of-work weeks that followed, George realized that his decision was rash, since he was a newlywed with responsibility. But he was also a man who refused to be put into a box and be told the only way out was to bend his principles. Though he was only twenty-five years old, George had set up boundaries for his life and he would stay inside them, he told Carol, even if they led to hardship.

His next work was for a bakery, soliciting new accounts, followed by a brief stay with a baby-food company doing the same. Neither gave him either security or dignity, but each had the decided asset of being outside. "You can't expect a man who has spent almost one-third of his life at sea to like being cooped up in a factory with no windows," he told Carol.

Eighteen months into their marriage, Carol became pregnant. She continued work for five months, then retired from Wall Street with no misgivings, no feeling that a career was being interrupted or ended because of motherhood. Work had been an interesting, necessary thing to do, a step to take, and now it was over. She would move willingly into the traditional role of woman. George, while he professed happiness over the news, felt panic that he could not put down.

I never really expected to get married, he told himself. I never thought I would have the courage to take the step, or find a good woman who would have me. I'm immature. I'm scared. I don't have enough money. I may never have enough money. I can't accept this new responsibility.

But he never told Carol these things. As it would always be with George, he kept his most private thoughts bottled up. On the surface he remained his extraordinarily cheerful self, rising each day and calling out happily, "Good morning! How are you this beautiful day!" Carol would frown and wave a limp hand in greeting. "I can't even speak until I get coffee," she would say, continually startled that her husband could be so ebullient at dawn.

Carol would discover that no matter what turmoil churned inside her husband, he would generally opt for harmony and peace. Driving home from a party at which one of the guests had been a little drunk and had found fault with everything George said, Carol wondered why her husband had not gotten angry with the man. "Why don't you get mad at people like that?" she said. "Perhaps I should have," answered George. "But the other guy was loaded and it was booze talking. I think it's easier to laugh things off and save getting mad for a really important reason."

The obstetrician expressed immediate concern over Carol's pregnancy. The strain of delivery, he warned her, could throw a damaging burden on her heart. This worry was compounded by the fact that Carol's blood was Rh-negative, and George's Rh-positive. A cardiologist was notified to attend the birth. The baby's delivery was predicted for June 6, 1954. On June 5, while the young couple dined at their favorite Italian restaurant, the one where they had courted, the pains began. George rushed Carol to the hospital in a taxi and, after several hours, the doctor appeared and told the expectant father to go home, because it would be a long time before the baby would come.

"Is she all right?" George asked.

The doctor nodded his head guardedly. "We're watching her heart," he said.

The next morning George returned to the hospital at dawn. The news was alarming. No longer could a heartbeat be heard within Carol's womb. There was fear the child was dying or already dead. During an X ray to see where the infant was positioned, George lurked outside in the hallway. When Carol was wheeled from the chamber, she saw her husband's anguished face, which he quickly tried to mask with a reassuring smile. But Carol went to the delivery room crying, believing her child to be lost.

With heart specialists gathered about the table, the obstetrician used forceps to pull the baby from the womb. When it emerged, they discovered that the umbilical cord was wrapped around its neck and that in a few days the child would have strangled.

The long and perilous labor tore strength from Carol. She had feared throughout the pregnancy that her baby would be born deformed, that she would pass on her damaged heart, or worse. When the doctor told her that the infant was normal in every way, she nodded weakly, not really believing him. She was encouraged when a nurse confirmed the infant's wholeness. But not until her husband appeared at her bedside with a bouquet of spring flowers and a face of joy and wonder did she believe.

George bent over and kissed Carol tenderly. "We have a beautiful redheaded baby boy," he said. "Thank you."

"Is he all right? I mean, is everything there?" Carol asked urgently.

George shook his head enthusiastically. He held up ten fingers to indicate that all equipment was normal. "He's perfect."

Later, when George was allowed to hold the baby, he rocked the tiny life in his hands. "Well, Momma," he said, "what are we going to call young Mr. Diener?"

Carol suggested Richard, after her father. Because Ring had no sons of his own, he would be flattered to have his grandson as namesake. George tactfully pointed out that *his* parents would be offended if that name were given. A compromise was reached. The baby would be called George Richard, after both grandfathers.

"But we'll call him Richard," said Carol.

George nodded. He pulled back the blanket to examine once more his child's face. He experienced that moment every first father has, the realization that nothing he had ever done or would ever do could best his production of a new life, the extension of his line, the plant of his own seed.

"Welcome to the world, Richard," he said. "Richie, my son."

PART TWO
Richie

Chapter Four

With fatherhood, George had a new job, work that brought him home to the tiny apartment exhausted each night. He had learned from a co-worker at the baby-food company of an opening in a similar line of work. Applying to a British food company that was expanding its American sales force, George was hired as a "merchandiser," which meant that he was on the road every day, the trunk of his car loaded with thousands of spice bottles. It was his responsibility to visit 250 stores each week in a large territory that stretched from Brooklyn all the way out on Long Island to the southern tier of burgeoning Nassau County. The pay was small, but if he worked hard enough persuading store owners to stock, and restock, his brands of everything from arrowroot to tarragon, he could expect, with commission, around $75 a week—adequate wages in 1954.

Though he did not reveal it to Carol for many years,

George at twenty-six felt pressure from many sides, pressure so severe that on more than one day he felt like finding a different highway and pointing his spice-laden car down it and running away. On one level, he liked his work because of the freedom, the freedom of not being confined in one place for more than a few minutes at a time, the freedom of being able to stop and revel in the beauty of a grove of cedar before the subdividers' bulldozers sliced them from the landscape. He would never lose his awe of nature. George was a conservationist a full decade before the idea became a national concern.

But he found it exceedingly difficult to push himself and his products in front of hostile store managers. When one of them would say that he had no desire to stock George's particular brand of tea, the novice salesman's initial reaction was to flee, to escape rejection. The insecurities of his teen-age years were still very much a part of the husband, father, and new salesman. He could bluff Carol into believing that he was genial and in control of his life. But at heart he was a quiet, frightened man in both business and social affairs. As a child he had used his fists and his daring to attend his anxieties and reinforce his identity, but they seemed useless as a man. The stability that Carol and their friends assumed was George's strength in truth was in those years a mask ever ready to fall off.

Often he would return to the apartment at night and find Carol crying, distraught over *her* new role. Richie himself was healthy, cheerful, and inquisitive, but his mother was encountering familiar problems. One night she threw herself into George's arms and wept, "I just can't take it any longer!" There had been a disagreement that day with George's mother, who had proclaimed that baby powder was bad for babies. "I used cornstarch," said the mother-in-law, "and believe me, it's better."

George put on one of his smiles. "Well," he said, "what do you want me to do?"

"Ask her to leave me alone," answered Carol.

George looked around the room. The walls closed in on him, as walls always did. It occurred to him that Carol was trapped as well. It was not like his wife to rage over such a trivial matter. She was at most times a gentle, soft-spoken woman. In the back of George's head was the dream of someday buying a house in the country, a place with trees and room for a family to grow. "When we can afford it," Carol had always answered. Even though there was no more money now, less even, than the day they married, George decided this night that they must begin their search for an escape.

One practical reason, he pointed out, was that if they could live on Long Island, he would be closer to his sales route and thus able to spend more time at home. It did not seem necessary to explain another. How could a man who had seen the cliffs of Dover expect to raise a family in the prison of a New York City apartment?

Carol was not enthusiastic. "He says he wants a better life for me and Richie," she told her sister, June, who by now had married a mortician and was living on Long Island, thirty miles from New York, in a village called East Meadow. "He so loves nature, trees, to be out in the woods. But I don't care for these things! I'd rather be close to my parents. George has less strong ties with his, he went away to sea so early."

Every Sunday George and Carol, with Richie crawling in exploration about the back seat, searched the expanses of Long Island, looking for a house they both liked and could afford. "Our maximum price," Carol kept saying, as she continued to keep the family books, "is $10,000. And our monthly payment with everything included can't be much more than $75."

On several afternoons, looking in the vicinity of West Islip, a good two hours from the city, they put down a ten- or fifteen-dollar deposit on a house. But on the long drive back to New York, in the torturous traffic that choked Long Island, traffic that would grow in annoyance with each passing year, first Carol, then George would find an excuse, an "out" to avoid the commitment. Finally one Sunday morning, looking in the storybook village of East Meadow where June lived, they encountered a little white and green cottage with three bedrooms, a handsome brick and shingle exterior, a patio outside the master bedroom, and a fenced yard with trees. The problem was the price, $12,500—too much, Carol said sadly. George nodded unhappily. He would usually defer to Carol in matters financial, and he rarely took any major step before winning his wife's approval. But standing in the backyard of the green and white cottage, feeling the quiet of the neighborhood about him, picturing his son running free in a nearby field with the youngsters whose faraway cries he could faintly hear, sensing his identity firming with ownership of a house and the earth on which it stood, George decided to take rare issue with Carol. Not only was the house accommodating to all their specifics, he said, the village was what he wanted. Its inhabitants were mainly young, working-class, the men veterans of the war. The taxes were lower than in other communities they had explored, because nearby Mitchel Air Force Base paid so much that home owners were less burdened. The ocean was near, a quarter of an hour away, close enough to catch a summer breeze, and there seemed to be a boat in every other driveway, strong lure for a man who had spent seven years at sea. Even the name was seductive. East Meadow! Certainly it sounded more fitting than nearby Levittown or Hempstead. George already knew that Algonquin Indians had lived there first, in their low and circular houses that looked like outdoor ovens. Pioneers from Connecticut had settled the lush green plains in 1643; later the Redcoats had occupied it during the Revolutionary War. Not until after World War II had it been much more than fertile farm land, a vegetable basket for the great cities of the Northeast. From 5,000 residents in 1941 to 28,000 in 1956, the year in which the Dieners stood in the little backyard, was remarkable growth, George pointed out. Not only would it be a proper home for his family, it would be an investment! Never had Carol heard George speak of anything with such longing. Still, she pointed out, the house was simply more than they could afford.

But when she put Richie down on the grass, the child tottered away with shrieks of laughter. "Well, *he* likes it, obviously," said George.

"I like it, too," said Carol, weakening. "I love it."

"Then we're going to buy it," said George.

The down payment was $300, which the Dieners realized with a little help from both parents, and the mortgage, on the GI bill, was $82 a month, including taxes and insurance. Thus in late 1956 George and Carol and their two-year-old son, Richie, left New York City and moved to East Meadow, unknowing participants in an extraordinary American drama, the flight to the suburbs that crested during the Eisenhower years. Hundreds of thousands of George Dieners came home from a war, took a wife, sired a child, felt the constriction of life in a crowded city, found the money that, combined with the largesse of a federal government eager to lend money at cheap rates to its voting veterans, was enough for flight. But all too soon they would learn that in escaping the vertical city, they were creating a horizontal one, with problems and agony yet to come.

Richie grew normally into a chunky little boy whose

fiery red hair and happy disposition charmed and drew
the attention of everyone who saw him. Riding in his
mother's cart at the supermarket, he would reach out and
tug a stranger's sleeve. "Hi, my name is Richie, what's
yours?" he would say. He attacked life with fervor, be
it walking, which he did at nine months without pausing
to crawl first, or the tricycle he rode with passion, or
the insects he caught and brought to his mother for uneasy
inspection. Carol lost count of the number of times her
small boy came into the house with arms and face and
legs puffed and angry from bee stings. The pain did not
deter him; he was trying to learn about them.

A neighbor was enchanted by Richie's ritual as he
walked down his street each summer morning to a friend's
house. The child had a greeting for every object he
passed: "Good morning, Mr. Maple. How are you, Mrs.
Rose Bush? Hello there, Mr. Bluejay." "It's extraordinary,"
the neighbor woman said. "He's not just a little kid chat-
tering and fooling around. He seems to personally know
each plant, bird, and puppy dog on the whole block."

Infatuation with nature was clearly the gift of his father,
and George welcomed it. On weekends he took his son
for long walks in the woods near the Vanderbilt Estate on
Long Island, explaining with patience the wonders of
birds' nests and woodpecker holes and how carpenter ants
can quickly fell a tree. While other children sat paralyzed
in front of television sets, Richie watched with fascination as beavers constructed a dam along an upstate stream,
or crouched on a beach examining—while asking endless
questions of his father—the beauty and mystery of a sea-
shell.

Richie's early report cards in school noted both his interests and a personality problem that surfaced early. In
1960, at the end of his kindergarten year, the teacher
wrote, "Richie is an active member of the group. But he

needs firm discipline. His interests are blocks, trucks, and ANIMALS!" A year later, the first grade teacher reported, "Richie tries to be cooperative, but he finds it hard. He is active and cannot discipline himself. His interests are two: things scientific, and animals. He continually amazes his classmates and especially his teacher."

In a conference with one of Richie's teachers, Carol learned that her son was tormented by some children in his class who teased him about his hair and his weight. He was still a plump little boy at seven, despite Carol's feeling that he would slim down as both she and George had done in childhood. Easily inflamed, Richie would hit anyone who teased him—something George could easily understand. The echoes of his own childhood would resound more and more with each passing year. The parents talked casually of their son's new reputation in school. Carol brought the subject up now and then, but George professed delight that Richie was not letting anyone push him around. It was hard for either parent to grow concerned, because Richie at home was a continual delight— energetic, inquisitive, and obedient. "He never even got very sick with childhood diseases the way other kids do," said Carol.

An elementary school teacher had mixed feelings as well on in the afternoon a little girl with blond pigtails began ragging Richie during art class. She pointed out that Richie was drawing "fat people" on his paper. "Fat people draw fat people best," she announced to those around her. Richie looked at his tormentor sharply, then coolly reached into his pocket and pulled out a small but violently wriggling snake. Either he had brought the snake to school and kept it all day, or he had found it during recess. Richie quickly deposited his snake on the girl's shoulder. "I scolded Richie, of course," said the teacher, "but the little girl was a stinker and she had been asking for it a long time. Besides, Richie kept saying, 'But I only wanted to *show* it to her' so convincingly that I had to bite my tongue to keep from breaking up."

Richie's second grade teacher reported that at eight, "Richie's mental ability is average to high average. His interests are anything that crawls, flies, or swims! I must point out, however, that his interests are not diversified. His only real love is wildlife. Has an *astonishing* amount of information in this area."

By the end of the third grade, a psychologist would have seen clearly a pattern developing within the child. The teacher commented, "Richie is above average in science and social studies. But he is also very talkative, tends to be disruptive, sneaky, and sometimes defiant of authority. Shrinks responsibility as much as possible. Lacks self-discipline. Only works on what interests him. Effort poor except when something interests him. Has many interesting things to contribute to class activities, but lack of control makes him a problem."

In retrospect, perhaps George and Carol should have sought professional counseling for their son. But a decade ago parents did not rush to the child psychologist when a school report indicated the boy was a troublemaker who lacked self-discipline. They would have been rare parents had they done more than worry a little and nurse the hope that the trouble was all part of growing pains. What concerned the Dieners more, but only slightly at that, was the fact that Richie scored in the top 20 percent of a nationwide testing of elementary grade children, but his regular school marks, save his predictable "excellents" in science and nature, were average or below average. "Oh, well," said George, "it's not news to anybody that I was never much of a scholar. I still have to pronounce words silently when I read a newspaper." Carol nodded. "I learned early in school that I could make passing 65's

without much effort," she admitted. "And I usually settled for that."

Carol did suggest that her husband at least *talk* with
Richie and try to improve his attitude toward school and
friends.

She always left the discipline to George. During Richie's
preadolescence, there were no more than two or three
incidents that so provoked her that she lost her temper
and hit the boy. Normally she would insist that George
punish Richie for the rare trouble he caused at home. And
when George did impose a punishment, usually nothing
more than ordering his son to stay in his room for a
treasured Saturday afternoon, Carol—the daughter of a
disciplinarian—would usually weaken. "I couldn't stand
him lying in there and moping around," she would say
to George. "When he started to cry, I let him go outside.
I know I'm a soft touch, but all my life I've gone out of
my way to avoid a scene." This inclination to revoke her
husband's will would lead—perhaps contribute is a fairer
word—to terrible moments beyond her imagination by
the time Richie reached his mid-teens.

In those turbulent later years, there would come criticism of George for having "forced his will" upon his son.
But from talking with those close to the Diener family in
the early 1960s, it seems more accurate to say that George
was not only a good father but an excellent one. "He was
never too tired to take Richie on weekend trips," says
June Marck, Carol's sister. "Nobody worked harder for his
family than George, but nobody cared about his son more,
either. He worshiped that boy. His whole face lit up
whenever Richie came into the room."

When walking in a forest, George would sometimes
stop and find a rock or a bed of pine needles to sit on.
There he would bring up the subject of Richie's erratic
schoolwork. "I only want you to do the best you can,"

he said gently. "You have so much more natural intelligence than me. You can be anything you want to be." But Richie's attention was not held by such talk. He was more interested in interrupting to find out why the maple tree turned red before the others in autumn. George usually let his lectures go with "See if you can do a little better, son."

George wished that he could be more eloquent with his son, because he was never sure that his words were meaningful to a developing child. Insecurity still gnawed him. Did he have any real wisdom to impart to his son? Even though he was now thirty-four years old and had been with the same food company for nine long years, he somehow lacked permanence in his life. The fresh revelation came and came again to George that he was actually a father, that he bore awesome responsibility for the boy who skipped after him in the forests. He could not express it to anyone, but it was within him. And though he loved Richie deeply, there still rose up the moments when he wanted to run.

The best way he could communicate with Richie was in basic endeavor, like climbing a pine tree until he was fifty feet above the ground, until he could almost touch the sunlight just beyond. "Come on up, son!" George would cry. "There's something wrong with a boy who can't climb a tree." And Richie struggled to follow his father. A stranger coming on the scene would have observed the grown man reaching for the sky, and, only halfway up the tree, a little boy reaching—perhaps in envy, perhaps in raw determination—for his father.

A second son, Russell, was born to George and Carol in 1961, and though his delivery was less grueling for Carol, his arrival in the green and white house was traumatic. Although Richie had no health problems in his infancy or childhood, Russell was a problem baby. From the day Carol brought him home from the hospital, Russell cried.

First there was colic that seemed never to go away, then his feet were discovered to be pigeon-toed and he had to wear orthopedic shoes. Later there were months of painful teething. The Diener house began to reverberate with the sounds of a screaming baby. George complained mildly that from the first week of his second son's life he never could hear a newscast. The family dinners, at which Carol had always served carefully prepared meals, turned suddenly into thrown-together affairs. Richie, who was seven, had looked forward to dinner because it had always been a time when he and his father could talk of rope knots and beehives. But now Russell clamored for attention—and got it.

"I spent a year parading up and down with this crying, screaming baby," says Carol in weary recollection. "He cried constantly. He'd be crying when Richie got up *and* when Richie got home from school. I did feel sorry for Richie, because instead of being able to get him ready for school and send him off with a good hot breakfast, I'd been up all night, walking the house with Russell. It got so bad that George started staying up nights to give me a break, and then he would have to go off to work exhausted. God knows we didn't slight Richie deliberately, but perhaps he felt he had lost our attention."

Russell outgrew his troubling early years and soon became a handsome, bright, and overwhelmingly energetic child. He was indeed *hyper*active, so much so that the family pediatrician prescribed amphetamines, a controversial treatment in which a stimulating drug works conversely on a young child and calms him down. Neither Carol nor George was enthusiastic about having pills in the house, for theirs had never been a medicine cabinet well stocked with pills. Believing in proper food and exercise, George spurned all medications, taking only a rare aspirin for a cold.

As his little brother stormed into life, Richie began to withdraw. One side of the seesaw bounced up, the other went down. Richie stayed more often in his room, which was fast becoming the lair of a naturalist. His library of science and animal books grew as George willingly ordered every book that Richie insisted he needed. The shelves filled with the entire *Life* Nature Library, plus encyclopedias of animal behavior. Carol's father, who was nearing retirement as a Westinghouse executive and who had more money than George could ever dream of, a fact that chewed at the son-in-law now and then, gave Richie a subscription to the *National Geographic*, which enchanted the child.

Often the mail brought wildlife catalogs that Richie had sent off for in his childish scrawl. Poring over them for days, he made copious notes and illustrations in sketchbooks. In one, Carol noticed a crow advertised from a mail-order firm in the Northwest. Secretly she sent off for one, paying $26 for an unusual birthday present for her husband. The day it arrived, the United Parcel Service delivery man brought in a crate with black tail feathers sticking out. "Well," said the man, "I suppose this is better than having your mother-in-law come live with you."

Father and son built a cage for the bird in the backyard. Richie set out to teach his pet—for he had assumed ownership—to talk. But the crow refused to utter a sound, despite Richie's diligent instructions. One night at four, a cat crept around the cage, and Richie's crow exploded with a torrent of sounds. Lights went on all over the neighborhood; Richie rushed into the backyard triumphant. His crow could talk when necessary.

One morning Richie went to the cage to feed his pet before leaving for school. He did not close the door firmly and lock it, and the bird pushed the entrance open, flying away before Richie could stop him, ignoring the child's tearful cries to come back. Richie could not bear to make immediate confession, and he went to school with guilt weighing heavily on him. That night he told George, asking punishment, but his tears were so heavy that his father could only console him.

The first animal in Richie's life had been his mother's Boston bull terrier, Boots. When Boots died at a noble age, Richie was so disconsolate that Carol found another terrier, almost a double, with the same black and white markings. She left it up to Richie to name the new pet, and he selected "Boots" once more. Boy and dog were inseparable. Richie talked to Boots, and, people swear, the dog talked back. When Boots was ill, Richie knew how to treat him. The child was becoming so expert at animal medicine that other youngsters in the neighborhood, who often excluded Richie from their games, began bringing their pets for him to examine.

Carol grew familiar with the touching sight of a small boy struggling down the street with a large dog in his arms, coming to see Richie. But that was the only reason they would come.

Chapter Five

After nine years of living in the green and white house, George and Carol decided, in 1965, that it was time to find a larger home. Their two sons, eleven and four, were "getting on each other's nerves," said Carol. She longed for a house big enough to give them separate rooms, preferably some distance apart. Richie in particular needed space for his increasing collection of books, animal skeletons, rocks, and leaves. George agreed, listing among *his* needs a full basement, which their first house did not have. He wanted a place to store his stock of spices and a work area to putter around in with do-it-yourself projects.

With Richie in the sixth grade and about to enter junior high school, Carol wanted to make the move immediately. She felt that children should not be uprooted after their secondary education began, once their more lasting friendships were formed.

There was also the implied consideration that George's ego would receive a boost by moving himself and his family into a more expensive home. It seemed proper to him that years of hard work and obeying the rules of the American game of life should be rewarded with a step or two up the ladder.

As they had done before, and with the same apprehension of getting into something they would not be able to afford no matter how much they wanted it, George and Carol set forth every Sunday afternoon to search the fast-growing village of East Meadow. When they had settled in the town in 1956, there were only 28,000 residents scattered about the 8.7 square miles of level land, streams, woods, and quiet lanes. Now the population was nearing 60,000, the roads were broad boulevards often crowded with automobiles, and new subdivisions were springing up rapidly. On more than one Sunday afternoon, the Dieners found themselves lost in their own town, at sea in a puzzle of circles, courts, and cul-de-sacs being carved from what not long ago had been potato fields.

During their explorations, Carol would keep her eye out for the "For Sale by Owner" signs in front yards, wanting to avoid the extra cost of a real estate commission. Their search went on for months until one Sunday they turned into a street marked by two white brick columns, down a gently winding lane lined with mature pine trees and maples. An older area of Cape Cod and ranch-style houses, it seemed to have been developed by contractors who had respect for nature. George liked it immediately. Many of the houses had small touches that pleased the couple; one builder had used flowing script to spell out the house numbers. The lawns were carefully groomed, with masses of azaleas and tulip beds and hedges trimmed and elaborately shaped. It impressed Carol as almost a suburb within a suburb, a place of permanence and peace.

On Longfellow Avenue, a street reached only by so

many twists and turns that it could have been the prize in the center of a maze, the Dieners found a fine house painted a sunny lemon. The architecture was nondescript, but within were all the things the family wanted.

Originally there had been three bedrooms, but a previous owner had taken the attached garage, enclosed the front, constructed a bay window, and created a unique fourth bedroom. Carol grasped Richie by the hand and showed him. "This will be your room," she said in a sales talk, for Richie needed convincing about the move. Even though his existence in the old neighborhood had not been a totally pleasant one, eleven-year-old Richie had never known another way of life. He was loath to swap it for an unknown.

Carol pointed out that Richie could be his own man in the new room, for it was almost a separate apartment from the rest of the house. One had to walk down three steps to enter it, and there was a private entrance off the kitchen that Richie could use. Between the kitchen and Richie's room were more steps leading down to a full basement, room enough for George's projects and Carol's washer and dryer and freezer.

Carol's sales talk was aided by the fact that Richie discovered a family of squirrels living in the large backyard, scampering across the branches of elderly trees. After seeing them, he told his mother that he liked the house and would be happy to live in the special room.

The Dieners sold their first house for $18,500, earning enough profit to make the down payment on the new one, whose price was $21,050. Monthly payments on the mortgage would rise to an ominous $165. As Carol did hasty arithmetic on the back of an envelope, George insisted, with a quaver in his voice that he tried to hide from his wife, that the budget could handle it. In 1965 he was making around $125 a week, and if necessary he could find odd jobs. During one Christmas season he learned how to do screen printing and in his spare time produced holiday greeting placards and sold them to neighbors and shops for a few hundred dollars extra money. In the mid-1960s "moonlighting" was a voguish new term. Magazines were running articles about thousands of Americans who held two jobs in order to pay for homes and freezers and cars and children.

Of course, Carol pointed out, she could always return to work if a crisis occurred, but she was reluctant to do so. Her feeling was that she was needed at home until both children were well along in school. In the other neighborhood she knew children whom she considered ill-mannered brats. The reason, Carol felt, was that both parents worked, with no adult at home when the children returned from school.

A few years later, when the Diener tragedy came under intense community analysis, there was gossip that one contributing cause was that George and Carol had been runabouts, involved in so much social and civic activity that their children grew wild. That was simply not the case. Not until Richie was sixteen did his parents even go away for a weekend without him, and their social life would not have alarmed a fundamentalist preacher. Mainly it consisted of dropping in for after-dinner coffee and cake at Carol's sister June's house, or to a neighbor's, and after an hour of conversation, home to bed early. Rare was the month when a baby-sitter was engaged to watch Richie and Russell while their parents took a late night out.

Both George and Carol did develop areas of outside interest, but neither seemed threatening to their children's development. Interested in her family history, Carol's sister, June, paid a genealogist to trace the line. The report revealed that the ancestors could be placed all the way back to a sixteenth-century English knight. Coming back up the line, there were Revolutionary War figures, enough for Carol to join the DAR. For a few years she attended

meetings of a Nassau County chapter and proudly placed
the certificate of membership on the living-room wall of
the yellow house, a rather startling object in her otherwise modest home. Some friends teased Carol now and
then about belonging to an organization whose reputation
was that of elderly and rich dowagers, and Carol would
hasten to defend the group, saying that there were plenty
of younger members like her and that the day of banning
Marian Anderson from Constitution Hall was long since
over. But in truth Carol did not feel comfortable in the
DAR. She knew she was the wife of a spice salesman
whose salary would barely cover the mortgage. She usually knew who she was, more than her husband did.

   To replace the DAR, Carol became a leader in the community's retarded children's charity, an unusual development because both of her sons were normal. The interest
began when Carol grew friendly with a neighbor woman
who had a son with brain damage. The child spent the
week at a nearby state mental institution, but he was usually home on weekends. The first time Carol encountered
the damaged little boy, her instinct was to turn her head.
"What a horrible thing," she thought to herself. "How
does she bear to have him in the house?" Sometimes Richie
would go with her, and when he saw the retarded child,
he would smile and show him whatever pet he had in his
arms that day.

   One Sunday afternoon, the mother of the retarded
boy asked Carol if she could help take him back to the
institution, as the father was unavailable. Carol agreed,
but during the trip, as she sat in the back seat with him,
the child fell into convulsions. At that moment the car
was on a crowded expressway and there was nothing for
Carol to do but endure the terrible few moments until
the mother could stop the car and climb into the rear. The
episode made Carol feel so helpless that she decided to
learn more about the retarded. She joined the Association

for the Help of Retarded Children, of which her friend had been a founder. "At first it was a meeting once a month, but only during the morning when Richie was at school," said Carol. "Then I started running bingo parties to raise funds. These were once or twice a month, but George was always at home those nights with the boys."

A willing worker, efficient and creative, Carol was elected president of the association in 1965 and reelected for four consecutive terms, so effective was her leadership. But even when she became president, Carol insisted, meetings were held during the day so she would not neglect her children. "Mainly the job consists of a lot of telephoning," she told George. On the few times a year when big affairs were held, Carol took Richie with her to help decorate. "Neither he nor Russell nor George could have felt neglected," said Carol. "I would have dropped my work in a minute if there was any indication of that."

When George was sixteen and a restless boy in Brooklyn, he served briefly in the New York State Guard. It was then that he fell in love with guns. A psychiatrist might suggest that any man only five feet seven would feel taller with a weapon in his hand, but George was certainly not conscious of this. He knew only that he enjoyed holding them, tending them, and firing them, a paradox for a man who held reverence for all forms of life. The few times he went hunting, he could not put down the feeling of revulsion afterwards that he had killed an animal, even though he could rationalize that it was in the scheme of nature to shoot for food. "Too many of those guys," said George once in reference to other hunters, "are out there just to kill." He would find another way to enjoy his guns.

One night in East Meadow, talking with new neighbors over coffee about his affection for guns, George recollected how he used to take Carol to Coney Island during their courtship and spend most of his time there on the rifle range, plinking away with a .22. And when he had been in the merchant marine, he enjoyed especially the port of Baltimore, because at shooting galleries there it was legal to use pistols—something forbidden in New York.

One of the neighbors made George an invitation. "Then why don't you join our pistol team?" George's reaction was puzzlement. As a native New Yorker he knew of the city's severe Sullivan Law. He had always assumed that private citizens could not own a pistol. "I thought they were taboo," he said. "I thought only crooks could get one. I come from the city, where nobody you know has one."

Dave, the neighbor, assured George that obtaining a pistol permit was easy, provided there was nothing sinister in his background. "As far as I know, I'm clean," answered George. "I've never been in jail." Then all that was necessary was for George to shoot qualifying rounds at the local club for a few months, during which the police would check out his background.

From his first night on the firing range, with headsets on to muffle the noise of fire up and down the line, target shooting was to become, as George often put it, "my joy." He entered competition enthusiastically, believing at the outset that his military training and the many evenings he had spent at shooting galleries would stand him in good stead for experience. But George quickly learned that target shooting in competition was a different matter. It requires, he told Richie, practice at least once a week if not more, intense concentration, even good physical and mental health. "A man can't fire a pistol well if his mind is all cluttered up. You stand there," he explained, "fifty feet from the target. There are ten men on a team, but only the top four firers count in scoring against another

team. You go from slow time, which is ten shots in ten
minutes, to fast time, ten shots in twenty seconds, to rapid
fire, ten shots in ten seconds."

"Can you do like this?" Richie asked, whipping out an
imaginary pistol and firing like a hired gun.

George laughed and shook his head. "That's only on
Gunsmoke," he said. He attempted to interest his son in
target shooting on a junior competitive level, but Richie
showed no interest.

The first year George scored poorly. But he was, if
anything, a man as stubborn as a terrier, and in the years
that followed, he became one of the most skilled members
of the Levittown Rod and Gun Club. One season he won
most of the medals. He was known as a superb marks-
man, a cool shooter who could hit what he wanted to hit
—quickly, efficiently, dead center.

The first gun he bought when his permit came through
from the police department was a .25 Colt automatic.
"She was a little gun from the Prohibition era, they used
to call them stocking guns because ladies carried them,"
George once said, for he remembered every detail of
every gun he had ever owned. "She was a beautiful piece
of work," he went on, usually using the feminine gender
to describe his weapons. Later there was a .45 that he
bought from a government surplus store, but during one
of the financially lean times in East Meadow George sold
it for thirty-five dollars to help make a mortgage payment.

One weapon for which he held great hopes was a .38
special that he bought for thirty dollars from a friend. It
was the kind of gun favored by most New York City
policemen. The original owner had been a doctor who
took exquisite care of it, and George's intention was to
use the five-chambered gun in competition, even though
its barrel was only two inches long instead of the preferred four inches. To his annoyance, George discovered

that because he had a small hand, the gun was difficult to handle. He could not cock, aim, and fire quickly enough in competition. A friend offered to buy it, but George decided against selling. He believed strongly in what he called "the Constitutional guarantee a citizen has to bear arms." In the closet the gun went, quickly available should the safety of George Diener's household be threatened.

Chapter Six

Richie was never really happy in the new home on Longfellow Avenue. When the Dieners first moved there in 1965, one boy of Richie's age lived on the block, and the two struck up a brief friendship. But when he moved away, there were only girls left in the neighborhood. Quickly they discovered Richie's temper, his embarrassment over his weight. At twelve, he was not quite five feet tall and an overweight one hundred pounds. Two girls of twelve or thirteen, chubby themselves and with raucous voices, took to springing out at Richie from behind bushes and shrieking "Fatso!" until he would rail at them and chase them home—he blustering and tearful, they angry and threatening vengeance.

Richie set out to explore the area in search of friendship, though he would never have admitted that was the reason. He soon discovered it was the custom of the neighborhood boys to scowl at alien faces. One day George idly asked his son why he looked so fearsome as a youth passed their yard. "Do you know that kid?" said George. Richie shook his head negatively. "Then why did you look at him that way?"

"I just don't like his looks," said Richie.

"How can you have friends if you act that way?" Richie had no response. He went inside to tend his animals.

Richie's lack of friends was becoming a matter of concern to Carol, although George insisted she was worrying unnecessarily. Privately George marveled at the many similarities between himself and his son. Were so many common traits passed on in the biology of his seed, or did a father unknowingly, *unwantingly* mold a child in his own image, a child who was so obviously lonely, who found solace in animals, who was so quick to raise his fists to defend his identity?

Both parents made continuing attempts to correct their son's unhappy social existence. But nothing worked well. Though she still remained busy in her work with retarded children, Carol took over as den mother of a Cub Scout pack, hoping that her role would have some status value for Richie. But the pack's membership, small when Carol became leader, declined even further. Families moved away. There were not enough boys of required age in the district. Meetings in their home were often disrupted by Russell, who had put aside the piercing cries of his infancy and was thunderingly embarked on his hyperactive assault on life. "I take the blame for the pack's failing," says Carol. "Richie didn't like it, and I can see why."

Throughout Richie's preadolescent years, Carol attempted to build his ego. Clever and imaginative in sewing, she fashioned elaborate masquerade costumes for Halloween and school parties. There are photographs of Richie as a solemn but plump French courtier, as a stout Argentine gaucho, as a well-fed visitor from outer space. He usually won first prize, but that was not enough in the cruel competition of childhood society. Nor were the fancy birthday parties Carol planned for him. "You're incredible," remarked Carol's sister, June, who had a son older than Richie and a daughter the same age as him. "I consider it well done if I buy a cake and have pin-the-tail-on-the-donkey." Carol dreamed up "theme" affairs, baking her own cake, carrying out motifs in table decorations and games and gifts.

George continued his weekend outings with Richie. Talk of nature remained their principal area of communication, and George happily bought scuba equipment and told his son that someday there would be a boat, or a camper, or both. In later years he would become both a leader in a Boy Scout troop—although Richie did not join—and an assistant coach for a Little League team, this time for his second son, not his first.

Richie had no interest in sports. Although he would lose his hated fat by the time he was fourteen and develop into a strong and well-muscled lad, he had not the slightest enthusiasm for athletic competition. He neither watched sports events on television nor read of them in the newspaper. Carol tried now and then to interest her son in sport, for she felt he would find friends in the camaraderie of a team. "Why don't you try out for baseball?" she'd suggest. Or wrestling, for he had strong arms and well-developed chest muscles. Or football, for despite his stockiness he could run like a forest animal. "I don't want to," Richie answered. "If I made a mistake out there and caused the team to lose, I don't think I could stand it."

Carol nodded and dropped the subject. Until that moment she had not realized the extent of her son's insecurity.

Richie's development as a loner did not entirely dominate the thoughts and lives of George and Carol. Despite the boy's moodiness, his middling grades, his flashes of temper and belligerence, his scraps on the school playground, he was, in sum, a satisfying, often affectionate, seemingly mostly normal youth. There were moments when Carol wanted to go into her neighborhood and tell the young people about her son and bring them home to be his friends, but such moments passed. It was easier to take the attitude, as mothers usually do, that Richie would outgrow his childhood pain, that the years would heal, that opportunities would come, that friends would soon be there. Every other mother she talked to had problems at home. They were almost typical in suburbia, she told herself, as if mumps and measles came and went, only to be replaced by stealing, dope, and violence—all of which she had heard of and none of which, mercifully, had touched her son.

Moreover, Richie seemed to have what most children his age did not—a direction. His deep interest in nature and animals continued to expand to the extent that Carol announced at dinner one evening that she felt she was dwelling in the middle of the Bronx Zoo. By the time Richie was twelve, he owned a thriving menagerie. For a time, a skunk named Cologne, a gift from Grandfather Ring, coexisted in the backyard with a tremendous gray rabbit named Thumper. It was Richie's intent to prove that different species could live compatibly in the same condition. But as the skunk grew elderly, it became hostile and snappish. Sadly Richie gave him away to the Frank Buck Zoo on Long Island. "This proves that my mistake was in raising Cologne in a pen," Richie told his mother. "If he had been brought up inside, like a puppy, he would have learned to act like a house animal."

The family of backyard squirrels that had so enchanted Richie on the first day he saw the yellow house multiplied and grew almost tame under his gamekeeping. The animals waited patiently for Richie to come home from school, knowing that he would feed them with cookies.

When a neighbor across the street threatened to have other squirrels shot because they were breaking the branches of her trees, Richie came up with a better idea. He took his Have-a-Heart trap, so called because it was able to capture small animals without seriously hurting them, and set it daily at the foot of the trees. Every afternoon for more than a week, Richie caught a squirrel and took it to a nearby forest.

From their field trips or from an East Meadow pet shop, George and Richie often brought home snakes of all varieties and installed them in pens. The grass snakes Carol did not mind, not even the pine snake. But the yellow rat snake, with its striking markings, grew melancholy and temperamental, unresponsive to Richie's ministrations, so much so that Carol suggested the creature be returned to nature. Richie read up on its natural habitat. Discovering that the species is indigenous to Maryland, Richie took the snake along on a family automobile trip to North Carolina, where Carol's parents had moved in retirement, near several golf courses where Mr. Ring played daily. Richie watched out the car window for a likely place, finally calling out for his father to stop. Somewhat sadly, Richie carried his snake to a brushy, rocky area, opened the box, and watched the pet slither away.

But, as she did with most things, Carol accommodated herself, even to the milk snake that, when dead of natural causes, was autopsied by George and Richie. They studied its innards and discussed possible causes of death. Then the skin went up on Richie's wall.

The boy's prize serpent was a boa constrictor purchased in infancy and carefully raised until it grew to be almost five feet long. Carol insisted, firmly, that *this* pet stay forever in Richie's room, in a secure cage. Richie obeyed, except for moments when he would appear at the dinner table with the boa draped about his neck, or when he would set the creature free in the kitchen and encourage it to glide into the dining room as Carol and George entertained neighbors with coffee and cake. The boa disappeared one day and, despite a thorough search of house, basement, and yard, was never found. Richie never told his parents that he had secretly taken the snake to a forest and let it go, perhaps relishing the mystery of a giant serpent haunting his parents' house.

By coincidence, Carol had a cousin by marriage who worked as a herpetologist at the American Museum of Natural History in New York. She telephoned and asked if Richie could visit her at work, explaining the boy's extraordinary interest in reptiles. Several times Richie was allowed to go to the museum, to private rooms in the research area where snakes were grown and studied. After each trip he returned to East Meadow with great enthusiasm. He explained to his counselor in junior high that he had decided to become a herpetologist. "The funny thing, Mother," he told Carol, "is that the counselor doesn't even know what a herpetologist is. He doesn't even know how to spell it!"

But going to New York City was a major undertaking for Richie, involving an expensive train ticket, or a full day for George or Carol of driving in and waiting and driving back. It simply could not be done as often as Richie would have wanted. If the Dieners had lived in the city, instead of an hour away in the suburbs that George had so passionately solicited for his family, perhaps Richie could have worked part-time at the museum, or at least had easier access. That "if," that "perhaps" were but two of the hundred others that Carol would someday remember, endure, and put away.

Suddenly George was forty. "The big four-oh," he said to himself as he shaved. Carol baked a cake, there were cards and gifts from family and friends on a geriatic theme. The evening passed pleasantly enough, but inside George was a gale as disquieting as those that shook him during his first weeks at sea. Introspection was not a word in George's vocabulary, but on this night he was deep within himself. He took stock of what, materially, his forty years had wrought. The inventory was brief:

One good house with three hundred monthly mortgage payments yet to fill and then it would be his and not the bank's. One secondhand car—could he ever afford a new one, one that another man had not first used? One portable, above-the-ground backyard swimming pool, value $400. Too costly, of course, but the children enjoyed it, and George liked the music of their laughter on long summer nights. One color television and six rooms of furniture, nothing elegant, but *all* paid for. George was comfortable in his living room, for Carol had decorated it in the colors of autumn in a forest—green pebble wall-to-wall carpet, Danish modern sofa and chairs in rust and gold. There were two large imitation oil paintings above the sofa, the kind found on motel walls, but they celebrated an imaginary landscape where man had not intruded on the mountains and the seas. The room was relentlessly middle-class, George knew that, and it did not approach the fancy decor with knickknacks that Carol's sister possessed across town. But he knew the slightly shabby, impeccably clean room somehow reflected him; it was the best he could do.

What else is there? George wondered this night. One company insurance policy on his life, one mortgage insurance policy on his life, but nothing personal to mark his financial importance to his family and his world. Perhaps $200 in the savings account. There was never more than $200. Even the $1,500 inheritance that Carol had received from her grandmother seemed to disappear as suddenly as it had come. Was $200 the ceiling God had put on him?

Of course there was his job; after fifteen years with the same company he was not likely to lose that. But he still plowed the same row, took the same spices out of the trunk of his car and put them in the same racks in the same grocery stores. Occasionally there would be a new product, a gravy mix, a white sauce packet to introduce, but this was the sum of his daily endeavor. George was a resident of Willy Loman country. The world did not and would not shake as he passed by.

His health? There George could take pride, even on a night when his life was half over. He did not smoke, not like Carol who puffed and coughed her way through at least two packs a day. Rarely did he drink, a glass of sweet New York State white wine when Carol loaded his table with lasagna and ravioli and the exquisite cheesecake she fashioned and baked in a springform pan. Occasionally he took a weak whiskey at one of her charity affairs. But alcohol meant nothing to him. The small cart beside the dining-room table contained bottles purchased chiefly for friends who dropped by. If he never took another drink, it would matter nothing to him. Never had a major illness felled him, and he was sure that one reason was his abstinence from pills and medication. He did not believe in putting foreign substances in his body. He kept it tough and sharp. Thirty push-ups a day on a wheel to keep the belly trim, this on top of the weights he lifted fifty times each morning, standing, crouching, and lying on his back. He kept his weights and exercise wheel under one end of the living-room couch, next to the American flag that stood in the corner, ready for the occasions when George proudly attached it to his front porch.

He could still climb a pine tree; he could still dazzle the children at the charity's summer picnic by standing on the bathhouse roof and leaping prodigiously across a chain-link fence into the deep end of the swimming pool. Someday he was going to take skydiving lessons. Why not? He was still young. "Like the man says," George said, "Life begins at forty."

But there had been other dreams early in George's nights, and none had lasted until dawn. A year or two before, during what he referred to as "one of my disaster periods, a time when I was depressed about my lack of success," George secretly signed up for a home study course in forest ranger work and conservation. When the books arrived, Carol grew irritated. She discovered that he had paid sixty dollars for them. "You threw sixty dollars away!" she accused.

George tried to explain. "Some days I feel I am growing old and life is passing me by," he said. "I've always had this real Walter Mitty thing about sitting on top of a mountain all by myself and watching the trees grow. I guess I thought I'd take this course and get a job and go to a forest somewhere and then send for you and the boys. And you would fall instantly in love with it, like me."

Carol was not excited by the explanation. "This will probably turn out like that book I bought you," she said. "Remember? 'Six Weeks to a Better Memory' and you forgot to read it."

George smiled ruefully. That was true. But the reason, he insisted, was not his lack of interest, only his difficulty in reading. He still pronounced words silently as he read. Mainly, his reading consisted of the New York *Daily News*, whose short, racy items and conservative editorial page he liked. He also enjoyed the *Reader's Digest* and *Plain Truth*, a conservative religious publication. Once, in an attempt to improve his reading ability, he enrolled in a speed-reading course at an East Meadow adult education program. But that project failed, too. "I just can't understand what's going on," he told Carol. "I can't make heads or tails of it."

But it did not hurt to float dreams, George told himself. They kept men going. Off and on during his life he had made little notes to himself, thoughts and fragments that he wanted to write down. They were private and no one ever saw them. At forty, George wrote:

Each decade is a disaster area. You worry that life is passing you by. I try to realize that I'm far better off than 80 percent of the world. But that's little solace when you realize that the world is slipping out of your grasp, that you're getting old, there's so little time left, and so many things are going wrong.

When I was young, I figured it was just a matter of time until I made it big. Then the realization sets in that life consists of work, boring work, work to pay the bills. You face reality. That's what it is. You work to keep up with the bills.

I always thought I would have my own business someday. My father told me to get a civil service job, one that would be security when I was 40. I couldn't imagine being 40! How could anyone live that long? How does everybody else make it this far? How do you go further?

Just before he went to sleep that night of his fortieth birthday, George considered the other entries on his list of assets, the human ones. Beside him stirred Carol, a woman still as slim, as attractive, as fragile as the day they had married. But George knew there was steel beneath the fragility. Her good humor, her patience, her hard work were cement that bound the family together. She was working now as a lunchroom attendant in the junior high school cafeteria, not very glamorous work, helping prepare and serve lunches for a thousand kids, but work she did willingly because the budget needed more than George could bring in alone. Somehow she managed to do this, be home by midafternoon to greet the boys when they arrived, fix a tasty dinner, keep her red hair teased and coiffed, make her own clothes, and still keep up with her retarded children's charity. The wall of the living room contained a new bronze plaque that attested to Carol's unprecedented five-year term as president of the group. It annoyed George now and then that his wife was not firmer with the boys, that either of them could get around her and escape chores and discipline. But that was Carol's way.

Their marriage—almost sixteen years now—was a good one. Only a few times over the years had there even been quarrels, "spirited discussions," Carol called them in recollection. And only once had there been the danger of divorce. That had come a few years earlier when Carol had fallen ill. For a time she had grown gradually tired, more and more, until she dragged about the house pale and weak. Listless and unresponsive, she had no interest in George's advances. For a time he wondered if *she* was having an affair, or, worse, had abruptly turned frigid in her middle thirties. When Carol finally went to the doctor and was put into the hospital for tests, George went out his first night alone looking for companionship. He considered it a "celebration," in fact. But when the doctor diagnosed in his wife a serious blood infection, probably related to her childhood rheumatic fever and heart damage, George was consumed with guilt. Carol stayed in the hospital several weeks and in bed at home for many more. She would have to take penicillin every day for years thereafter.

When she was able to get out of bed and resume her role as wife and mother, Carol discovered a pair of women's gloves in the family car. They were not hers. George made earnest confession and promised it would never happen again. It had not. Nor would it, he told himself. He could listen to the "Lothario tales" of his fellow salesmen and companions on the firing range with ease now.

Above all the assets, there were his sons. They were the riches of his life. There is joy in a daughter, but there is power in a son. They were the mirror that reflected the image he most wanted to see. Russell, often rowdy, always rambunctious, possessed zest for each day that was difficult to penalize. He was, moreover, an extraordinarily handsome youngster with thick brown hair, a strong physique (like his father!), and friends who crowded the house with their laughter and pranks. So different from his older brother, Russell adored sports and was almost a social lion among the young of Longfellow Avenue.

Richie? Richie was improving. No doubt about it. Signs of maturity were present, beyond his deepening voice and the faint line of hair on his upper lip. He would never be a scholar, but his junior high school grades were solidly average, with those high marks in science that had become routine. He ranked in the top 10 percent for reading ability in a nationwide test of ninth-graders. The natural intelligence was obviously there. He was not following his father in *that* department. Richie knew who he was. He knew what he would become. He was giant steps ahead of George, who had never known, who wondered even now.

Even Richie's social difficulties seemed to be easing, as Carol had so hoped they would. He had met a girl named Sheila whom he seemed to be interested in; at least, they talked on the telephone for hours at a time. Sheila was a pretty little thing, skinny as a board, but with long black hair she kept clean and straight.

Moreover, Richie seemed to have a new pal, a neighborhood boy named Brick he had met at a Methodist church outing. For a few months Richie had attended services, long enough to be confirmed, which satisfied Carol and both sets of grandparents. George had not yet met Brick, but Richie talked about him often. He lived a few blocks away and he had decent, hardworking parents who lived in their own home.

All in all, George thought to himself as he drifted off, things aren't going too badly. A neighbor child even chose George as the subject of his school English theme: "The Adult I Would Most Like to Be."

Chapter Seven

With a pierced heart dripping blood tattooed on one arm and a coiled serpent on the other, and with a scraggly beard under cultivation, Broderick (Brick) Pavall looked, at first sight, totally villainous. It was an image he carefully nursed. When Richie first saw him close up at the church retreat, he was startled. What was Brick doing in a place like this? His milieu was the street, where he walked with a swagger, where he drove an ancient Plymouth with pocks in fender and doors but the carefully tuned roar of chariots from the exhaust. During a lengthy prayer, Richie glanced at Brick and saw that he was pantomiming a cigarette at his lips, one that made his eyes roll and his shoulders quiver. Richie knew what kind of cigarette Brick was dramatizing. By the time a boy reached fourteen in East Meadow, in the late 1960s, he would have been unusual if he did not know what marijuana was, what it smelled like as it burned, what it cost, and where to get it.*

Richie had been offered puffs on the playground and after class in junior high, but he had not been interested. He was not offended, just not interested.

Richie had often seen Brick in the neighborhood; he lived three streets away. Richie further knew, since Brick was talked about in the area, that he had dropped out of high school, that he was working as a gas station attendant, and that he had a pack of kids glued to him.

What Richie did not know was that behind the tattoos, beard, and swagger was a desperately immature youngster who told his mother more than once, in moments of agonizing self-honesty, "I'm nothing. I'm shit. I'll never amount to anything." Mrs. Pavall, a strong-willed, effusive woman who worked part-time as a bookkeeper for mom-and-pop stores in East Meadow, embraced her son on those pained occasions and always reassured him, in uncertain tone, "No you're not! You're a good kid. You'll find your way. You just need a little confidence."

Brick's mother would descend into hell to help her son. During one of his many encounters with the law, she pathetically searched the halls of the courthouse, trying to borrow the extra fifteen dollars she needed to bail him out. The sum was fifty dollars; she had but thirty-five dollars in her purse, and that had been intended for Friday night groceries. In another, she stood ashamed while a judge scolded her boy. "I hope you come back before me," the judge said in granting Brick probation on a

---

* *A study made by two psychiatrists in 1970 of eighth- and ninth-graders in East Meadow showed that 23 percent were using illegal drugs. Two years later, a survey of New York State indicated that more than 45 percent of young people under the age of eighteen used "psychoactive" drugs, with marijuana included in the category. District Attorney William Cahn of Nassau County was more alarming in his early 1972 estimate. He said that upward of 75 percent of young people in his county had at least tried some form of drugs.*

minor drug matter. "I want the opportunity to put you away for a long time. I feel sorry for the girl who marries you. I feel sorry for your parents. I feel sorry for anybody who comes in contact with you."

One spring evening in 1969, when Carol and George were down the street having coffee after dinner, Richie sat on the deck of his home with Brick and a rail-thin kid named Hammer. Warm, with thunder rumbling in from the nearby sea, the night promised an April downpour. When Richie felt the first drop of rain fall on his face, he suggested they move to his room. Brick refused. He was enthusiastic about the thunder. So was Hammer, a boy of fifteen who would two years later, being involved in cocaine selling, vanish from East Meadow.

"I wanna keep this going," said Brick, looking at the troubled sky and reaching into his windbreaker. He produced a joint of marijuana, lit it, pulled in a deep drag, and handed it to Hammer, who enthusiastically followed him.

Brick routinely handed it to Richie, who looked at the fast-burning cigarette and shook his head.

"Why not?" said Brick.

"I don't wanna get started," said Richie.

"You don't know what you're missing," said Brick. "Right, Hammer?" Hammer nodded with gusto. "I never heard thunder quite this way," said Brick, lifting his face to the darkening sky and closing his eyes.

Midway through his second joint, Brick again handed it to Richie. "Come on, Richie, take a few puffs," he said. "You're not going to turn into a dope addict."

Abruptly Richie seized the cigarette and puffed it. Instantly he choked and his eyes began to water and turn red. Brick laughed. "Take a little at a time, the first time," he instructed. "Here." Richie watched and then took a few more discomforting drags.

Finally he shook his head. "It doesn't do anything for me," he said.

"You're fighting it," said Brick. He offered what was now a quarter-inch butt to Richie with a strip of match-book cover wrapped around it as a holder. Richie shook his head. He was firm.

But a few days later, this time when Brick's parents were away, Richie accepted another joint. More than likely, he had no real interest in what the grass would do for him, only a desire to prove to his new friend that he could behave maturely. This time he tried to keep from cough-ing, even when the acrid smoke burned his mouth and throat and made his eyes water. But he kept the smoke down. He held his breath tightly to keep from exploding. He fell silent after a time. Then he giggled, over nothing.

"You know what, Diener?" said Brick, with a knowing grin. "You're stoned."

Richie shook his head to deny the surprising pro-nouncement. But in a few moments he leaped up and circled the room. "I'm high," he said, "I'm really high!" A few nights later Richie asked Brick for a joint, rather than wait for an invitation, and within a month was routinely using pot once or twice a week. He was fourteen years old. Brick congratulated Richie and wondered why he had waited so long. "I started when I was twelve," bragged the older boy with the scraggly beard. "And even then I was late. I know kids eleven, ten years old who use grass. I heard of one kid in the second grade who comes to school stoned."

From the beginning, Carol did not approve of Brick, though she had no idea what had transpired on the deck outside her dining room the night of the spring thunder. Chiefly she objected to Brick because he was almost three years older than Richie. Moreover, she did not like the fact that he had dropped out of school, nor did she relish the hoody aura about him, despite his politeness and good manners when he came to her home.

The Brick relationship and the vague malaise it stirred within her were but one reason Carol brought up the subject of summer camp for Richie as June neared in 1969. She handed George a folder advertising Camp Red Cloud Lake in the Adirondacks. Her sister planned to send her daughter, Susan, there, and from all reports it was an excellent place for youngsters.

George examined the folder and seemed responsive until he came to the price.

"Eight hundred dollars!" he said, shaking his head. Need he remind his wife that the sum was more than he made in six weeks' hard work?

Carol pressed her point. The previous summer had been difficult not only for Richie, she said, but for her. While George was at work all day, she had to stay at home and cope with two boys who either said there was nothing to do and moped around sulking because Carol would not chauffeur them at every whim, or, often worse, would so fill her backyard with noisy friends that her head throbbed. She made a poignant commentary on suburban life. "You move to the suburbs for your kids," she told George, "and then you find out that nobody wants them on their lawn. They might spoil the rosebushes and the grass. There's no place for them to play, so they end up over here. I'm the neighborhood softie."

"I can sympathize with that," said George. "And the camp looks like a beautiful place. You don't have to sell me on the advantage of spending eight weeks in the mountains. I'd like to spend the rest of my life there. But where do we get eight hundred dollars?"

Part of it could be borrowed from her parents, Carol suggested tactfully. Mr. and Mrs. Ring had often come to the aid of their daughter and son-in-law in times of financial emergency. The rest could be found by saving, sacrificing, eliminating a planned family vacation, she would even cut down smoking if necessary.

George fell silent. Carol saw that he was weakening. What better place could there be for Richie, she said, almost pleading, than the mountains and forests he had so long adored?

"Is it that important?" George asked.

Carol nodded.

George borrowed eight hundred dollars from his bank as a personal-signature loan to pay for Richie's stay at Camp Red Cloud Lake. It was the second largest expenditure of his life, after the mortgage on his house. When George sprang the exciting news on Richie, the boy was receptive, but not overly so. "Why doesn't Russell have to go, too?" he wondered. The second Diener son, now eight, refused even to entertain the idea of camp, which was just as well, because George could not have found another eight hundred dollars.

As Carol launched enthusiastically into the motherly ordeal of assembling camp clothes, sewing in name tags, and packing a trunk, George received a disturbing telephone call exactly one week before Richie was due to leave. The Juvenile Aid Bureau of the Nassau County Police Department was on the line. A bicycle had been stolen from the home of an East Meadow policeman, and Richie Diener was suspected of the small crime.

Two juvenile officers stopped by the Diener house late that afternoon to talk to Richie. Almost indignantly he denied knowledge of the theft, as he had done when George questioned him.

"If I was going to steal a bicycle, which I wouldn't," he said, "I sure wouldn't pick a cop's house."

Because there was no evidence to connect Richie with the theft, the investigation was dropped. A folder, however, bearing the name of George Richard Diener was opened in the Juvenile Aid Bureau. It did not contain the news that Richie had indeed stolen the bicycle and had sold it to Hammer for five dollars' worth of marijuana.

A little more than one week after Richie had gone away to the Adirondacks, George received a second startling telephone call. This time it was the owner of the camp, an East Meadow woman, whose voice was distraught. She came straight to the point. Richie was abusive, disruptive, and interfering with the order of her camp. Moreover, he had threatened a counselor with physical assault. And he had been caught smoking marijuana. Could George come immediately and fetch Richie? Most of the tuition would be refunded.

Stunned by the indictment of his son's behavior, George made the long drive to upstate New York alone. Richie greeted his father with no sign of embarrassment. But George, humiliated and very angry, made a hurried apology to the camp owner. He watched as Richie said good-bye to his friends.

On the day-long drive back to East Meadow, Richie was eager to defend himself. The counselor with whom he had feuded, Richie said, was disliked by all the kids. He had teased Richie and accused him falsely of putting holes in the wall beside his bunk. "They were already there from last year," Richie insisted. "And when he said I cussed him, well, all the kids cussed him."

"But you were the only one who threatened to get him at night when he was sleeping," said George, who had spent a private hour with the camp owner. "And you were the only one who threatened to tear up his car. I think you're a little too quick with your big threats of vengeance and retaliation and getting even. I've seen this before in you."

For an hour, George was quiet. He was not as concerned about Richie's trouble with the counselor as he was about Richie and marijuana. How could he best bring *this* up? If he wanted to nip it in the bud, it was necessary that his guidance be well thought out. Finally he spoke. But all he could manage was to blurt out, "How can you use this marijuana stuff? I think it would take the worst kind of person in the world to do this."

Once more Richie sought safety in numbers. "All the kids" were smoking it, he said. It grew wild in woods about the camp. What Richie did not say was that his knowledge of nature and expertise in plant identification made it easy for him to spot the weed. He also did not reveal that the counselor in question had caught him with a bag of marijuana and demanded that Richie turn it over. When Richie refused, the counselor threatened to turn him in. "Give it to me and I won't squeal on you," the counselor said. Richie finally handed over his bag— only to discover that the counselor had appropriated it for his own use. This had been fuel for the fire between them. But Richie could not tell his father that piece of news.

As they neared East Meadow, George glanced over at his somewhat chastened son. "Well, I tell you what's what," he said. "You're going to have to straighten up. I don't care what all the other kids are doing. In my house, marijuana is illegal, because the law says it is."

Richie nodded.

"One more thing," continued George. "You can start shaping up by getting your hair cut. You look like a sheep dog."

Probably expecting more severe rebuke, Richie readily agreed. He would have his hair cut the very next day. But when he returned from the "hair stylist," a new term to George, the father shook his head in disbelief. "*That* cost $7.50?" he said. "It looks like they combed it, nothing more. You walk outside in the wind and it'll be like you never even went."

That telephone call from Camp Red Cloud Lake in the summer of 1969 and the long drive back from the mountains were the first clues George Diener received that his son was caught up in radical change. But George did not recognize them as such. They came at the crest of Richie's adolescence—and George could well remember the agony of his own teen-age years. They came at a time when newspapers were commenting on the widespread popularity of marijuana among the young. George gambled that Richie was only going along with the crowd, that the infatuation would be no more lasting than the occasional pimple that erupted and faded on his son's face. Had marijuana been around twenty-five years ago, George told himself honestly, I might have tried it. Perhaps at that moment there was nothing more than a crack between the father and the son, but over the remaining months of the summer, and in the autumn that followed as Richie began his sophomore year in high school, the crack became a gulf. And George and Richie would stand on opposite sides of a tragic new world.

Richie's interest in animals started to wane. He gave away his snakes and hamsters, or let them go. When Boots, the family's second Boston bull terrier, died, Richie had neither grief, nor attention for the large gray poodle, Bridget, that Carol bought as replacement. The squirrels still waited for Richie to come home and feed them, but more and more he ignored them or told Russell to do it. His room, for so many years a naturalist's lair, underwent a dramatic change of character.

The extensive library of nature books went onto the top shelf of his closet and began to gather dust. Once they had been all over his room, open on his desk, on his bed, their pages thumbed and underlined. In their place came the decor of the youth culture: posters of rock stars, ticket stubs from pop concerts, a display of drawings from an underground artist whose work seemed drenched in drug-induced horror. Specializing in monstrous creatures, he drew modern half-man, half-animal grotesqueries with electrified hair, claws for hands, and violence as avocation. One such apparition was drawn seated in a bathtub with daggers and blood about him; the impression was that he had disemboweled himself.

Richie carefully stapled these drawings on the paneled wall directly in front of his bed. As he lay there, he could look at them without moving his head on his pillow. After attending one of his mother's charity dances, Richie delightedly collected the white styrofoam balls that had been used for decorations. Splashing them with Day-Glo paints, he hung them from the ceiling of his room. Somehow he found money to buy a black light, which, switched on, transformed his chamber into a sanctum of psychedelia. Everything was precise. The mementos were not thrown helter-skelter on the wall. Richie placed them with almost geometrical care. His decorative labors produced the desired effect. One friend told Richie, "You have the best room of anybody." They began to come, as Carol always said they would.

To only a few of these, his new friends, did Richie show the prize attraction of his quarters—a small storage chamber at the back of his closet that he had discovered one day by accident while putting his shoes in a neat row. There was an opening about eighteen inches square covered with a nailed piece of plywood. Removing the plywood, Richie was elated. Within was a small secret area, perhaps an architectural blunder, a place big enough for him to lie in—six feet long by three feet wide by four feet high. To improve it, Richie lined the walls with crinkled aluminum foil. On the ceiling he placed rock posters. On the floor went a cast-off single mattress. The opening to the private place he disguised with his shoe rack.

He took to entering his hideaway and lying on the mattress, with only an eerie crack of light from the closet and the glow of his pot pipe to illumine him. There he could escape his parents' calls. Often Carol would announce dinner, knowing that Richie was in the house, hearing the rock music from his room that announced his presence, but puzzled when he did not respond. When she went to his room, he would not be there.

Finally George discovered the place and dismantled it, annoyed that Richie would crawl inside a wall to hide from his parents. Pulling down the aluminum-foil walls, he found a small cache and, in it, a piece of hardened substance in a plastic sandwich bag.

"What is this?" George demanded, suspecting it was important because of the elaborate method by which it had been hidden.

"I don't know," the boy replied. "Mud, I guess."

"I'd guess it's more than that," said George. "Or you wouldn't take such pains to hide it."

"It's hash," Richie finally said, explaining that it was hashish he was keeping for a friend. "It isn't mine," said Richie, "I swear."

Whatever, George angrily threw it out, despite Richie's protestations that he had no right to destroy someone else's property. And he nailed up the secret place.

One autumn afternoon in 1969, Richie and Hammer smoked two joints after school, and they both became hungry. Hammer looked at his watch. If he did not get home and rake leaves, his father had threatened to ground him for a week. Richie shrugged, for he had the same work to do. He went to a Carvel ice-cream stand alone. When he had finished his dish, Richie continued to sit at his table for more than an hour. Finally the owner asked him to leave. Richie refused, announcing that by paying for his ice cream he earned the right to occupy a table for as long as he wanted.

The owner said that if Richie did not leave immediately, he would be thrown out. "Try it," said Richie coldly. Two young countermen thereupon seized the red-haired boy and threw him bodily out the door.

Richie picked himself up, went across the street, found a large rock, and threw it into the eight-foot-wide plate-glass window. Enraged, the owner sent his employees after Richie. They chased him for several blocks before one caught him with a flying tackle. Pinned to the ground, Richie spat out his name.

Later that day, notified by the store owner that the window would cost $250 to replace, George muttered an apology and said his insurance would cover it. But when he sat Richie down that night and received his explanation—Richie contended that he threw the rock because he had been "manhandled"—George was distressed to see his son's lack of remorse. Richie seemed, in fact, proud of what he had done.

The next day, George notified Nassau County Family Court that he had decided *not* to submit the claim to his insurance company, that he wanted the drama played out before juvenile authorities. "I think Richie needs a hard lesson right here and now," George told Carol. She agreed.

The case dragged on for several months, with the store owner filing a "criminal mischief" complaint. But when he failed to appear for three hearings, the charge was dropped.

Richie was annoyed at his father for making him go to Family Court. "Then don't throw any more rocks through ice-cream store windows," suggested Carol, concerned that a coldness was setting in between her husband and her firstborn child. George daily drove his sales route, yet no longer did he look forward to the dinner waiting for him at home. Once it had been the hour of lively talk between him and his sons. Now only Russell piped in with news of his day. Usually Richie ate in silence, shoveling his food in hurriedly, bolting from the table to go to his room, where the door would slam and the music would swell. Once George rose and followed Richie and stood outside his door and started to knock. But he put his hand down and turned away with a look on his face that touched Carol's heart. Richie had moved into his own world at fifteen, and he was denying his father admission.

During another dinner, Richie did mention that he had seen a coatimundi in the window of an East Meadow pet store. The animal was so unusual, "so cute," said Richie, that he stood and watched it for almost an hour.

The next day George went to the store and priced the foreign animal. Eighty dollars, far more than he could justify. But practicality and parsimony were not in his mind at this moment. All he could think was that if he bought the creature for Richie, perhaps it would rekindle the boy's enchantment with wildlife, perhaps it would even open the door to his room. Perhaps it would restore his son to what he had so recently been. With a poignancy understood only in America, George reached into his wallet and bought the coatimundi and charged the eighty dollars on his Uni-Card. Where else could a father attempt to stop the clock, to shove back time on a thin strip of plastic credit?

But in a month or two Richie grew disenchanted with the animal and gave it away to the Staten Island Zoo. "Snoopy" or "Nosey," as he alternately called the inquisitive creature that crawled along Carol's drapery rods and hid next to the exercise wheel under the Danish modern couch, held his attention only briefly. Richie had discovered something else to seize his fancy, something that George and Carol would not discern for a long while to come, not until the yellow house on the peaceful street was a battle ground, not until the owner and his son were in open war.

Chapter Eight

The political evolution of George Diener ran parallel to the deteriorating relationship between the salesman and his son. As Richie moved into his new territory with lime and fuchsia balls dancing over his head, with rock music shaking the house, George made a hard turn to the ideological right, where the principal colors were black and white, the only factors right and wrong. There was scarcely an issue of the day for which George did not have an opinion, reinforced by those after-dinner coffee hours with neighbors as conservative as he. It was as if the camera of his life saw everything outside his home in sharp focus; only in self and family portrait did it take images blurred around the edges.

Curiously, there would never be an intellectual clash between man and boy, with Richie participating in the peace movement or voicing militant notions alien to George's thinking at the dinner table. For Richie had no such commitments. The price of pot was more important to him than the purpose of Vietnam.

The trouble with his son was but one of the sores festering on George's back. He needed not only a villain to explain Richie's shift of life-style and the boy's puzzling truculence, but one to blame for the taxes on his house, which had tripled in the five years he owned it, from $400 to $1,200, for crime in the streets, for any and all assaults on the country that he had been bred to respect, fight for, and adore. George lumped all the symptoms together in a virus called liberalism.

" 'Liberal' to me is a dirty word," he often said to friends across his table. "I just don't see how anybody can be liberal. Look what they've done to our country with their permissiveness." Perhaps George could have said, "Look what they've done to me," for that was what he believed.

It had not always been so. Political thought was late in coming to him. His first presidential votes were cast for Eisenhower, not, certainly, because Ike represented conservative points of view, but because he was a hero, a military leader, and an object of inspiration to one who had embarked on a fruitless pursuit of heroics at the age of sixteen when he left Brooklyn for the sea. Seven years under the regimen and traditions of a ship, preceded by a childhood at the hem of Catholic nuns, had chiseled respect for authority in George.

In 1960, however, he switched to a Democrat, John F. Kennedy, not because the young Massachusetts senator was young, or possessed of grace, or bent on drastically changing the tone of America. And certainly not because he was liberal, because George lacked the sophistication to place him on the political spectrum. George's favor was bestowed on Kennedy chiefly because he was Roman Catholic—"one of our boys." "All my life I'd heard people say, 'There'll never be a Catholic President,' and I wanted

to help disprove that," he often said in explaining a vote
that in a few years would become unthinkable to him.

Because by 1964 George would vote for Barry Gold-
water, and in 1968 for George Wallace. From the benign
embrace of fatherly Eisenhower to the strident dema-
goguery of George Wallace was not an uncommon change
of direction in George Diener's world. He had allies up and
down his street: a cop next door, a telephone repairman
across the way, the butcher a few doors down. Even
though he wore a shirt and tie and suit on his daily spice
circuit, George dressed figuratively in the blue collar of
America's working class. And the decade of the 1960s
traumatized everything he held dear. Harsh criticism of
the American way of life set off sparks in his eyes. If a
man belongs to Rotary and someone says Rotary is foolish
and cruel, then that man is going to be angry. If a man
like George belongs only to a nation, then that is his
fraternity.

Though he never joined the John Birch Society, whose
name, address, telephone number, and leader's name are
conveniently published each year in the community di-
rectory put out by the East Meadow Public Library (the
listing is between those of the Auxiliary Police and the
Fire Department Ladies Auxiliary), George often said he
had a "sympathetic nerve" for what the extreme organization preached.

By 1970 George had a firm posture for the issues of
the day.

Blacks? "I'm not anti-Negro," he would say when conversation in his living room turned to rumors that a black
family had been seen pricing houses not far away in the
community that was 97 percent white, or that more and
more black students were coming into the East Meadow
school district to take advantage of its very good tech-
nical training. "I get accused of that, but I sincerely and
genuinely like blacks more than a lot of these liberals who

profess so much. But I like only good blacks! I'm talking
about a black man who works hard, pays his taxes, obeys
the laws, and brings his children up like I try to do."

Crime? "No wonder it's growing. You look at the crime
statistics, and you see that murder and rape and drug
addiction are going up. The reason is that the liberals don't
want to punish criminals anymore. We pamper them now
and forgive them because they had a 'difficult' childhood.
We turn them loose on society. If by some miracle they
do go to jail, the Supreme Court turns them loose."

Taxes? "Now, legitimate taxes don't bother me. But
what about your waste in welfare, for example? There
again, I don't mean to take welfare away from somebody
who really deserves it. But there are too many people who
cheat and chisel. And I help pay for it!"

School taxes? "They keep rising to pay for a school
district that has decided to let the kids run wild. Maybe
some intellectuals can handle it, but 98 percent of the
kids simply cannot. Richie does not have the maturity for
his kind of school. The ACLU even comes into the high
school and hands out pamphlets telling the kids what
their rights are. What right does the ACLU have to do
this? No wonder kids act the way they do; they realize
nobody can touch them."

Integration? "School integration is being jammed down
our throats by vote-seeking politicians. I wish integration
could come about normally, like in Hawaii where they
have four or five different colors that mingle and get along
without any trouble. There's no pushing or rushing over
there! But here, we push, and pushing is never for the
reason that the liberals profess. Integrating schools to 'improve education' is a farce. It's for *politics*, for *votes*,
nothing else! I would prefer separate but equal schools
for blacks and whites. It's a shame we have to worry
about integration, but we do. It's a shame we're not in-
tegrated naturally, but we're not!"

And, of course, guns. "The gun control laws they're trying to push are stupid. They'd only hurt the law-abiding citizen. The kind of gun control law I believe in is the kind that should punish people, not guns. In New York City, which already has the toughest gun law in America, the authorities never prosecute the use of a gun in the commission of a crime. They catch somebody like that and right off they drop the gun charge. They let the criminal plead guilty to the lesser charge of burglary. If I had my way, a person caught with a gun while committing a crime should first get twenty years in jail for carrying a deadly weapon. First! Then when that sentence is finished, they should serve time for the crime. A few sentences like that and I think the criminals would think twice about carrying guns. And bleeding hearts would leave the legitimate sportsman or the fellow who needs to defend his home alone."

When he delivered himself of such opinions, and when he allowed that his favorite film star was John Wayne and his favorite television program was *All in the Family*, a visitor newly in earshot might brand George a right-wing extremist, Archie Bunker defending the Alamo, one of those peculiars who stayed up nights telephoning talk shows, or leading parades against sex education in schools, or indoctrinating his children with hatred of Earl Warren and love of J. Edgar Hoover.

Such, however, was not the case. In the cloth of America, George was not the fringe, but the middle of the bolt. In the anatomy of America, he was not the brains, but the bone. There was no poetry in his life, no classic literature, no bookshelves in his house except for those that once held Richie's nature books, not even great ambition, for he had long since accommodated himself to the fact that he would always labor for the Friday paycheck from some other man. But there were values, ideals to which he clung tenaciously. He could not have articulated them to a Gallup polltaker, but they were his bedrock. They had brought his ancestors from Germany to Brooklyn, and they brought him from the malt and hops store of his birth to the expansive home with trees on Longfellow Avenue. And he would not relinquish them, even in the hurricane of social change.

He believed in hard work—eighteen hours a day did not tire him during those holiday seasons when stores sold extra spices to housewives baking pies and preparing special feasts; in love and respect for woman—a small elbow-digging remark of sexual innuendo was allowed, but no profanity in front of a lady, *ever*; in honor for the law—men smarter than he wrote laws, and he was taught to obey authority; and in the likelihood that his children would be better off—he expected no financial tribute from his sons when they were grown, but the rays of their success could warm the dark corners of his life.

Herman Kahn, the think-tank oracle, said in the early 1970s that "67 per cent of America is square and getting squarer." Although George had never heard of Herman Kahn, he would have agreed with the man, quickly positioning himself in the comfort of that vast majority. His hair remained short, his ties stayed narrow, his pants—with cuffs—tended to bag and the pleats went to the waist. A man's business, reasoned George, was neatness, not fashion. He had no interest, not even the secret prurience of salesmen with nothing better to do on a fruitless afternoon, in the new morality. Once he had liked movies, but they had become, in his fifth decade, either too expensive—or too dirty. The only film that George and Carol went out to see over a two-year period was *The Sound of Music*. Once he had enjoyed taking his pretty wife out to a romantic Italian restaurant, where he could watch her red hair glow in candlelight and take public pride in having won her. But now, more often than not, all he could manage was hamburgers for four at McDonald's.

Once he had been able to throw his arms about his oldest son and embrace him. But now, even though his heart yearned to do it again, to tear down somehow the barrier suddenly erected between them, something held him in check. The monstrous creatures stapled on Richie's wall were symbols of the dangerous forces trying to change his America. Already they had come into his house and captured his son. The only plan available to George was to harden his stance. He was too set in his ways to try and understand Richie.

And he was too old to cry.

Chapter Nine

"My main problem," Richie told Brick Pavall one autumn afternoon in 1969, "is finding a place to hide my pot." At first he kept his marijuana, carefully wrapped inside a sandwich bag, at the bottom of his desk drawer. But fearing that his mother would find it when she cleaned up his room, or his father on one of his dismantling expeditions, Richie began shifting the bag to random hiding places— under his mattress, behind his school books, in an old jacket pocket. "One night I was stoned and I wanted to roll a new joint, and I couldn't even remember where I'd hid my stash," complained Richie.

"Don't be so paranoid," suggested Brick. "People are always paranoid when they first start smoking. You see shadows and you think the cops are coming into your room to bust you."

Brick suggested a hiding place outside the house, not frequented by Richie's parents. Elated at the idea, Richie found a loose plank in the tool shed, and there, for several months, he kept his paraphernalia.

During this autumn of 1969 there developed a shortage of marijuana not only in East Meadow, but in much of America. It was probably due to Operation Intercept, the attempt by President Nixon to close the Mexican border to marijuana smuggling. With a flurry of headlines, television lights, and regular press releases, the project promised—with the cooperation of the Mexican government—to seal off the principal avenue of marijuana into the United States. While Nixon earned the politically attractive reputation of a foe to marijuana—a few arrests were indeed made and several thousand kilos of grass discovered and confiscated—an ironical development occurred.

During the brief American marijuana famine—it would take two or three months before illegal traffickers could develop alternate lines of supply from Colombia, Jamaica, several African countries, and by new routes from Mexico —some of the drug's regular users looked for a substitute. This flies in the face of those advocates who contend that using marijuana absolutely does not lead to the desire for something else, something more potent. In the majority of cases, this is no doubt true. In Richie's case it was not.*

Brick encountered the grass shortage of 1969 when he met with his regular dealer, a youth named Corley who worked now and then as a roofer. Later Corley would become a heroin addict and, while trying to work with a head full of the narcotic, would fall off a house and land

---

* *Dr. Victoria Sears, a psychiatrist who had worked with youngsters at the Nassau County Drug Abuse Council since 1966, noticed something of alarm in the autumn of 1969.*

"During those several weeks when marijuana was scarce, and expensive," she says, "a lot of kids out here turned to amphetamines, barbiturates, and even heroin. These were solid middle-class youngsters, not delinquent blue-collar gang members. The fact of the matter is that a lot of addicts I am treating today, in 1972, date their use of harder drugs from Operation Intercept."

squarely on his head, causing permanent brain damage. After that the kids called him Zombie.

At the time of their meeting, Corley had no marijuana to sell.

"Wanna try some ups instead?" suggested Corley.

Brick shook his head. He had bought some amphetamines a few months earlier and they had done nothing for him. "I can't get off on ups," he said.

"You can on these," said Corley. "These are Dexedrines, real pharmaceuticals." He showed Brick the capsules, brown on one end, clear on the other. "You know they're real when they have SKF printed on them."

Brick bought twenty. At the time they cost five for one dollar. On his way home, he popped five into his mouth and, when no more than ten minutes had passed, was startled at how rapidly the rush had come. "It's far out," he told Richie that night. "Faster than grass and a helluva lot better."

But Richie declined to take any. It was the pattern of his drug experimentation that he always declined, vigorously, any new plateau.

However, as his pattern also went, a few days later he weakened under Brick's salesmanship. The two boys were at the home of a girl Brick knew, sitting on stools in her kitchen.

While the girl watched with interest, Brick pulled five Dexedrines from his jeans and ate them with ceremony. Then he offered three to Richie. His outstretched palm was clearly a dare.

Brick later related the story to a friend:

"Richie grabs the ups and eats them quick. Then we sat there looking at each other. The chick was waiting for something to happen, like maybe our hair was supposed to stand on end, or our eyes would turn red and spin like a merry-go-round. Pretty soon the chick's mother comes into the kitchen, and, about that time, Richie and me got off. Pow! We were getting paranoid quick. I could see Richie was scared, but I couldn't stop talking. About everything and nothing. You do that on ups. You rattle on like crazy. This old mother was staring at us, like she knew something was happening. Something was, man. We were in outer space.

"Richie flashes me a signal he wants to get out of there fast. We go over to my house, and my mother insists on both of us having dinner. She always fixes a big meal. Richie stares at this heaping plate, and he gets one tiny piece of lettuce and a little bit of meat down when he pulls his chair back and runs out of the room. I follow him, and he's upstairs white as a sheet. He's trembling. He throws up all over my room. Jeez, he'd only taken three. Then he starts crying and I don't know what to do."

Richie was frightened. The next day he told Brick he did not like "the feeling of ups" and that he would never take them again. "I don't dig being hyperactive and para-noid," he said. "Grass is better."

His attitude toward ups was reinforced when Brick, unaffected by Richie's disavowal, went on a two-week binge. Taking an astonishing fifty amphetamines a day, Brick whipped about the neighborhood as if shot from a cannon. He told Richie he felt like a rubber band stretched so tightly it might break. "When it breaks," Brick said, "I'll come down." But deep into his two-week trip, Brick began to hallucinate. After forty-eight hours of no sleep, he telephoned Richie in panic. "I get in bed," he said, "and I turn off the lights, and I close my eyes, and I try to push out all my thoughts to get my mind totally blank—only then I suddenly think to myself, 'I'd like to see a monster,' and I think on this, and, sure enough, the monster appears on my wall. In color, too!"

At the end of the binge, during which he lost thirty pounds (amphetamines are sometimes used as diet pills),

Brick swore off them. But a few weeks later, Corley the roofer offered his good client some "downs," street slang for barbiturates. Other names are "reds," "rainbows," "blue devils," "peanuts," "yellow jackets," "goofballs," "double trouble," and "nimbies."

"These are Seconals," said Corley proudly. "The best." He pointed out the tiny word *Lilly* printed on the bright red, bullet-shaped capsules. Seconals, a brand name for secobarbital, are made by Eli Lilly & Co. They are powerful pills with various reputable medical uses, chiefly to induce sleep. One can usually not only knock out an adult for a full night of hard, deep slumber, but give him a slightly groggy head the next morning. In the late 1960s the drug culture discovered that a unique, albeit frightening alteration of the mental state could be obtained from using secobarbitals, often heightened by washing them down with whiskey or wine. But the rite was perilous; one too many of the capsules and the celebrant could sleep forever. The combination of barbs and alcohol could also be fatal.

"You must be lame," said Richie, when once again tempted by Brick. The two were walking from Richie's house to an enormous discount house in a shopping center one mile away.

"You're the one who's lame if you don't try these," said Brick. He walked over to an ice-water fountain at a service station, filled his mouth with water, and waited until he was a block away to take five Seconals. He had three left, but Richie remained adamant.

"I'm scared of downs," he said frankly. "I don't wanna OD or something."

"You're not gonna OD, dummy," said Brick. "I'm with you. You'd have to take twenty to OD, anyway."

Richie shook his head once more. "I'll stick to grass."

"Grass is good," Brick agreed. "Great grass is fantastic. But you can't always depend on it. You can always get downs. They're around. And there's less hassle. You told me yourself you still hate the smoke when you do grass. Downs are cool. You see a cop walking toward us and you've got a joint in your pocket, what are you gonna do? Eat it? You'd vomit. But you got downs on you and you *can* eat 'em. Fast. If the cop saw you, he couldn't prove anything. You could say they were M&M's."

Brick's proselytizing was typical. He was not trying to seduce his friend into becoming addicted to pills and thus dependent on him for supply. He was not a pusher in the classic sense, for the sallow man in the overcoat lurking outside school fences had disappeared, if indeed he ever existed. Kids turned one another on in East Meadow in 1969, for little reason other than social reinforcement. Brick needed an ally for his adventure, as any man does when venturing into an unknown.

A Nassau County narcotics officer once said that the thing that puzzled him most about the drug culture was "the glamour attached to it." How, wondered the cop, did drug-taking cease being a dark affair and suddenly transform into "a phenomenon of teen-age status"? *

Brick Pavall's testimonial and the dare contained in it were effective, as they always were with Richie. The younger boy suddenly stopped on the road and faced his friend. "Gimme those mothers," he said. He put the

---

* *In a 1972 magazine article called "The Suburban Hustlers," writer Jack Shepherd interviewed a teen-age drug salesman who lived not far from Richie Diener. The quotes he elicited from the youngster were chilling: "When I first started getting high in Freeport, there were maybe 15 people in town who also got high. It was really a new thing. Now, in all these towns everybody's getting high. It's all over. Seven years ago [in 1965] out here, it was like the real suburbs. Kids were still into surfing and beer drinking. Drugs were unheard of. In fact, kids who used drugs were put down by other kids: 'Ah, he's a junkie.'*

"Now, it's the opposite. Kids say, 'Don't worry about him; he's cool, he's got good connections.' It's the complete reverse. Now kids say, 'Ah, he don't get high. Don't hang around him. He's lame. He don't know what's happening.'

"Everything's inside out. The suburbs are the city now."

three red capsules into his mouth, one by one, swallowing them without water.

Twenty minutes later, Richie and Brick were, to use their favorite word of behavioral description, "wasted." The two staggered down the street in swerves and arcs. Later that night Brick telephoned Richie to see if the downs had worn off. Richie said they had, but not before he had difficulty getting through dinner with his parents. "They kept looking at me like I was a freak show," said Richie. "All the time I was afraid my head would fall in my plate."

"They shoulda seen you on Hempstead Turnpike about four o'clock," said Brick. "You couldn't walk, much less talk good. You were like some old drunk. Doing downs is the same as being drunk, you know. You either get in a rowdy mood, or a nice, mellow mood. Me, I get courage and I can talk to any chick in Ryan's bar and try to make it with her."

Richie yawned. It was only a few minutes past nine, but, he said, he could hardly keep his eyes open.

"You'll sleep well tonight, that's for sure," said Brick. "Me, I'm gonna take some more downs. I like to take about five around this time and stay up till one. I'll wake up tomorrow morning early and take two more—only I get off better and quicker the next morning on only two than on five the night before."

"It was really a weird thing that happened this afternoon," said Richie. He started to begin another sentence, but he yawned once more, said good-bye, and hung up. Barbs are, after all, sleeping pills.

Brick, buying more downs from Corley in a few weeks, told him about Richie. "Some people like ups, some people like downs," Brick said. "Richie likes downs. They seem to hit him quicker and deeper than most people. The only trouble is, he gets sort of smart-aleck and wise-ass. Instead of dropping out, like most people do with downs, Richie gets all fired up. He's king of the mountain, or he thinks he is. If Richie was doing downs and a dog ten feet tall came into the room, Richie would say, 'I'm gonna kick shit out of that dog,' and he'd go over and do it. He ain't afraid of anything."

Richie's reputation as eccentric and unpredictable grew in the late months of 1969 and early 1970. His classmates at East Meadow High passed around tales of his antics. Such as falling asleep in the middle of the Pledge of Allegiance during home room. Or walking in a neighborhood near his home and suddenly picking up an operative water sprinkler and tossing it through an open living-room window. Or the sandwich caper. After buying overstuffed turkey sandwiches at a delicatessen near his home, Richie and a friend strolled along Newbridge Avenue eating them. Abruptly Richie decided to enter a large catering restaurant, a vast, ornate place of stone, glass, and neon that specialized in wedding receptions and bar mitzvahs. Strolling into the lushly carpeted lobby, Richie stood defiantly among the mirrors and gilt. An employee in decorous suit and manner approached him. "May I help you?" he asked.

"Fuck you," said Richie, throwing the turkey sandwich in the man's face. The two boys ran out, Richie fleeing across a nearby yard. As he approached a fence to scale, Richie stopped long enough to kick an aroused, barking German shepherd.

Psychiatrists believe that in most human beings there is a repository of violence and aggressive behavior, but the brain throws up a barrier, a fence, to keep such in check under normal conditions. Secobarbital acts quickly upon the central nervous system to depress it. The drug will, of course, induce drowsiness and finally sleep. But it can also, through overdosage, rip down this mental fence and permit hostility, even violence to rush forth. In hospital operating rooms, personnel often must cope with the patient who, having received sedation for surgery, suddenly rouses from his half-sleep and tries to attack a nurse, or climb off the table with a torrent of curses. In his normal life, the patient could not conceive of such behavior.

In the first few months he used downs, Richie rarely took them before occasions when he would have to face his parents. Usually it was before going out with Brick, or on the rare evening when Carol and George were out. Thus the parents did not witness the sudden flames that leaped up within their son. Richie used barbiturates for more than a year before George and Carol became aware of them. There were no needle marks on his arms for a mother to spot, only troubling changes in his attitude and behavior. But were these different from any adolescent's? wondered the parents. That communication with Richie was becoming more and more difficult George passed off as the generation gap he read about and saw dramatized so often on his color TV.

During the year that Richie took barbiturates without his parents' knowledge, there *were* ample clues, but perhaps valuable only in retrospect. One came on a warm spring day in 1970. Richie and two friends were hitchhiking on an East Meadow boulevard. Thumbing was and is a common method of transport among the young of the town, particularly for those not yet old enough to own a car. East Meadow has only one bus line, which runs infrequently and covers but a minor portion of the sprawling area. But hitchhiking is illegal, and a passing patrol car stopped to so inform the three youths. They were instructed to get in the back seat of the car for a small lecture.

As the officer spoke, Richie suddenly flung open the door and ran away, across a nearby field. Annoyed, the policeman elicited Richie's name from his friends. They said he frequently hung out at a drive-in grocery where kids gathered around a cold-drink machine in the afternoon.

The policeman went later to the drive-in and saw Richie immediately. He was easy to spot with his shock of red hair. Richie also saw the police car. For a moment, he endured panic. In his pocket were four downs, purchased fifteen minutes earlier.

Richie quickly turned his back to the approaching car, threw the pills into his mouth, and washed them down with soda. Then he ran. The policeman yelled after him, shouting his name to let Richie know that he was identified. But the barbiturates were moving through his system. He felt, he told Brick the next day, "as if I could fly." When he did downs, Richie conceived that he could step outside himself and view himself as if he were another person. As he ran this day, he could *see* himself running. He was an impala, leaping great distances, leaving the cop far behind.

Another man had joined in the chase. By coincidence he was an off-duty policeman who saw the uniformed officer giving pursuit. The two doggedly chased Richie and watched as the red-haired youngster cleared a six-foot chain fence like a hurdler.

The off-duty policeman took the fence as well, but coming down he fell and fractured his kneecap. The other officer made the jump more cautiously. Ahead Richie ran with abandon. He began to laugh, his merriment at the fallen cop floating back on a spring breeze. Then Richie stumbled and pitched forward. A very angry officer pounced him, as the second hobbled up.

Driven home by the police, Richie was presented to George. No crime was suspected, the officer said, other than hitchhiking. But Richie had run. Twice! Flaunting all cries to stop and heed.

Sitting quietly, looking at the floor, Richie endured the scolding. George nodded in absolute agreement with everything the lawmen said. When left alone with his son, George asked Richie why he had run.

"Because I didn't do anything," he said. "When that first cop told me to sit in his car, I just got nervous and ran away."

"If you didn't do anything," said George, "you shouldn't get nervous. You must have looked suspicious or they wouldn't have wanted to talk to you."

"They're pricks, all fuzz are pricks. They're out to persecute kids." Richie turned to go to his room.

George stopped him. *Now* he was irritated. He had obtained a special permit to serve as a free-lance security guard to bring more money to the house. Often he moon-lighted, sometimes patrolling the parking lot at one of Carol's charity affairs. He felt kinship with policemen. "There may come a day when you need a cop," said George. "They're here to protect you, not persecute you. Don't ever forget it. This is a society of laws, and we must have police to enforce the laws."

"What law is it that says a cop can bust a kid for doing nothing?"

"You weren't busted. Now go to your room and get ready for dinner."

The next day George was called by a caseworker from Family Court who was investigating the report on Richie. The officer had added the episode to Richie's file. George said he was worried because Richie's birthday was only nine days away. "Then he'll be sixteen—and an adult under the law," said George.

The caseworker appreciated George's concern. He had just been talking to the high school to ascertain Richie's academic record. The school reported that Richie was not an attendance problem, not a disciplinary problem, but his intellectual progress was disappointing. "He's not doing anything close to what his aptitude shows he can do," said the caseworker.

George said he knew that. He was Richie's father. He saw Richie's report card. Richie was failing three major subjects, doing poorly even in science, a subject he had always excelled in.

George could no more understand this development than he could fathom why Richie, in the midst of a back-yard quarrel with his father over a task not done, suddenly picked up a pitchfork and flung it against the $400 above-ground swimming pool, puncturing its side.

In the instant before his fists clenched and anger flooded his face, George felt bewilderment. He wanted to cry out, "But the pool is yours, son! Don't you understand I bought it for you?"

Chapter Ten

It would have been difficult to live in the United States in the years from 1964 to 1972 and not possess a considerable storehouse of information concerning that cursed, celebrated trinity of drugs—marijuana, heroin, and LSD. Not only did they become magazine covers and newspaper series and sermons and political issues and thundering speeches in the halls of Congress and presidential declarations and tens of thousands of educational brochures multiplied by tens of millions of warning words scattered like propaganda leaflets into every school of the land; they also became song lyrics and theatrical plots and the axis on which works of literature turned. The film industry made so many drug movies—most of them commercial failures —that the subject finally became anathema. Surely any parent worth the bronzed baby shoes atop the television set could recite the symptoms and certain doom of youthful drug-taking as quickly as rattling off the seven signs of cancer.

But somehow the barbiturate story did not get around. Rather like a tumor growing quietly and unnoticed in the leg bone while doctors worked on something else at the neck, barbiturate use and abuse multiplied in the late 1960s and early 1970s until the malignancy metastasized throughout the body of America. "There are supposed to be 500,000 heroin addicts in this country," says a Nassau County narcotics officer. "Then there have to be a million barb freaks." A Los Angeles psychiatrist, testifying before a Senate committee, reported in 1972 that barbiturates were the number-one drug problem among the young of his county, surpassing marijuana, heroin, and LSD. He predicted that 1972 would be "the year of the Barb."

"Why is this so?" asked this psychiatrist, Dr. Sidney Cohen, chief of UCLA's Center for Study of Mind-Altering Drugs and among the nation's more sophisticated minds in the field of youth and pills. He was testifying before Senator Birch Bayh's Senate Subcommittee on Juvenile Delinquency, which held hearings on barbiturates in late 1971 and early 1972. "For the youngster, barbiturates are a more reliable 'high' and less detectable than marijuana. They are less strenuous than LSD, less 'freaky' than amphetamines [speed], less expensive than heroin.

"A schoolboy can 'drop a red' and spend the day in a dreamy, floating state of awareness untroubled by reality. It is drunkenness without the odor of alcohol. It is escape for the price of one's lunch money."

Other testimony before the Bayh subcommittee (which, incidentally, did not get as much press attention as the senator had hoped) revealed so many startling statistics, so many gothic tales of insanity, death, horror, and sorrow that by simply reading statements and Q. and A.'s at random one began to fantasize a drugged young America, lulled by a bellyful of sleeping pills, blissfully "down" save for those irksome streaks of violence before euphoria wrapped its cloak around.

Throw a dart at the map of America and almost anywhere it struck, there seemed to be a barbiturate crisis:

—A survey of one middle-class suburban community in Southern California concluded that 40 percent of a *fourth grade* was using barbiturates. Fourth graders, need it be pointed out, are usually around ten years old.

—In New York State barbiturates were being used in 1971 by 1.5 million workers, with more than 350,000 of these suspected of being addicted. Among the group 17 percent obtained their pills without prescription. Or, putting it another way, 83 percent got them legally!

—In Stamford, Connecticut, population 108,000, police seized one shipment of 92,000 illegal secobarbital capsules.

—Nationwide, arrests for barbiturate possession among minors jumped almost 1,000 percent from 1967 to 1972.

—In Fresno, California, police seized 760,000 illegal barbiturate pills in 1970, enough to supply 4.5 doses for every man, woman, and child in the city.

—In Nassau County, New York, District Attorney William Cahn, whose jurisdiction includes East Meadow, observed: "For the past ten years we in law enforcement have noted the steady increase in the availability of these pills on the streets and the dramatic upsurge in their use among our young people. No longer is there just a steady rise. Our communities are literally flooded and the trends of barbiturate abuse have reached epidemic proportions."

—In Los Angeles in 1970, 971 people died from barbiturate causes, almost four times as many deaths as those related to heroin. Many, of course, were suicides. But many others were not. Also in Los Angeles in 1970, more than 6 million illegal barbiturate doses were seized by police.

—In numerous American cities barbiturates were either

the principal cause or a contributing factor in an estimated one-third of major traffic accidents. "It is impossible to tell how many innocent people are killed in car wrecks by kids driving around with their heads full of sleeping pills," said one officer. "But there would have to be thousands."

—In Little Rock a federal district attorney reported alarming increases in the number of youngsters who inject, rather than swallow, barbiturates into their veins—causing not only a faster "rush," but a coincidental number of gangrene and amputation cases. The pattern was noticed elsewhere in the country.

—In Santa Fe, New Mexico, with a population of only 40,000 people, less than East Meadow, there was one death from drug causes every three days in 1971, more from barbiturates than heroin. The youngest death in Santa Fe that year was a baby who, thirty days after its delivery from a barbiturate-addicted mother, went into violent convulsions and died.

Barbiturate is the family name given to drugs whose ingredients include barbituric acid and whose purpose is to depress the central nervous system. This family has two branches, sedative-hypnotics and tranquilizers. A close relative is alcohol, the most widely abused depressant of all. Indeed, it is difficult to distinguish between a drunk and a barbiturate addict because both behave in the same manner. "Barb heads are the sloppiest freaks I encounter," says one caseworker in a Nassau County drug clinic. "They're always bumping into things, crashing their cars, falling down on the sidewalk, getting into fights. Same as mean old drunks."

In the sedative-hypnotic branch, there are many valid, historic medical uses for barbiturates, ranging from the long-duration types such as phenobarbital, often administered in the treatment of convulsive disorders and high blood pressure, to ultra-short-acting ones such as thio-pental, which are used by doctors as intravenous anes-thetics of brief duration.

The branch of the barbiturate family most favored on the street is the kind known as short- or intermediate-acting. The three most popular in this group, their trade names as familiar as breakfast cereals to a good percentage of America's young, are secobarbital, which Eli Lilly & Co. manufactures under the brand name Seconal; pento-barbital, which Abbott makes under the brand name Nembutal; and amobarbital, which Lilly puts out under the name Amytal.

Here, then, was one reason why the barbiturate story did not crackle across the public conscience so rapidly in recent years as did the tales of other drugs. Barbiturates are not grown like marijuana on the sunny mountain slopes of Mexico and brought across the Rio Grande; neither are they born in the opium poppy of Turkey and shipped to clandestine laboratories in Marseilles or Beirut for conversion to heroin and put in the false bottoms of suitcases to slip past customs in New York; nor are they cooked up by a college chemistry dropout in a Haight-Ashbury kitchen.

Barbiturates rarely have sinister parentage. They are, in fact, usually pure, carefully produced products of great American industry. They are enormous profit items for distinguished pharmaceutical houses. They account for 20 percent of all prescriptions written in the United States in 1971. They are supposed to be obtained only by doc-tor's prescription, sold only by pharmacists, kept under lock and key until dispensed.

But somewhere, somehow, something went awry because in 1970 the drug houses of America, according to President Nixon in a speech before the AMA, churned out five *billion* barbiturate pills. Of these almost half, enough to put the entire country to sleep forever, were unaccounted for and were presumably distributed on the street.

An angry man named Eugene Gallegos testified on May 3, 1972, before the Bayh committee. He introduced himself as an attorney from Santa Fe. As a director of that city's St. Vincent's Hospital, and of El Vicio, a drug treatment and rehabilitation center, he possessed sophisticated firsthand knowledge of barbiturate use among the young.

After revealing his city's unpleasant barbiturate statistics —a drug-related death every three days, 40,000 illegal pills flooding Santa Fe every few weeks—attorney Gallegos laid blame at some powerful doorsteps:

> In my judgment, it would make little sense to concentrate efforts toward the arrest of the disorganized "nickel and dime" dealers in secobarbital, those who are addicts or users themselves. We have staggering rates of unemployment . . . in Santa Fe and throughout New Mexico, and the supply of potential dealers necessarily is a large one.
>
> I believe we should identify and stop the major suppliers of, and profiteers from, the illicit barbiturate traffic. As an initial step in confronting the problem, we should identify those who profit most from black-market sale of barbiturates. In my judgment, those profiting most . . . are not Turkish farmers, corrupt communist politicians, or the Mafia.
>
> On the contrary, those profiting . . . are an otherwise respected, successful, powerful group—the American pharmaceutical corporations who simply must know what they are doing, and know the ugly consequences of their over-production.
>
> From my contacts, I am advised that it is all too easy for pharmaceutical manufacturers to overpro-

duce vastly the legitimate market for barbiturates, and to "dump" their excess production into the hands of irresponsible drug buyers outside the U.S. Questionable pharmaceutical operators in Mexico evidently have played this role vis-à-vis the Southwest, purchasing great supplies of barbiturates "legally" from American manufacturers, and then routing them back into the Southwest black market through Juárez and El Paso, and Tijuana and Los Angeles.

As indicated, I am not moved by the familiar protests of either innocence or unawareness by spokesmen for the pharmaceutical industry. . . .

I also am not moved by the laxity shown by the U.S. Justice Department in giving the black-market barbiturate problem sufficient recognition and priority, in informing the public, and in providing leadership in seeking solutions. In my opinion, this implies the potency of that industry's political contributors and lobbyists.

Narcotics officers on both federal and state levels would have agreed with attorney Gallegos on several of his points. That the pharmaceutical houses are powerful in Washington is undeniable. Not only are they generous contributors to campaign war chests, their lobby ranks in prestige and influence right alongside the gun and labor interests. That a substantial percentage of United States-manufactured barbiturates are shipped to buyers outside the country who in turn smuggle them back into America for street sale is also well known. Mexico has been a popular way station for American pills, because it has far less stringent laws relating to regular purchase of drugs.

The drug corporations sent their presidents and counsels to Washington for testimony before the Bayh committee, and each predictably insisted that their security regulations rivaled those of a missile site. Many stated that, alarmed at illegal barbiturate traffic, they were no longer exporting barbiturates to foreign countries and that their domestic policing of the pills was being tightened in every sector. Well and good. But, significantly, most *opposed* Senator Bayh's bill that would put barbiturates under Schedule II of the Controlled Substances Act, moving them up a notch from the less severe Schedule III. Under Schedule II, which controls such drugs as opium, morphine, codeine, and the family of amphetamines popularly called "ups," production and distribution of barbiturates would come under strict federal guidelines. These range from forcing drug manufacturers and wholesalers to keep such products in self-locking safes and vaults to insisting that doctors prescribe them only in writing and prohibiting refillable prescriptions. One drug-house president complained to the Bayh committee that if barbiturates were moved up to Schedule II, his company would have to construct the required security vaults and consequently raise prices—hinting darkly that the legitimate patient in need of barbiturates would have to pay the piper. Senator Bayh expressed no sympathy.

In the barbiturate matter, attention must be paid to America's doctors. As skilled as they are, as technologically rich as they are, they overprescribe sleeping pills. A recent survey of New England doctors asked the question: "Do you think *other* doctors overprescribe barbiturates?" Two-thirds answered yes, they thought *other* doctors certainly did. A staff physician at New York Hospital commented, "Anybody who walks into his doctor's office, in fact it doesn't even have to be his own doctor, it can be most any doctor, and says he has insomnia and is under tension or is facing a job crisis and must get some rest, presto! He'll have a prescription for secobarbital as fast as the doctor can write it. You can even ask the doctor to make it refillable."

There is a saying that medical students have fun with, one that seems to fit in here. "If a doctor had to depend upon sick people for patients," the saying goes, "he'd starve."

The American Medical Association sent its representative to Washington for testimony before the Bayh committee. He was Dr. Henry Brill, a proper, carefully spoken physician whose credentials included being a director of Pilgrim State Hospital on Long Island, New York, and a member of the AMA's Committee on Alcoholism and Drug Dependence.

Dr. Brill agreed that "drug abuse and drug dependency in this country represent a serious and growing problem . . . of such proportion as to represent a major public health problem."

But his succeeding remarks were frankly astonishing to those who would seek at least to slow down the flood of downs washing across America. Dr. Brill pointed out that barbiturates have a wide number of legitimate medical uses and that many patients require them. That remark goes without contention. He went on to say, however, that if the federal government placed such medication under the more stringent Schedule II, such action might not be a good idea.

"To add to the present restrictions on barbiturates so as to reduce medical overuse would be a disservice to patients who need them," said the man from the AMA. "Not only would it be more difficult to prescribe and administer such drugs in the treatment of numerous illnesses and disease, it would inevitably raise the costs of hospital care in direct proportion to the additional record-keeping and reporting that would be required of these institutions, where so great a proportion of sedatives are used in therapy."

This AMA statement should be dissected more carefully than a freshman medical student's cadaver. Does any doctor or hospital encounter difficulty in prescribing and administering a drug such as Demerol, a pain-killer, which is on Schedule II? Or even Dexedrine, a stimulant, also under the same strict housekeeping rules? As to the warning that charges would rise, this is a familiar bugaboo that the AMA has thrown up before. In opposing Medicare, they warned that additional paper work forced on doctors would drive up charges to the patient. Costs have indeed gone up, but rare is the doctor who, deep in his heart, now opposes Medicare. Most have been enriched by the federal program.

Dr. Brill further aroused the Bayh committee with this comment:

"Although we have no substantiating data, it is our impression that physical dependence is far less frequent with barbiturates than with heroin or other opiates, even among persons who take barbiturates chronically for medical reasons."

The jury is not yet in on exactly how addicting barbiturates can become, but there is little disagreement that physical and psychological dependence on barbiturates can be more severe than addiction to heroin. And that *withdrawal* from barbiturates is a trip more hellish and potentially fatal than any a heroin addict ever took. Even under hospital supervision, the barbiturate addict undergoes an excruciating journey of purge. Dr. Burton Angrist of Bellevue Hospital in New York has guided patients on such. On day one, the patient suffers tremors, shakes, a splitting headache not unlike a walloping hangover. On day two, there are generalized seizures. The central nervous system has become so depressed by the barbiturates that when it is suddenly deprived, it bursts through with a sort of eruption. On day three, hallucinations often appear. The patient hears people planning to kill him and he screams out his fear. Dr. Angrist once sat for hours comforting a patient who was being ravaged by an imaginary killer, an assassin who was whispering, "I'm going to hurt you and torture you and kill you." On day four, confusion, anxiety, apprehension rack the patient. There are auditory-visual hallucinations. He sees enormous bugs creeping across his body. He becomes incoherent. But he is nearing the end now of withdrawal. If he does not suddenly spike a fever of 108 that can cook his brain and send him into fatal convulsions, he will complete the course. "I know of little in medicine that compares to this," says Dr. Angrist. "It is sheer horror."

Dr. Brill, the AMA spokesman, also discounted testimony from district attorneys and narcotics officers who had told the Bayh committee of enormous seizures of illegal barbiturates in communities all over America. "The claim that billions of doses of barbiturates are diverted annually into the black market for street use, however," said Dr. Brill, "has never, to our knowledge, been documented."

Maybe not billions. When numbers become astronomical, there is always room for error. But as long ago as 1967 the U.S. Bureau of Narcotics and Dangerous Drugs reported that 117,558,000 dosage units of barbiturates were "unaccounted for." And the pharmaceutical industry, in 1971, manufactured 1,052,386 *pounds* of barbiturates, according to the BNDD. Of these, said its director, John E. Ingersoll, 73,000 pounds were exported, 130,000 pounds used in manufacture of rocket fuels, and more than 250,000 pounds, to use an industry catch-all phrase, were "consumed in wastage and additions to inventories." How much was wasted, exactly what "wasted" means, and how much was added to inventories would be interesting disclosures, because a quarter of a million pounds of barbiturates is enough to make around two billion doses of sleeping pills.

Dr. Brill's position, one in which he has a large number of well-meaning allies, is that no amount of fright statistics, warnings, scary stories, and even tougher laws will do much to alter the attitude of the American young toward drug-taking. In the last half of 1960, when the glare of publicity and public attention was focused on the drug culture, its members multiplied in biblical proportions. What might help things more, claim all the Dr. Brills of the land, are massive educational programs for society as a whole, a turning around of the Madison Avenue pill ethic in which television commercials demonstrate a hundred times a day how to ease most any human torment by easy-to-purchase, easy-to-use, quick-acting potions, and—paramountly—studies into *why* youngsters pop pills.

Valuable all, such suggestions. But to wait for them might be as tiring as to wait for Consciousness III to green America. A more immediate step would seem to be (1) stop making so many barbiturates, and (2) better police those that are made.

As for Richie Diener, who lived in East Meadow, not too far from Dr. Brill's own hospital, Pilgrim, just a few downs a week were sufficient. Here there can be no dispute whatsoever. He rarely had trouble getting them. If he could find the money, he could find the downs.

Chapter Eleven

Rarely did the Diener family take summer vacations, for the simple reason that whatever extra money was available usually went for items like the backyard swimming pool or a new animal or piece of scuba equipment for the two boys. But when Richie was sixteen, he and his little brother and George and Carol spent a summer fortnight in North Carolina, where Mr. and Mrs. Ring had moved in retirement. During the stay, Richie was well-mannered and polite, and he gave no hint to his maternal grandparents that there was trouble at home in East Meadow.

On an early-evening stroll with Richie in some fields near his home, Ring gestured idly toward a weed patch. "That's some sort of locoweed," he said to his grandson, knowing of his interest in nature. "Farmers try to keep the cows from eating it because they act crazy."

"Is that right?" said Richie, busily making mental notes as to the exact location of the weed patch. That night he returned and harvested what he had quickly recognized as prime marijuana, already in flower, six feet tall, and ripe for drying and smoking.

When he returned to East Meadow, the stash of grass turning from green to grayish brown in his suitcase, Richie could hardly wait to telephone around with news of his incredible fortune. Right away he dialed Sheila, his more or less steady girl friend at the time. Sheila, who lived with her divorced mother in a neighboring village, was two years younger than Richie and would date him for almost four years. She planned to be a nurse if she could get through high school, for her grades were as poor as Richie's. Less than five feet tall, she had delicate features and enormous black eyes, "twice as big as they should be," she always told Richie, "so they see twice as much as anybody else."

Sheila listened appreciatively to Richie's tale of the North Carolina discovery. His words were slurred as he spun it out.

"Are you stoned now?" she said.

"Can't you tell?" he answered, making his voice dance like a violin string breaking.

"On what?" she said.

"On Grandpa's grass. I told you."

"Just make sure it's grass and nothing else," said Sheila. "Don't start on me."

Sheila often worried about Richie's infatuation with downs and usually slipped it into their marathon telephone conversations each time they connected. Before the North Carolina vacation, she had threatened never to go out with him again if he did not renounce his pills. No puritan, Sheila smoked pot occasionally, but had grown both sick and frightened the few times she experimented with the pills Richie offered. "I can stop anytime I want to," Richie had answered in response to her warning. "In fact, I'll stop tonight. . . ." He giggled. "Because I don't have any." But a night or two later, taking Sheila to a rock concert, Richie popped reds again and fell asleep in the middle of the show, a considerable accomplishment in light of the decibel level.

On the way home, Sheila had repeated a position Richie was weary of. "I don't mind grass," she said. "In fact, I dig it now and then. But pills are a scary scene."

"Look," Richie said. "I do downs when they're around. You don't get hooked on downs, a person can't become a pill freak when he does them as little as I do. I'll never stick a needle in my arm, that should give you some consolation."

When he talked on the telephone, as he did the night he returned from North Carolina, Richie usually began his conversation in the kitchen, where the Diener phone was fixed to the wall. Then he would take the extension cord and move as far as it would go, either to the doorway of his room, or to the top stair of the basement, keeping his voice as confidential as possible. But Carol, working in the kitchen only a few feet away, could not help but hear snatches of conversation.

She heard Richie's brag about the North Carolina marijuana, and the next day, despite Richie's insistence that she stay out of his room, she went into the paneled chamber of black light and dangling colored balls. She found a large plastic bag of what she could now recognize as marijuana. Into the garbage it went, Carol burying it at the bottom of the bag under eggshells and coffee grounds.

To forestall a confrontation between her son and her husband when the loss was discovered, Carol told Richie that she had found the bag and thrown it out.

"But it's mine!" said Richie.

"It's against the law," said Carol. From the start of this marijuana business more than a year ago when the call came from Camp Red Cloud Lake, she had left the warnings and the lectures up to George. Not only did she dislike having to discipline her son, she reasoned that with one parent taking a hard line, it was better for the other to keep the flame turned down as low as possible to prevent the kettle from boiling over.

"Don't worry about it," said Richie, a comment he invariably used when the subject came up. Carol was weary of it, so weary that she almost flared at her son.

"Of course I worry about it," she said sharply. "I worry about it because I love you."

Richie cleared his throat by coughing several times. He spit phlegm into a tissue. The coughing was another sound Carol was growing accustomed to, and she suspected it was from his smoking pot. "Clamming," the kids called it. When four or five youngsters were in Richie's room and all started coughing at once, it sounded like a tuberculosis ward. Here was something a mother could safely challenge, a threat to her boy's good health.

"You're coughing too much," said Carol. "How can you smoke this stuff when you constantly scream at me about getting lung cancer from cigarettes?"

It was true. On the family trip to North Carolina, Richie had fussed every time Carol lit a cigarette. Demanding that the windows be kept open so he could breathe fresh air, Richie kept up a running lecture on the perils of tobacco.

Somehow, however, he drew a line between two different kinds of smoke. "Pot's different, that's why," Richie answered his mother.

Carol shook her head. It made no sense to her. "Maybe I could understand it if you'd only tell me *why*. Why do you smoke marijuana? What does it do for you?"

How could you expect to understand, said Richie's wordless glance. Carol would not accept his silence, no matter how it was decorated. She stood on the steps of his room, waiting for a reply.

"Because," Richie began, then, turning away so that his

words were almost lost, "because it helps me talk to girls." Carol was touched by the confession. She doubted if this was the principal reason, but there was surely a particle of truth here. Once she had seen a book in his room entitled *How to Talk to Girls.*

When George came home, Carol told him of what she had done and of her conversation with Richie. Instantly he tensed and started for the boy's room. "Wait," said Carol. "Bring it up at dinner, gently."

When the meal was over, George sent Russell, the younger son, out to play. Richie rose as well, but his father stopped him. "Sit down," he said. "Your mother told me what she found in your room. I think we'd better talk about it."

Richie stood behind a dining-room chair, drumming his fingers on its back. He gave the impression of being inside a soundproof chamber, that no words were going to reach him.

"There are a few things I want you to know about your marijuana," began George. "The first is this: it's against the law. I don't care if it's good or bad or if it helps you talk to girls or makes you sing and dance. Dammit, it's illegal! In this state, it's a felony to possess and use marijuana. You are past sixteen now, and you are an adult in the eyes of the law. You get arrested with this stuff, and you get a permanent criminal record. Then you can't become a doctor or a herpetologist or anything that requires a security check. Not even a cab driver can have a record. You certainly couldn't become a forest ranger, because they check those guys out good to get a federal job."

George hoped he would touch a nerve here. Several times in recent months he had tried to rekindle his son's interest in the outdoors. During one such conversation, George had spoken with deep conviction of his own unfulfilled desire to work as a ranger. Richie had seemed interested—so much so that George initiated the idea often. Rangers are set up for life, he said, "If I knew at your age what I know now," George had said, "I'd become a forest ranger. These people make a comfortable living and they have a beautiful life. Very little pressure, out in the woods all the time. Usually the housing is free. You work for the government so the job is secure as long as you want it. And, who knows, the woods might not even be around too much longer unless kids your age try to protect them." Richie had seemed impressed by George's suggestion, enough anyway to tell his sophomore counselor at East Meadow High that he wanted to study conservation in college and was headed toward a career with the National Park Service. But that idea had flared and died and Richie did not respond when his father tried to resurrect it this dinner hour.

George nonetheless warmed to his lecture. Point two. "And, even more important, you may be affecting your mind."

Richie looked up incredulously. "There's nothing wrong with it. Can't you read?"

"The verdict isn't in," said George, his voice rising. "I've read enough articles by prominent doctors to say that it *can* affect your brain. It's possible."

Richie shook his head in disbelief. He turned from the table.

"I haven't given you permission to leave," snapped George. "I'll tell you when I'm finished talking to you."

With a sigh of impatience, Richie stopped.

"Has it ever occurred to you," George went on, "that those places which have an open policy of marijuana, like Africa and the Middle East—well, just look at them. The people have no incentive, no ambitions, the countries make no progress. Isn't there a lesson to be learned here?"

For an instant, George thought he had gotten through, that he had scored a point. Richie seemed to be interested in this line of reasoning. But if he was, he only put the charge away in his head and returned to drumming the tattoo on the chair back. His face did the talking. Are you finished?

George, weary, nodded. Richie left the room.

That night, just before they went to sleep, Carol held her husband's hand tightly. She could feel the tightness in him. Ever the peacemaker, she spoke softly. "I still think it's just a phase he's going through," she said. "He's experimenting with marijuana because the other kids are, and if we don't make a fuss over it, maybe he'll get tired of it."

"I hope you're right," said George. He was silent a long time. Then, just when Carol thought he had fallen asleep, he spoke quietly, almost to himself: "I just don't understand why it's happening here. To us."

There is a widely held theory among those who work with drugs and the young, as either police or therapists or doctors or educators, that the drug process is a cyclical one, faddish in fact, with great waves of favor for one particular substance moving across the country, only to be displaced in a year or two by a new one. East Meadow, like any community its size existing in the shadow of a great city, followed the course with predictability.

Marijuana came first, in late 1963 and early 1964. History will note that two disparate events occurred during this period, and it is interesting to speculate if either or both were midwives to the birth of the grass culture. One was the assassination of John Kennedy, surely a President of the young. The second was the emergence of the Beatles and Bob Dylan as their troubadours, commentators, and prophets.

"At first," noted Frank Saracino, dean of students at East Meadow High, "pot use was of the 'weekend warrior' type. It was unthinkable to bring it into schools."

Saracino heard stories of a few youngsters "getting high" on weekends, but their attendance and behavior at school during the week was normal. By 1965, however, grass was as much a part of middle- and late-teen culture as a clandestine beer had been thirty years earlier.

"Kids are very fad-conscious," says Saracino. "They struggle to be identified with peer groups. They may mouth around that they want no part of the masses, that they want to be individuals and do their own thing, but they can't deny the comfort of the group.

"Suddenly out here it wasn't the bad guy using drugs, the hood, the wasted kid. It was youngsters with status in the youth community. It was kids who could influence others, kids who had direction, who were college-bound, whose prognosis was success in life."

In 1966 there was a brief infatuation with drinking codeine cough syrup and glue-sniffing, followed by a two-year season of LSD. Amphetamines, or "ups" as they were known, rushed into favor in 1969–70, only to be replaced by barbiturates.

"Where we are now," said Dr. Victoria Sears of the Nassau County Drug Abuse Council, "is, quite frankly, a horror." She was speaking in 1972, which, by early autumn, was scarred by not only the same national outburst of barbiturate abuse, but by alarming increases in favor for cocaine, and, surprisingly, alcohol. "I'm seeing kids who are turning from barbiturate users to acute alcoholics in less than six months."

East Meadow does not have an independent police force, nor do any of the some seventy villages and towns wedged together in the huge county. They depend upon the Nassau County Police Department for law enforcement.

Before 1963 there was no separate division to deal with drug offenses. Such investigation was under the arm of ordinary detective work. Only fifty-odd arrests were made in the drug category that year. It was considered less of a community problem than shoplifting.

When police noted a disquieting increase in both using and selling drugs, a separate Narcotics Bureau was established. Growth of this bureau is the most graphic testimony to drug activity in the county where all the George and Carol Dieners had put down new roots.

By 1971 the Narcotics Bureau of the Nassau County Police Department was the *largest single agency* of the force, its personnel far outnumbering those in homicide or robbery or even traffic, astonishing in one of America's wealthiest counties, where there seem to be more automobiles than humans. The number of drug-related arrests rose from less than 50, in 1963, to 3,257 in 1971, and even that latest figure was down from the year before because the Narcotics Bureau shifted its arrest emphasis from the individual user to the bigger fish of the trade.

A cop named Jim Henderson bossed the bureau during the years it swelled with men and arrests. A tough-looking man with a bristling crew cut, a ruddy face, and a brusque voice whose tone was that of a police report, he kept a large map of Nassau County behind his desk, with colored pins clustered together to mark scenes of narcotics arrests. Some of the villages were completely covered by purple-headed pins, indicating one kind of drug, or pink or green for others. East Meadow was heavily pinned, but by no means more so than a dozen other towns within a few miles of its borders.

When a visitor to his office in the winter of 1972 commented on the map, Chief Henderson thumped his fist against the wall. A shower of pins fell out and onto the floor. "It's not current anymore," he said as he leaned

over to pick up the pins. "We've simply run out of space."
He juggled a handful of pins. Each perhaps was a memory
for him, for he looked at them as a man browses through
a family album. "Right now the kids favor pills," he said.
"Barbs, chiefly. Pill-taking is so widespread, I sometimes
think we're only scratching the surface no matter how
many arrests we make. We don't know what's out there.
You'd need a crystal ball."

When Richie Diener first began using secobarbitals in
1970, he was not among the avant-garde of his community. For almost a year before, Henderson and his squad
had been encountering puzzling popularity for both ups
and downs. One November, four high schools reported
OD's in the same week. One child was carried out of
school on a stretcher. Such events came in rashes, noted
Henderson. When a big shipment of illegal pills hit his
community, he could expect overdoses for weeks thereafter.

During one such siege, Henderson was annoyed to hear
that a high school principal had gotten on the public
address system of his building and announced to the student body that "adulterated and contaminated" pills were
being sold on the street and it would not be a good idea
either to buy or to use them. "This seems like strange
psychology to me," barked Henderson to the officers who
brought in the report. "Why the hell didn't he get on his
PA and tell those kids that barbs are dangerous and potentially deadly?"

When Henderson addressed civic groups or student
organizations, he had a catalog of horror to relate. He did
not believe that youngsters could be frightened out of
drug use, but he did feel justified in letting people know
a few of the tragedies going on around them.

Two youngsters burglarized a drugstore near East
Meadow and stole 250 barbiturates. They decided to get

high. They sat down in front of the living-room television set, turned it on, and took two pills each. Checking their watches, they waited fifteen minutes. When that time had passed, they took two more because nothing interesting had happened. And, fifteen minutes after that, two more. So on and so on until each had swallowed twelve. Suddenly one of the boys said, "I feel chilly." He *was* chilly. He was dead. The other, discovered and rushed to a hospital where his stomach was pumped out, survived.

Another teen-age boy, known as a "garbage head" because he would take anything to get high, popped barbiturates and went into his mother's kitchen seeking something else to extend his high. He drank half a bottle of lye. The autopsy was particularly grim. One detective on Henderson's squad attended and reported back that the boy's esophagus looked as if moths had been eating at it.

In Roslyn, one of Nassau County's wealthiest towns, Henderson kept his eye on a poignant case. A father there was afraid to go home. His son, a pill freak, waited each night and tried to throw the older man down the stairs.

Occasionally a parent would ask Henderson how the pills get around and why youngsters take them. For the first part of the question, he had a detailed answer. "Just a few days ago," he recounted in early 1972, "we caught up with one local kid, nice boy around fifteen, who had phonied up a federal drug license and somehow obtained a pharmacist's number and began ordering large quantities of pills from drug houses. The day we arrested him, he had just received 15,000 pills in the U.S. mail. His total investment had been around seventy-five dollars. At three for a dollar on the school playground, you figure out his profit.

"He wouldn't have had difficulty in selling them, because the marketplace is any school, public or parochial, in Nassau County—or any other metropolitan area in the

U.S. for that matter. It's also the neighborhood street corner, the baseball diamond, the parking lot of the hamburger stand where kids hang out.

"So far the dealers in pills around here seem to be mainly kids or young adults, with no big guys from the city moving in—yet. We have no evidence that organized crime is involved. The main reason, I suppose, is that the profit margin is smaller than with heroin.

"Another source is the family medicine cabinet. If a kid gets into using barbs, a lot of them start their habit at home. All these mamas out here in suburbia who can't sleep have no trouble getting a bottle of secobarbital from the family doctor. And with a hundred pills in the jar, is she going to miss the ten or twelve her kid steals?

"Then there are forged prescriptions. A kid visits his doctor on a sham, and when the doctor turns his back, the kid grabs a pad of prescription blanks. He can read *The World Almanac* in his school library, to learn medical abbreviations in a prescription. We have kids going into hospitals and stealing prescription pads from nursing stations. We have burglaries of hospitals and drugstores and pharmaceutical houses. One drug manufacturer in Plainview came to work one morning and discovered he had been hit bad. There was even a trail of pills leading out into the parking lot."

After hearing Henderson rummage mentally through the colored pins on his map, one parent asked the second part of the question. Why?

Henderson shook his head. A tiredness always then swept his face. "I've talked to thousands of these kids," he answered. "None of them feel they're going to get hooked. All of them feel they're smarter than the drug. I've heard the story so many times. 'I took it first on a Saturday night and planned never to do it again.' Only by the next Wednesday, he's feeling a little low and he tries it again."

But these are logistics and statistics. *Why* do the children put, not beans in their nose, but pills in their mouth? "Hell, I don't know," he said. "Ask them. Ask a psychiatrist."

Dr. Victoria Sears never saw Richie Diener around the Nassau County Drug Abuse Council, although his friend Brick Pavall and parents attended group therapy sessions for more than a year. She never met George Diener, either, or Carol, but she counseled daily with their counterparts. Always their questions, those troubling ones, were "Why?" and "Why here?"

To answer, the brunet psychiatrist had numerous options. She could have quoted from the Second Interim Report of the Nassau County Probation Department's Continuing Research Study of Drug Abuse, a thick green report full of statistics. It held that drug use stemmed from three factors: (1) environmental and cultural change rapidly altering the face of suburbia and causing social pathology, social instability, normlessness; (2) the "vicious circle" concept, in which users need more drugs, and when more drugs come into the community, more users are created; or (3) the law of probability or chance, meaning that the mere fact of drugs being in the culture creates a risk situation for many nonusers, with certain individuals being more vulnerable than others.

More specifically, Dr. Sears could have drawn on any of the hundreds of case histories poured out in stops and starts and silences across her desk since she began drug work in 1966. At the very moment George Diener tossed in his bed and murmured bewilderment to Carol, Dr. Sears was counseling a twelve-year-old girl who was the adoration of an affluent, high-powered family. "She was a big hit in elementary school," said Dr. Sears, "a leader, popular, a good student. But when she got to junior high, she wasn't that much of a hit. She struggled awhile before she found 'popularity' and 'acceptance' through pills. She found that getting stoned won her a place in at least one circle of friends."

But that was only one child and one set of circumstances. When Dr. Sears drove her car through the gentle, groomed neighborhoods of the community where she both lived and worked, she noticed more universal reasons. These gave her cause to drop the clinical demeanor of a professional and speak more as a troubled resident and parent when she discussed them:

"In a healthy society, people don't use drugs. People have an identity, a purpose. People are too valuable! Fifty or a hundred years ago in America, kids would have been called upon to work for the family, to bring money to the house, to contribute someway, or—if they felt like it—to ship out on a whaling boat or look for gold or find something to do with excitement and dignity. There isn't that anymore. Kids feel that nobody needs them, nobody really wants them, that they are just another possession. There's nothing important for them to do!

"After the war, young couples flocked to East Meadow and its equivalents, full of dreams and bursting with enthusiasm. Everything was going to be great. A philosophy developed here—Achieve! Progress! Win! The pressure for achievement and the parental anxiety for their children to achieve became so great that many kids began to believe, 'I'll never please anybody. I'm bad. I'll get stoned.' They walked around East Meadow and they saw houses just alike, block after block, and there was nothing to do, no place to go.

"I've had kids say to me, 'If I don't do drugs, I'll be nothing. I'd rather be a dope fiend than be nothing.'

"I've had parents say to me, 'I wish my kid was dead.' Parents see their kids as extensions of themselves, and when the kid acts bad, they would destroy him.

"I've seen kids on barbiturates go into a 'Kill! Kill! Kill!' state—attacking people twice as big as they are."

When the Diener case broke that February of 1972, Dr. Sears was saddened. But not shocked. She was, in fact, privately surprised that such a tragedy did not occur more often in the little villages that nudged one another in Nassau County. "Richie Diener," she said, "was unconsciously demonstrating to his father, 'Here's what you are! A failure!' It must have been an awful time for them both."

PART THREE
George and Richie

Chapter Twelve

On a hot summer night in 1970, the front screen door of the Diener home flew open and Richie burst forth, leaping the concrete steps, bolting across the freshly mown lawn, his face consumed with anger. Seconds later, George erupted in pursuit. In his right hand he held a threatening small piece of rubber hose. For a moment he debated whether to chase his son to the corner, where Richie was racing to be swallowed up by the mob of kids hanging out there, draping themselves across lawns and car hoods, tape recorders shattering the languid July heat.

But he stopped. There were neighbors outside, this early evening, people leading normal lives, mowing lawns and sipping drinks. He did not want them to witness the spectacle of him sprinting down a sidewalk in pursuit of his son, who by now was surrounded by allies. Wearily, George turned and went back into the house where, once again, Carol's dinner had been ruined.

She was sitting alone at the remains of her half-eaten food, staring at the row of family pictures on the wall beside the dining-room table. The one common denominator in all the faces framed in gilt and fine woods, thought George, is a smile. Richie is smiling. I am smiling. Carol is smiling. If I came into this house and saw this gallery, I would envy the people who smile in these photographs. Where have they gone?

Carol quickly rose and started clearing the dishes. George knew that she did not want him to see the sadness that welled in her eyes after the last moments of this latest quarrel.

As he walked to the bedroom to put away the piece of rubber hose, George muttered to no one, "I told him he couldn't leave the house." George dropped the hose into a drawer; he had cut it a few weeks earlier during another confrontation and brought it out now and then as an exclamation point. Thus far he had only brandished it. Often he wondered if he could actually crash it down on the body of his own son.

George sat down on the bed and put his head in his hands. They come regularly now, he thought to himself. Almost like some grotesque play with performances scheduled regularly in the theater of my living room. I cannot even remember the opening scene anymore, only that they commence from nothing, build to something, building, every one of them, building to the conclusion of yelling and slammed doors and disobeyed orders.

Joining Carol in the living room, he could hear the noise from the corner. Perhaps he would call the police again and beseech them once more to break up the teen-age congregation that gathered each summer evening a hundred feet from his home. The first time he had called police headquarters to complain about the mob of fifty kids tearing up the sanctity of his neighborhood, dancing, taunting passing motorists, wrestling on the grass, the officer who took the call said that there had been other complaints, and that the nightly occurrence was being watched. A police car moseyed about the neighborhood, and a few youngsters scattered, but the next night they were back.

"Brick Pavall is the pack leader down there," said Carol. She gestured with her head toward the sounds, strong enough now to come through the closed front door and interfere with the television dialogue.

"I saw him," said George, grimacing.

Carol said that neighborhood rumor had it Brick threatened his parents, and that the bearded boy, now eighteen, was hiding out in somebody's garage. "He sent some little kid over to his mother's house for some clothes with the message that if she didn't do as she was told, Brick would burn the house down." Carol related the story dryly. She added, almost hesitantly, the information that Russell was swiping apples and cookies from the pantry and taking them down to feed Brick.

"Well, he doesn't stay holed up in any garage very long," said George, "because he's down there right now throwing eggs at cars and shouting profanity at anybody who is unlucky enough to drive by."

Pretending to become absorbed in television, George watched the program. But Carol, crocheting, knew that he had no interest this night in anything but the spectacle so close to his home.

At that moment, Richie was telling Brick of the fight he had had just to get out of the house. "Did you see my father chase me into the yard with the rubber hose in his hand?" said Richie loudly. "He stopped because there were neighbors around and he didn't want them to see him take after me with a hose."

Brick wanted to know what had caused the blowup.

"He said he didn't like you," answered Richie informatively. "But don't feel bad. He doesn't like Mark or Peanuts, either. Or me, for that matter."

"We all got hassles," said Brick.

"But not on Blackstone Avenue in the summertime, right?" put in the boyish soprano voice of Mark Epstein, who with Peanuts Coleson had formed an inseparable quartet with Richie and Brick.

The "Blackstone Summer," as it came to be known, was a phenomenon that lasted only a few weeks, but one that tore at George for months afterward. It seemed to symbolize to him the rot setting in, growing within his son and his community. So abhorrent did George find the gatherings that Richie for the most part obeyed his father's order to stay clear of the corner. Only rarely did Richie go there, and then by a circuitous route that he followed for several blocks, slipping carefully into the rear of the group, keeping an eye and an ear open for his father's house, so very near.

Long after the Blackstone Summer was forgotten by most, someone asked Mark Epstein what it had been like those hot months of 1970. The boy's face lit up in happy recollection:

"Nobody knows how it got started, but a bunch of kids started hanging on the corner, a few doors down from Richie and Brick. We used to sit on the lawns, sniff glue, nail polish, whatever we could get. Brick ran around with a can of Krylon in his hip pocket. Everybody saw it, everybody knew what it was for. It was a spray enamel, but Brick wasn't buildin' model airplanes, that's for sure. You'd spray it into a paper bag and put your head inside and get a quick high.

"The cops never liked the Blackstone scene. But everybody was there. Word got around. If you needed a place to hang, you'd just bop over to Blackstone Avenue and you'd find everybody you knew, sittin', smokin', sniffin', humpin'. . . . The music was good, pussy was always around. Everybody tried to make it with everybody else's girl. But the girls were tough. Like boys. They used to wrestle us.

"Brick used to kick cars and throw eggs and yell 'Fuck you' at any grown-up who drove by. The grown-ups would yell back, 'You seventeen-year-old degenerate!' Everybody knew Brick.

"If you were a kid and you hung out on Blackstone Avenue, you'd have had the time of your life. It was like a white ghetto. But it got heavy toward the end. Too many weirdos started coming around. If it didn't die out when it did, there would have been a lot of trouble."

Mark's memory went blurry when asked if he could recall what caused the Blackstone Summer to "die out." "Somebody got stabbed or something like that," he said. "I don't remember the details, except it was some hassle over the Chalkbuster album."

Was Richie involved?

"No." Mark answered quickly. "He didn't hang with us too much on Blackstone Avenue. His old man said he would beat the shit out of Richie if he caught him down there, and I think Richie believed him. I think that was the summer Richie started hating his old man. At least, it never got any better between them."

Before they went to bed the night of the chase with the rubber hose, Carol spoke with George. She wanted an end to the hostilities. "I think we should all promise to lower our voices around this house," she said, although hers was never at the pitch of her husband's and her son's. "I simply cannot stand all this yelling."

George agreed. "I just can't get through to him anymore," he said. "It's those kids he's running with. They're a great influence on him. Brick is everybody's favorite, and Mark and Peanuts are no prize, either."

"These kids come and go," said Carol gently. "They

always have. They fall out of favor with each other. School starts soon and maybe he'll find some other friends. Besides, anything is better than that Harold kid."

Again George agreed. The Harold incident had frightened him and made Carol almost hysterical.

It had begun in late May or early June, when George had first set up the backyard pool. Richie asked his mother one afternoon if he could bring a new friend, a boy named Harold, home for a swim. Carol quickly granted permission. She still remembered well the years when Richie had few friends, and she encouraged him now to bring classmates home.

But when Harold arrived, Carol was a little taken aback. Harold was a gangly black youth, with a mushrooming Afro haircut. He was the son of a pastrycook in nearby Hempstead. But he was polite and well-mannered, and Carol put aside her initial discomfort. "I reasoned with myself and decided it was all right," she told George, who allowed once more that he held nothing against responsible black people.

Richie and Harold started hanging together, to use the voguish East Meadow term. They became so friendly that Brick faded from Richie's room, which satisfied both George and Carol considerably. But the assistant principal from East Meadow High telephoned one afternoon and told Carol, "Don't get alarmed, Mrs. Diener. Richie has been in a fight and has a bloody nose."

Questioning her son, Carol learned in bits and pieces that there had been a fight in the school locker room. Richie suspected Harold of ripping off a rock concert ticket. Harold heatedly denied the charge, in turn accusing Richie of stealing his Afro hair pick. When Richie denied this, saying that he had no need for a "nigger comb," Harold pulled a knife. The black boy and the redhead squared off as a crowd gathered. In fury Richie charged Harold, knocking the knife from his hand and landing a punch square on his mouth. His opponent managed a few defensive blows, but Richie pinned him under a bench and pounded his face.

When someone yelled that the vice-principal was on his way, Richie let Harold up. Wiping the blood from his face with a towel, Harold said, "It ain't over, Diener. I'm gonna get you. It's not gonna be at school. It's not gonna be when you expect it. You won't ever know when. But I'm gonna get you."

Carol absorbed the story as best she could. She asked if marijuana had been in any way involved. Richie shook his head vigorously. "Nah," he said. "It was just a fight."

For the next few nights, every time Richie left the house, Carol fretted. "I die a hundred deaths until he comes back in that door," she told George. He dismissed her fears. It was only a falling out between kids, he said. And he was pleased that Richie had defended himself so well.

Then Harold moved away to another village. The tension eased.

One night soon after, Richie came home with welts on his arms. He had been jumped by "two black kids" working for Harold. They had sticks and they had beaten Richie severely. A night or two after that, Richie was surrounded by a gang of black youths as he rode his brother's bicycle in the neighborhood. Police who were coincidentally passing by broke up the "ambush," as Richie called it, before anything happened. Then a neighbor called Carol to say that several black youths rang her front-door bell in mistake, looking for Richie.

Carol begged George to intervene, but he was reluctant. The situation, he said, was something Richie should work out for himself. Besides, the less conversation he had with his son, the less opportunity there was for a confrontation. "My new policy," said George, "is silence."

Richie spent hours on the telephone eliciting the support of his friends. He told his mother that "horrible things are going to happen to Harold and his gang." Carol feared a suburban gang war was about to break out.

Her son reeled off so many promised acts of vengeance that Carol *insisted* George speak to him. She was so worried that he agreed. "I don't know what this thing is all about," said George to Richie, "but one thing I don't like is all these threats. All this talk of revenge and 'getting people.' I've heard this too long out of you."

Richie looked surprised. But he was interested in what his father was saying. George continued.

"The thing about threats," George said, "is that if you make too many and don't follow through on them, nobody is going to believe you. I hear you on the telephone threatening holy hell. I hear you saying, 'I'm gonna get so-and-so. If he comes after me, I'm gonna pull a knife on him.'

"Let me tell you something about weapons. Never pull a weapon unless you are prepared to use it. Because if they do come at you, you've gotta use it. When I was in the State Guard having riot training, I was supposed to be seventeen but I was really sixteen, I remember them telling us, 'Never fire over the heads of a crowd.' If you've got to fire, fire low, but fire to hit them. If they think you're just trying to scare them, you're lost."

George's remarks must have affected Richie in some manner, because he stopped announcing his intentions of taking care of Harold. In fact, the situation deteriorated and went away. Carol never knew why. She was only glad that her nights of waiting, "a nervous wreck until Richie came through the door unhurt," were over.

Toward the end of the Blackstone Summer, George and Carol were watching television when a man rang the doorbell. Answering it, George encountered a stranger, a man distraught and near tears. He identified himself as a Mr. Craig and he had a teen-age son who had just been stabbed on the corner of Blackstone Avenue.

Instantly George tensed. He dreaded the next question. He could almost mouth it silently as Craig asked, "Is your son Richie here?"

"I don't know," said George. His face was glass, ready to break. "Is he involved?"

Craig shook his head. "No. I'm trying to find out about the boy who did it. Apparently Richie knows him, or at least somebody down there says he does."

George felt the relief rushing through him. "I've ordered Richie to stay out of that jungle on the corner," he said.

"He wasn't there tonight. Some kid named Oscar told my boy to go to a record shop over on the Hempstead Turnpike and steal a certain album for him. When my son refused, this Oscar pulled a knife and pushed it against his chest as a threat. He kept pushing and pushing . . . and my boy's in the hospital."

Now George had enormous sympathy for the shattered father standing in his doorway. Here was another member of the bewildered parents league. "I'll find out what I can," promised George, "but in the meantime I urge you to call the police. Have this thing investigated. For some reason, parents seem unwilling to call in the police when their kids are involved. But we've got to stop what's going on out here. Please. I urge you. Call the police."

As Richie began his junior year of high school in the autumn of 1970, there existed in the Diener household a fragile period of tranquillity. The summer's violence—the episode with Harold, the stabbing on the corner, the flaring quarrels between father and son—acted as an emotional purge for the family. George and Carol took a few steps to extend the welcome calm.

Uncharacteristically for her, Carol laid down a bill of particulars for Richie with a firmness that surprised him. First, his weekly allowance of two dollars was suspended. Indefinitely. "Whether you get spending money will depend upon your attitude around here," she told her son. "On whether you mind your father and me, whether you do a little chore now and then. It won't kill you. You're a part of this family."

Secondly, Carol announced that Brick Pavall was not welcome in her home. "I can't keep you from seeing him on the street, obviously," she said. "But I can keep him out of my house. And tell him not to call here, either. Because I will hang up on him."

Richie opened his mouth to protest. He could usually soften his mother's orders, if not erase them altogether. Carol allowed him no entry. "And I want you to stop thinking your father is Simon Legree or something. He loves you very much and he would do anything in the world for you. All he asks is a little respect. I'm thirty-seven years old, and to this day I wouldn't dream of answering *my* father with a fresh mouth."

George went along with the suspended allowance idea, but he wondered if Carol would stick to it. "Richie has always gotten around you," he said.

A fatigue had settled over George, a hardness etching his eyes. Carol saw that the ugliness of Blackstone Summer had deeply marked him. The malaise was aging him beyond his years. He was only forty-two, but the thick curly hair of his youth was thinning and graying, and wrinkles not of time but of discontent creased his face. His good humor seemed cut off, a fountain suddenly dry. He read his newspaper in silence, put it down, looked about the living room, and said, "This country's getting as flabby as the tattoo on my arm." In more than two decades, the American flag had stretched and faded on George's biceps. For all the years of their marriage, eighteen now, George had welcomed each morning as a gift. Now, more often than not, he arose with the same mask of worry and weariness that he had worn to bed the night before.

At the dinner hour, which was the critical period of the day in which the whole family sat together, Carol tried to keep conversation pleasant and light. She took to storing up bits of family news, neighborhood gossip, some accomplishment that Richie had mentioned to her—a promising grade on a paper, a remark of praise from a teacher—and she would carefully deposit them up at the table, like hard-earned dollars put into a savings account. Failing that, she would encourage Richie to tell the plot of a television show she had heard him laughing over. Anything, reasoned Carol, anything at all to bridge the silences.

George saw clearly through his wife's careful plans. He knew Carol had placed herself as anxious buffer between him and his son. But he went along, as anxious as she to seize an hour of calm.

It worked for a while, only to be shattered when an argument broke out at her table over—over what, she could rarely even remember. Only the orchestration was the same, building to a crescendo of George ordering Richie not to leave the house, and Richie, eyes afire, disobeying and hurrying out the side entrance next to his room.

One night Richie asked the friend who was bringing him home near midnight to stop the car a block away from his house. "Can we just sit here and talk for a few minutes?" said Richie to his companion. "My old man'll be in bed in about ten minutes, and there won't be any hassle then."

But George *was* waiting for Richie. He heard the side door open and close quietly. He heard Richie's soft steps into his room. He waited until Richie had had time to ready himself for bed, then George knocked at his son's door.

Feigning sleep, Richie did not respond. George walked to the bed and sat beside his son. He spoke in the darkness of the room.

"There's something between us that I don't want," said George. "I don't know how it got there, but let's work together and get rid of it. We used to have such great times. Remember them? There's no reason why we can't bring them back. I was thinking that maybe next weekend, you and Russell and me could go up to the Vanderbilt Estate. Trees should be pretty this time of year."

Awkward gaps dwelled between George's words, for his lines were difficult to speak. He had rehearsed this scene, he had wrestled with himself and decided to make a heroic effort at "communication," but now that it was being played, he could not speak his words as he had planned then. He jumped at random from subject to subject, remembering to keep his tone low and conversational.

"This school year is important to you," he began again. "The junior year really counts. You said you'll be taking your college boards soon. I never even *thought* about college when I was a kid, and my father couldn't have paid the bill anyway. But if you decide to go, and if you've got the grades to get in, I'll help however I can. You'd have to get a job, but that wouldn't hurt you, would it?"

Richie shook his head in agreement. George reached over to his son's desk and turned on the study lamp. The small pool of light spilled over to throw shadows on Richie's face. How young, thought George, how very young is my adversary.

"The generation gap or whatever they call it isn't new, you know," said George. "We had it back when I was a kid. Even over music. My sister and I, we had to hate Kate Smith, we had to hate Bing Crosby. We had to hate any of the stereotype establishment figures of the time."

"Why?" asked Richie.

"Because they were establishment. My father put Bing Crosby practically on the altar. I'd say, 'Boy are they terrible,' and he'd get furious. I'll tell you something else. I experimented a little myself. When I was your age, the temptation, the big deal was whiskey. I remember trying to drink two quarts of beer straight down in my basement and getting sick for days. Then I tried straight whiskey and I still remember the foul, terrible taste. Even now I can't drink it straight."

George paused. He had hoped this would become a dialogue, but thus far he had done all of the talking. He waited for a response, but none came from the boy.

Now George made confession more honest than any he had told the priests of his childhood. "I'm only a salesman, son," he said. "I guess I'd still like to be a forest ranger, on top of the most remote mountain you could find. But I know now that will never be. I've been a salesman for seventeen years and I'll always be one. Maybe I didn't have the potential to be anything else. But *you* do. You can be anything you want to be. If you don't let drugs and those friends of yours mess it up."

Richie raised himself on his elbows. "What about my friends?" he said, his newly deep voice testy.

"You know how your mother and I feel about Brick. He's two years older than you, a high school dropout. I heard he got busted for marijuana. And it does seem unusual that Mark and Peanuts what's-their-names are two years younger than you. We just wish you'd find some friends your own age."

Richie shook his head slowly. "But you can't pick my friends for me," he said.

"I'm not trying to," said George, his anger stirring.

"Yes you are," cried Richie. "I don't tell you who to run around with."

"You're sixteen years old," exploded George. "And until you get big enough to move out of my house, I can tell you what I want to tell you!"

"Why don't you just get the fuck out of my room and leave me alone!" Richie pulled the pillow over his head.

George checked his voice, for it was about to ring with fervor for the neighborhood to hear. "I'll be happy to," he said, "and you'll be staying home all weekend. Is that clear?"

"We'll see," said Richie. "We'll certainly see." But perhaps George did not hear the last, for he was gone, slamming the door behind him, regretting his attempt at man-to-man. There would never be another moment approaching tenderness between them.

The next night, a Friday, Richie left the house before dinner and did not return until well after midnight. During those hours, he encountered Brick at a hamburger stand and spat out the scene with his father.

"That shithead made me so mad I ate two downs," said Richie. "Oh, and by the way, whenever you call me at home, use the code name Tommy in case one of my parents answers. Tell Mark and Peanuts not to call for a while."

Brick nodded. He said he had problems with his father, too.

"Not like my old man," said Richie. "I'm gonna fix him some day."

Chapter Thirteen

After writing two paragraphs of a history composition in his junior year of high school, Richie broke off his train of thought, took a red felt-tip pen, and angrily drew large X's across his work. Flipping the paper over, he drew three long, precise columns. Under the heading "People I Like," he listed eleven names, led by a boy named Bob Simmons, a clean-cut, popular youngster who was well into his senior year at East Meadow High, preparing to attend college and medical school. In the next column, entitled "Chicks," Richie made three entries, leading off with Sheila. Under her name, in parentheses, he printed in capital letters, "SOMETIMES."

In column three, under the title "People I Can Count On," he listed three again—Brick Pavall, Mark Epstein, and David (Peanuts) Coleson. Then he crumpled the paper into a ball. Later he attempted to smooth the wrinkles away by slipping it into his history workbook to keep. Obviously it was important to him, this document of friends and their rankings in his young life.

Between Richie, Brick, Mark, and Peanuts was a powerful relationship, one that endured spats, three against one, two against two, bitter denunciations, accusations of thefts and conspiracy against one another, and adventures that brushed them perilously close to the outstretched fingertips of the law. But they held together, glued not by their smallish size—all five feet seven more or less—or their lonely childhoods, or their poor marks in school, or, except for Brick, their high intelligence and natural aptitude, or even their parents—men and women from the same working-class mold who fled New York City to establish respectable homes a few hundred yards from one another in East Meadow where their flowers and children would bloom.

In their middle teens, the four young men built no rafts to float down a river of exploration, found no tree limbs to hang from and warm their bodies in an August sun, marched in no parades to save the earth, possessed no vision of who they would be or where they would go when the world proclaimed them adult. They held but minor interest in cars, none at all in sports, and little more than peripheral curiosity, embellished by bravado talk, in girls.

As George suspected, and as he would one day confirm through some curious albeit laggard detective work of his own, the weld was drugs. What Is Available? How Much Will It Cost? Where Can We Get Off? And, for days thereafter, What We Did When We Were Stoned! The actual consumption of the drug was perhaps not as rich in experience for the four as anticipation and post-mortem discussion. "It's our thing," Richie once explained to Sheila in defense of a drug escapade so filled with intrigue and violence that it alarmed her. "This is what we do."

The growing turbulence in George and Carol's home was not unique. Had they not elected to try and work out their crises alone—they would not seek outside help until the situation deteriorated much further—they could have perhaps gained strength, or at least solace, in learning that the same angers raged in each of the houses that Richie telephoned each day.

Brick Pavall telephoned his mother from the car wash where he had a part-time job wiping windshields clean. "I'm sick, Ma," he said. "Can you come and get me?"

Mrs. Pavall hurried there and saw her son jump down from an elevated place to meet her. Pale and trembling, he said, "I must have a virus." He walked unsteadily, like, thought Mrs. Pavall, a drunk.

"You look awful," she said on the way home.

"You would, too, if you'd been throwing up as much as I have," answered Brick.

At home, putting her son to bed, Mrs. Pavall brought up a question with studied casualness. Had Brick been smoking pot? In the morning? Brick shook his head quickly. "Nah," he said. "I took some pills." He felt so ill, his body was so convulsed with retching that he needed to make confession.

"What kind of pills?" Mrs. Pavall was alarmed.

"Downs. Seconals."

"How many?"

"I dunno. Three. Four maybe."

Mrs. Pavall grabbed her son's wrist to feel his pulse. She could not find it. His face was white and doughy. My God, she yelled to herself. He's going to die right before my eyes. He's OD'ed himself.

Her family doctor suggested on the telephone that Brick be taken to Meadowbrook Hospital, a large county health institution in East Meadow. Brick was kept there under observation in the emergency room for the rest of the day. While this was going on, Mrs. Pavall prowled the corridors and offices of the giant hospital, saying, "What do I do now? Where do I go from here?"

Spotting an intern writing medication, she rushed over and blurted out her story. "What can I do about my boy?" she begged. "He's taking pills."

The young doctor looked at the distraught mother with frank boredom. "They're all doing it," he said. "Your boy's nothing special." He returned to his writing.

Mrs. Pavall was not to be denied. She had seen the serpent in her garden and she was going to kill it. That the serpent had lived there for more than a year was something she did not know.

By collaring "everybody in the hospital," as she told her husband that night, Mrs. Pavall discovered the existence of the Nassau County Drug Abuse Council, which was less than ten minutes from her home. She ordered Brick there, despite his protestations that he could stop taking pills, stop smoking pot, that he could do anything she suggested if she would only leave him alone.

"If you don't go to Drug Abuse," she said with an authority Brick understood, "I will take you before Family Court and get an order forcing you."

Mrs. Pavall even persuaded her husband to attend. "There must be a *reason* why Brick uses drugs," she insisted. "Maybe we are factors." For more than a year, the parents attended weekly group sessions in which other mothers and fathers spilled out the problems of their homes and lives. Brick dutifully went for two years, with results that were at best mixed. Principally, there were fewer shouting matches between Brick and his father, not due so much to therapy but to the fact that the older man, a warehouse foreman, arranged his work schedule so that he would not arrive home until well past his son's dinner hour, and by then Brick was usually out with Richie and the others. This meant Mrs. Pavall had to set two tables, but it was a small price to pay for quiet in the house.

Brick told his mother that the two-year attendance at Drug Abuse did help his confidence. "I can talk to people now," he said. "I express myself better." That pleased Mrs. Pavall. She always felt that Brick's lack of confidence was the root of all his evil.

But Brick told Richie that the therapy sessions were "a farce." He went to them, he said, because "it's a good place to cop," meaning a place to buy drugs. "When you get that many heads together in one place," said Brick, "the parking lot's a fucking dope bazaar."

David Coleson, who as a baby possessed a large round head, a wisp of hair, and a look of world-weariness, drew the nickname Peanuts, after the comic strip. He could not shake it when he entered adolescence. By then he wore a look of solemnity, of wiseness, that would have suggested —falsely—that he was a scholar. Of the four, Peanuts was the quiet one, living in a land of silences. Richie would telephone Peanuts and ask, "What are you doing?" for that was the invariable opening line of every conversation, and there would always be a pause, a period of time that stretched so long that Richie would get annoyed and bark, "Shit, Peanuts, you asleep?"

Once, in fact, he was. He had taken four downs before the phone rang, and he dozed off with the telephone in his hand. Richie hardly noticed, for he, too, was afloat in secobarbital.

Peanuts was the only son of a cabinetmaker, whose home was a warm, beautiful place of color and rich paneling, bookcases, hand-crafted furniture. He dated his first experience with drugs exactly one week after Richie initially turned on, the night of the spring thunder.

Somehow in that first week when Richie, then only fourteen, originally turned on, he came into possession of a tiny piece of hashish. He urged Peanuts, almost thirteen, to join him. It took little persuasion because Peanuts had been exposed to the drug culture at home. His older sister, Vivian, then sixteen, was so deeply committed that she not only smoked whatever she could get, she eagerly put any kind of pill into her mouth, any kind of needle into her arm, any kind of powder into her nostrils. Richie called Vivian "super head" and, when Peanuts was not at home to take his call, engaged the girl in long, meticulous conversations as to the merits and demerits of various drugs. Vivian was a principal contributor to Richie's drug education, although he rarely even saw her.

During one conversation, Vivian hurriedly broke off because she could see from her window policemen coming up the front walk. Frantically she ran to where she hid her hypodermic needles, pills, and assorted drugs, only to find that her eighty-three-year-old grandmother had beaten her to them. The elderly woman snatched up the cellophane bags and equipment, secreting them carefully in *her* musty room, amid shawls and needlework and family pictures in swirling gold frames. Only then did she open the door for the law, berating them with the crustiness allowed the very old, indignant at the suggestion of drugs in her house.

Richie and Peanuts and a boy named Karl, who would soon fall from favor in the group and be pronounced hopelessly "lame" (the prevailing adolescent term in East Meadow to denote stupidity and unawareness), began spending the precious hours after school hanging around a supermarket. George and Carol Diener had spent their Brooklyn childhood in and about a candy store only ten feet wide. Their son—as did his friends—filled his languid time within the grounds of huge shopping centers.

The most remarkable change in Richie was the quickness with which he gained influence over people. For someone who had hidden from social contact during his childhood, he burst forth in adolescence to make his will known. Some of it was bluster.

He took to sending Peanuts and Karl into an Associated Food Store on what he called "errands." At first the errands were to steal fruit, or candy, followed by more detailed shopping expeditions to obtain, say, a certain color of fluorescent paint to decorate his room.

"Richie had considerable influence over Karl," remembered Peanuts, speaking with a dry wit to match his solemn face. "He persuaded Karl to steal some albums for him. He did this by hitting him with a brick. Karl quickly agreed."

Peanuts did not think Karl was shrewd enough to steal a paper clip, so he accompanied the tyro thief to a department store while Richie acted as "lookout" from another part of the floor. "I still don't remember how Richie managed to persuade us to take the risk while he was going to own the albums," said Peanuts, "but we did."

A security guard saw the two boys stuffing albums under their shirts and arrested both. Karl said a "redheaded kid *made*" him do it. While the two boys stewed in a locked office, guards searched the massive store and found Richie, furtively making his way to the exit.

Richie was taken to security headquarters, squirming all the way, shouting curses at the officers. He figured he could beat any charge of record theft, but in his pocket was a half-ounce of hashish, cut up into dimes (ten-dollar chunks). As the officer began to question Richie, he was called away for a telephone call. In his absence, Richie hurriedly hid the hashish behind a shelf of books.

All three boys' names were taken, and three sets of parents were informed. Rather than face his father, Richie ran away—but only to Peanuts' house. He stayed there a few hours until Carol called. And he went, gratefully, home.

During his hours at Peanuts' home, Mr. Coleson happened into his son's room and met Richie for the first time. "Nice boy," he told his son later. "He's polite."

Peanuts nodded in agreement. It did not seem appropriate to tell his father that at the very moment Mr. Coleson entered the room, Richie had broken off discussion of a scheme to somehow get back into the security office of the department store, find the bookshelf, and regain the hidden hashish.

Mark Epstein was the youngest, the smallest, the loudest, the most coarse, and somehow the most appealing of the four. Frail, with a rib cage barely concealed beneath almost translucent skin, girlish-looking with long hair falling to his shoulders, he could almost be called beautiful—except when he talked, which was most of the time. Talk poured from his lips in torrents: profane, imaginative chatter so swathed in fanciful deeds and plots that it was difficult for Richie and the others to know when Mark was on the level, if ever. Because he spoke in a choirboy's soprano voice even at fifteen, and because he possessed a remarkable gift of imagery in his language, it gave an incredible tone to the dark sides of his life.

One thing was certain. Mark had more drug experience than Richie, Brick, and Peanuts put together. And he wore it as a badge of elusive manhood. With no beard on his baby-smooth face and no more than 110 pounds on his stringy frame, when Mark talked drugs he was basso profundo and a heavyweight belter.

Mark entered Richie's circle during the Blackstone Summer, though the two youngsters had spent previous months scowling at one another in the neighborhood tradition. Immediately Mark presented his credentials to Richie. The stocky redhead sat spellbound as the skinny boy rolled out his history.

Like Richie, Mark was born in New York City, son of a father who moved through several speculative businesses —discount jewelry, "ranchettes" in New Mexico—before settling into becoming an exporter's representative. Mark was not exactly sure what the job entailed, only that it seemed to bring in money. "My old man makes bucks," said Mark in describing his father's occupation. "He paid $52,000 cash for our house in East Meadow, I saw him write out the check, and now he's going into condominiums in Nassau. He's religious, too. I go along with it —up to a point. I got $1,600 in checks for being a good bar mitzvah boy."

Thus establishing his family's financial position, Mark asked if Richie turned on. Getting an affirmative nod, Mark continued in breakneck fashion. "I must have been about nine when I first tried grass. Dug it! All these dudes who lived in Brooklyn near me hung together and we used to chip in and buy a nickel [five dollars' worth]. Then I had this uncle move in with us—he's twenty-two now and pretends he's clean, but I know better—but back then he was into everything. I used to sneak downstairs, find his stash, and snort it or smoke it. He was so stoned he couldn't catch his breath, much less me."

At thirteen, Mark said, which was a year and a half prior to his meeting Richie, he moved to East Meadow. "I didn't like the neighborhood," he said, "so I went into the crime business."

Systematically he began to rob every house on his block. He explained: "It's so fuckin' easy, Diener. You find a window at the back, and you tape it up, and you smash it and you crawl in. You look for things that are easy to fence. Like mink stoles, diamond rings, cash, of course, checkbooks, credit cards, savings passbooks, small TV's."

But Richie wanted to know, how do you get rid of it?

"For a while my fence was the ice-cream man," said Mark. "He deals dope, too. Cool guy named Monk. It's important to have a fence you can trust. I know this kid who stole two diamond rings worth $29,000, and he sold 'em to a nothing fence for only forty bucks, and he got caught. With a score that big, he should have found Monk."

Since Richie had never possessed more than ten dollars at any one point in his life—that sum either as gift money from relatives or for helping his mother set up tables at one of the retarded children's charity affairs—his mind leaped at the sums.

Robbing, explained Mark, was how he met Cantrell.

"Who's Cantrell?" asked Richie.

"Only the biggest and best dealer on Long Island," said Mark.

Cantrell was a Vietnam veteran in his mid-twenties, short, wiry, and a karate expert. "He can destroy people with just his feet," said Mark. "I saw him attack a guy once and his feet were flying all over the place, like propellers." Cantrell kept his wife, his baby son, and a large, variable supply of drugs in an expensive home on the North Shore of Long Island.

"I was there once and he had like 25,000 fucking Seconals," said Mark, who had quickly learned from Richie the name of his drug of choice.

"How did you meet him?" asked Richie.

"That's weird, too," said Mark. "I was standing on a corner looking at this row of houses and studying them so I could rob every one of them, when I see this guy. He says his name is Cantrell and he asks me what I do and I say I am a robber. He says that's a coincidence, because he wants a color TV. I say, 'Wait here a minute,' and half an hour later, I had him a Zenith portable, which he buys from me for seventy-five dollars."

After that, a relationship was forged in which Cantrell would accept Mark's stolen goods in exchange for drugs. "He's really a cool guy," insisted Mark. "Anytime I need anything, I go to Cantrell. He has everything a head would want—everything but heroin. But you have to know him before he'll deal to you. In fact, he has to like you."

Briefly into their friendship, Mark asked Richie to meet him on the corner of Blackstone Avenue. Maybe they would encounter Cantrell somewhere in the village. Richie said he wanted very much to meet Cantrell, but on this particular evening he was grounded. "My old man and me don't get along," said Richie.

Mark nodded sympathetically. "I can dig that," he said. "I stole a book of blank checks from my father and managed to forge $1,500 worth of little ones. Then I made a big mistake. I forgot to intercept the bank statement in the mail one month and he caught on. You think you and *your* old man don't get along."

By early 1971, the four boys were, to use Richie's word, "together." After several disastrous blunders Richie evolved into the natural leader, perhaps "chairman of the telephone" would be a better term, for he presided over where the group would meet and when, what they would do, and who was in favor at the moment. His were the talents of organization, usual good humor, and a bull-headed willingness to attempt anything. He was also the best-looking, a factor that, among the young, contributes to leadership. Brick brought a car and the veneer of a tough guy, which was valuable particularly with strangers who were persuaded by his heft, tattoos, and beard. Peanuts was the element of reserve, of wait-a-minute-and-think-this-over, coupled with a cold meanness when necessary and a sister usually so stoned that she could be ripped off when no other drugs were available. Mark was fancy, imagination, charm, and experience. "You act high when you're not even stoned," said Brick in summation of Mark's character. Peanuts estimated that if Mark did only one half the things he bragged he did, "You're still the biggest and youngest gangster on Long Island."

The year to follow, as Mark would often describe it, was "everything a kid would want it to be, a new adventure every fucking day."

Typical was one that came early in the quartet's being. One Saturday the four sat around Richie's room listening to music, debating how best to pass the rest of the day. Richie wanted to go to Roosevelt Field, the massive shopping center a few miles from East Meadow. Mark wanted to smoke pot and go look at the breakers crashing against the South Shore of Long Island. Peanuts didn't care. Brick, at eighteen the only one old enough to drive legally and the only one who owned a car, made the decision.

"Let's drive into the city and look around," he said, looking at Richie for confirmation. Richie nodded. Pleased, Brick produced a small wad of aluminum foil from his pocket and opened it carefully. There were downs for everybody. Richie went into the nearby kitchen and got a large glass of communal milk to wash down the pills.

Within ten minutes, Brick was driving on both sides of the street, careening within a hair of cars parked at the curb. The boys found it amusing at first, Mark crying, "It's bumper cars!" Then Richie cut into the laughter.

"Can you see, Pavall?" he demanded. Brick's eyes were half-closed and fire red.

"I'm blind," answered Brick. "But *I'm* driving. Shut the fuck up, Diener."

In the back seat, Mark produced a hash pipe and worked to keep it lit. Quickly he passed it around, Brick lifting both hands from the wheel to take a deeply contented draw. With that, the car lurched toward a parked automobile. Richie grabbed the steering wheel and prevented at least a sideswipe.

Suddenly the quiet voice of Peanuts came from the rear. "Fuzz," he said. Brick's drooping eyes flew to the rearview mirror. A police car was behind him.

Richie hissed, "Put out that pipe!" He opened the windows to let out the hash smoke.

"Oh, shit," said Brick.

"Beat his ass," encouraged Mark, making a suggestion Brick found hilarious. "In this?" he answered, starting to giggle, picturing his '62 clunker pitted against a 1971 police car.

The police car—sirens on and lights flashing—forced Brick over. He shook his head vigorously in a futile attempt to clear it.

Richie was on the floorboard, trying to hide a small piece of hashish.

Brick jumped out of the car and walked unsteadily to the policeman, a young officer who greeted him.

"Hello, Brick," he said.

Brick looked at the patrolman. He had been stopped by him before. "Something's wrong with the steering mechanism," alibied Brick. Strolling to the car, the officer looked down at the three boys cowering within. Had he stuck his head inside he would have smelled hash smoke.

Finally the officer spoke again. "Better get that 'steering mechanism' fixed," he said. Brick nodded hurriedly, edging back to his car.

"One more thing," he said, stopping the boy in his retreat. "I'm letting you go this time, but I want a few favors. I'll be collecting, Brick. Understand?"

Nodding quickly, understanding that he owed the cop a due bill good for names or information later, Brick got into his car, thunderstruck at his good fortune. He could never predict how a cop was going to act. "He's cool," said Brick, starting the car and attempting to drive a straight line down the broad avenue.

"I wonder if he ever saw four heads stoned at eleven in the morning before," said Peanuts, who had found the whole scene funny.

"To think I almost tried to eat this," said Richie, retrieving the piece of hash from its hiding place under the floor mat.

"You'd've thrown up if you were lucky," said Mark, the expert on everything. "Else you'd be dead."

Chapter Fourteen

After the initial commitment is made to drugs, the second decision to be faced is an economic one. For a few months Richie lived off the charity of Brick and Mark, who usually had a few dollars in their pockets, or a joint of grass to share, or a few pills to lend that had to be paid back promptly.

Richie's only dependable source of income was the fifty cents Carol gave him every day to buy a hot lunch at school. He often used this instead to buy drugs. There was always a girl who would share her sandwiches, or a cafeteria lady who knew Carol and could be counted on to slip Richie something to eat when he said he had lost or forgotten his lunch money.

But $2.50 a week would hardly buy a solid Saturday night trip, much less the other six nights and days during which Richie increasingly wanted a joint or some downs. By the spring of 1971, as he neared seventeen, Richie's dependence on barbiturates was growing. He told Peanuts that he would take one or two a day if he had the money. "Who wouldn't?" agreed his quietest friend with a solemn shake of his head. Richie was not yet at the stage where he actually needed the pills to function, but he found the dry stretches of days or weeks when he had no money and thus no drugs increasingly difficult to get through. It did not occur to him that both physically and psychologically his need was building. None of Richie's group believed downs were addictive.

Richie argued with Carol to restore his allowance, but she refused. However, as George predicted, his wife often softened when Richie insisted he had to have five dollars for a date with Sheila. When four or five days of relative tranquillity went by in the Diener house, Richie was smart enough to learn, then his chances of getting money out of his mother were good.

George noticed Carol giving the boy a five-dollar bill one Saturday evening. As soon as Richie left the house, he took issue with his wife. "Richie has absolutely no financial responsibility," he said. His voice was sharp, a tone he never used with Carol. "He's probably going to use that five dollars to buy marijuana."

"He has a date," said Carol. "Seventeen-year-old boys do go out with girls, you know. Besides, I think he's doing better."

George shook his head in exasperation. How could he convince Carol that, to his way of thinking, the only way to deal with an errant son is to maintain a united position of parental firmness, an unbroken hard line until months—not days—of improvement could be experienced.

"You're a very good person, Carol," he said. "You're the kind of person who thinks that giving a child everything he wants is the way to show love. I say that's the worst possible thing. We can't reward Richie just because he behaves himself for half a week. If he needs money, let him get a job. He's old enough. Other kids his age are working. If he can't find a job, then there are chores to be done around here."

Carol nodded, not so much in agreement as in termination of the discussion. She wanted peace with her husband, too. Life to her was not a continuing thread, but bits and pieces, a day to be gotten through, a meal to be cooked, clothes to be washed, a meeting to be attended, a letter to be written. She did not often look forward or backward as George did. There were no dreams, no fantasies in her life; she sought only calm. She was tired enough without disturbing fantasies when she got into bed each night. Above all, she sought calm. If she did not make trouble, then there would be no trouble. If she could buy five days of sun with five dollars, it was a small price to pay. And there were always memories of her own childhood, of how grateful she was to her mother when Mrs. Ring tried to soften the unrelenting sternness of her father. If a father is steel, believed Carol, then a mother must be velvet.

Carol did agree with George on one issue: Richie should have a job. She read the classified ads of the Long Island newspaper, *Newsday*, and she kept her ears open for possible employment in East Meadow. Hearing one day that a large discount house was hiring, she telephoned and received confirmation that young people were being seen for stock-room jobs.

Richie was pleased with his mother's piece of news. Together they planned what Richie should wear for his interview and how he should respond to the employment manager's questions. "You'll have to tell him that you don't have any experience," said Carol, "but that you're willing to work and that you want the job."

Carol drove her son to the store and parked the car in front. She looked over at Richie to give him a smile of confidence and a motherly pat, but the boy was suddenly frozen in his seat, his hand locked white and trembling on the door handle.

"What's the matter?" asked Carol.

Richie took several moments to respond. "I . . . I just can't go through with it," he finally said. "What if they don't take me?"

"You'll never know unless you go in there and apply," said Carol, worried that the old insecurity was flaring again.

Richie sat for several more pained moments. Then he shook his head. "I can't. Mother, I'm sorry, but I just can't. Maybe tomorrow."

That night, when Carol told the story to George, she fretted over their son's inability to go through with a simple job interview. "He has so little confidence in himself," she said. George did not agree. "He has plenty of confidence when he needs it," groused the father, "like when he talks on the phone all day long to those wonderful friends of his."

Inspired by Mark's sagas of easy crime, Richie tried burglary twice in the spring of 1971. His first attempt was on a house in East Meadow whose owners appeared to be away on a long trip. The lawn was overgrown, the shutters closed, yellowed newspapers clustered on the front porch. Following Mark's instructions, Richie taped up a rear window, hit a pane firmly with a rock, and reached inside to unlock the catch. Gaining entrance, Richie found the house, as expected, dark, gloomy, and musty. But to the fledgling intruder's shock, the house was not unoccupied. An aged old man suddenly appeared, ghostlike, from a back room. In a panic, Richie seized a broom and swung wildly at the ancient resident. He missed, and the old man kept coming at him with no sign of fear whatsoever. Searching desperately for an exit,

Richie found the front door locked. He ran wildly about the house, the man shrieking curses at him. Finally a rear door appeared in Richie's path and he charged through it, crashing against a window pane as he burst outdoors. A block down the street, running as fast as he could, Richie saw drops of blood on the sidewalk. He had cut his hand on the pane. The cut was not serious, but the experience dampened his enthusiasm for burglary.

"You're really lame, Diener," said Mark, when Richie told him the news.

In the first place, explained Mark, the seasoned young thief with the choirboy voice, you do not break into a house just because it looks deserted. A lot of families in East Meadow have aged relatives tucked away in upstairs bedrooms. It was true. An elderly aunt lived in Brick's house, and Peanuts' grandmother was the character of his home. After you find a likely house, instructed Mark, you get the name off the mailbox, look up the telephone number, and call. If there is no answer, then you go to the house and ring the front doorbell.

"What if some old man answers?" asked Richie.

"Then you say you're collecting waste paper for the ecology drive, or selling cookies, or that you've got the wrong house. Shit, Diener, don't you know anything?"

The second house fitted all of Mark's specifications. Only when Richie gained entry, he couldn't find anything worth stealing. Even the television set was chained to the wall. About to give up, he noticed a cigar box on a bookcase. Inside the box were twenty silver dollars, which Richie happily took. He expected to be able to sell the dollars for marijuana, but he discovered that none of his sources would take the money. "They're hard to get rid of," he told Brick. Finally Richie sold them to a small boy in his neighborhood for two dollars in bills. With that he swore off conventional burglary.

One night in Richie's room, the four boys got off on

downs. As he usually did, Richie underwent a burst of energy for half an hour or so before he faded under the power of the barbiturates. During his spree, he danced alone to the rock music coming from his record player. Then, seizing an imaginary guitar, he pantomimed the lead singer. Now he became Jackie Gleason, sagging his body, making it heavy, flapping his arms like an insane penguin swooping about the room. A remarkable mimic, particularly when stoned, Richie had the gift of evoking laughter in others, holding his three friends enthralled until the juices ebbed. He sat down in a corner and withdrew into himself.

An hour later, perhaps more, perhaps less, for the passage of time is tricky when deep sedation blankets the mind, Richie announced that to his thinking these downs were particularly good. They were not Seconals, for the "Lilly" trademark was missing. Nor could Brick vouch for their parentage, only getting assurance from his dealer that they were "respectable" downs.

Brick was pleased that Richie had gotten off so well on the dubious downs. "You're really enjoying your head," he said.

Richie nodded. If he could have one wish, he said, it would be for a large grocery sack full of Seconals.

Talk turned, as it so often did, to the dealers that the boys used as sources of supply. Tales of their rapid wealth were legend in the East Meadow drug culture.

There was, for example, a seventeen-year-old boy named Fritz who took orders for drugs on the telephone and then delivered them on his bicycle. After a few months, he moved up to a sports car and had enough money for tuition at Columbia University.

Another well-known dealer got a job at a large Long Island distributor of pharmaceutical products. As the story went, he stole a quantity of morphine powder, sold it at five dollars a hit, and earned enough in one week for a Kharman-Ghia automobile, a vacation in Florida, and a lavish wardrobe. While on holiday he met a beautiful girl and married her, still on the proceeds of his one week's drug sales. "He has a kid now and is totally straight," said Brick.

Mark's friend Cantrell, the Vietnam veteran with the karate chop, remained the most dependable source of marijuana and pills, but—as Mark frequently pointed out— Richie almost ruined the connection. Richie had never met the famous dealer, but Mark had once pointed him out on the street. Later, Richie went up to Cantrell and asked if he could buy downs.

"What the fuck are you talking about?" hissed Cantrell. Richie backed off quickly, fearful of the karate feet. "Get away from me, shithead," shouted Cantrell.

It took Mark several days to pacify his dealer, and he scolded Richie for having tampered with him. "I told you that Cantrell doesn't sell to just anybody," repeated Mark with annoyance. "I told you he has to *like* you."

The very downs that affected Richie as he sat in the corner of his room, with his friends stoned and scattered about him, had come from Cantrell. Mark had been "fronted" with one hundred dollars' worth of Seconals by the dealer, which meant that Cantrell trusted the youngster enough to let him have the drugs on consignment. When Mark sold them, he paid Cantrell the asking price, pocketed a small profit, and had enough pills to use himself, and to give to his friends as he had done.

Richie had a question. From where did Cantrell get his merchandise?

Mark did not know for sure, but he suspected the next step up the ladder was another young man, about twenty-three, who was often seen around East Meadow in a beat-up, nondescript Dodge. "I saw him once at Cantrell's," said Mark, "a real bum-looking guy, but he had like fifty pounds of hash in the trunk of his car. It was all in fertilizer bags stamped IMPORTED FROM LEBANON."

Beyond him? "It's somebody big in New York," speculated Mark, "somebody rich and quiet and unknown."

Brick perked up. It was difficult for him to talk when stoned because his words slurred together in a guttural groan. Usually he would lose track of what he was saying in the middle of his anecdote, and the others would have to remind him where he left off. Once, Brick said, he had been taken by a friend to a large and rambling house in the fashionable Westbury area of Long Island. "This older guy owned it, about forty-five," said Brick. "He took us to this back room and there was a secret wall. Like in the movies. Behind it were garbage cans full of dope—pot, pills, whatever you'd want. Like thousands, man, like tens of thousands of everything!"

"What'd you do?" asked Richie excitedly.

"I got sick just thinking about it."

"Why don't we rip him off?" said Richie.

Brick looked blank. For the moment he could not figure out who Richie was speaking of. "Who do you mean?" slurred Brick.

"That dude. The one with the garbage cans full of dope."

Brick frowned. He was back in focus. "You'd get dead very quick if you messed with this guy."

The two boys ambled through the sprawling covered Roosevelt Field shopping center, a few miles from East Meadow, stopping in front of a boutique where teen-age girls danced in and out, to the tempo of rock music blaring from speakers. In youthful lettering, the store's name was "Ups 'n Downs," which on one level meant pants and tops. But both Richie and Mark smiled at the *double entendre.* "I may open a shop called 'Reds for Heads,'" said Richie.

At the department store that was their destination, Mark hesitated before going in. He had briefed Richie several times, but he wanted to make sure, as commanding officer, that his instructions had been absorbed.

"First," repeated Mark once more, "we make sure this chick is working today in the record shop." His reference was to a girl he knew who "looked the other way" when Mark walked out of the department with a bulge under his jacket. "If my connection isn't there," said Mark, "we just look around and leave—without taking anything."

Richie nodded, impatiently. He was getting bored with Mark's battle plan.

"Wait," said Mark. "Remember, you walk around casually, like you were browsing. You pick out a record, you go into the listening booth. Maybe you pretend you don't like it, and you put it back neatly. After a while you start selecting the ones you want to rip off. You keep them under your arm. The most I ever ripped off was thirty, but don't take more than you can fit into the crook of your arm."

Mark demonstrated how to slip the stolen records under the left arm. "Then you slip your jacket over your shoulder. Don't try to put it on, because it won't work."

"I know . . . I know."

"Most important," instructed Mark. "Don't take all the records out of one slot, like all of the Stones. Don't, repeat, *don't* take the whole category. You've gotta be cool—or you'll blow this girl for everybody."

Strolling into the record department together, Mark and Richie split by plan and began browsing. In less than fifteen minutes, Mark glanced up and saw Richie almost bulling his way out of the store, exiting in a hurry with a huge bulge beneath his jacket.

Mark's eyes quickly swept the counter where Richie

had been "shopping." Two full categories—Led Zeppelin and Paul McCartney—were gone. Only the dividing partitions with the artists' names remained in the rack.

Outside the store, at their prearranged meeting place, Richie waited eagerly for Mark, who approached with noticeable anger. With pride, Richie displayed the twenty records under his jacket. Mark looked at them with disdain. "I told you not to rip off whole categories," he said. "The manager's bound to notice, and if that girl gets fired, the whole thing is blown forever."

Richie was dismayed. He had expected congratulations from his captain. "I got nervous," he said. "I saw this guy in a suit watching some other kids."

Later that day Mark took the records to his fence, a nineteen-year-old East Meadow boy of rich parentage who paid $2.50 for each new album, provided he liked them and provided the cellophane wrapper was still intact. Sometimes he even gave Mark shopping lists of music he desired. When the youth rejected albums, Mark offered them to Cantrell in exchange for marijuana, or, failing that, peddled them to youngsters in his neighborhood for fifty cents, a quarter, anything they would bring.

Despite Richie's gaffe, his share of the escapade earned him eleven dollars, which he used to buy a quarter ounce of marijuana and a handful of downs. Within days he exhorted Mark to try again. Richie lacked the courage to attempt the job by himself, and he did not yet know the all-important girl clerk who would "look the other way."

Mark agreed to give his friend one more chance. A few Saturday afternoons later, they entered the record department. The shop was crowded with young people, which pleased Mark because this would make his exit more graceful. He tried to keep one eye on Richie's meanderings, another on the shop manager, and at the same time browse nonchalantly. Suddenly Mark saw Richie taking advantage of a crowd of people at the cash register, using them as cover to sneak out with records under his jacket. Only a few minutes had passed, not enough for Richie to conduct a leisurely shopping tour. Irked once more, Mark left the record department without taking anything and caught up with Richie at the elevator. Richie unzipped his jacket enough for Mark to glance quickly at the albums inside.

Once again Richie had taken an entire category—every Jefferson Airplane album on the display counter. Mark anxiously looked back toward the record department. Two men in business suits were pointing toward the elevator, pointing at them.

"Shit," snapped Mark. "Now you've done it." Fortunately the elevator doors opened, and the two boys leaped inside. Mark hammered on the Close button to make the doors shut. Directly before him, the two men approached purposefully. When they were only twenty feet away, when Mark was trembling and a very frightened little boy, the doors glided together. On the next floor up, Richie took his stolen records and shoved them under a pile of remnants on a sale table.

"Don't look back," said Mark. "Take your jacket off like you were hot and sort of carry it." Richie did as he was told. The two boys managed to leave the store and disappear into the afternoon shopping throng outside without being stopped.

"That's it," said Mark. "You're a hopeless robber, Diener."

By the end of the day, Mark had told Brick and Peanuts how Richie bungled the rip-off. He expected a point or two of status to come his way, he being the master thief trying to manage the incompetent apprentice. But Mark was the weakest member of the quartet, and his disapproval of anybody was worth little.

Richie remained silent a few days in face of Mark's

criticism. He refused to discuss the matter with Brick or Peanuts, either. But one night, late, he telephoned Mark and came icily to the subject.

"I hear you've been talking about me," Richie said. His voice was flat. Mark knew he was stoned because there was a floating, disconnected tempo from Richie. But he had never felt his friend's wrath before. "I may not do things your way," said Richie. "But that ain't necessarily the best way." He hung up.

When several more days passed without a phone call from Richie, when even Brick and Peanuts ducked his calls, Mark's insecurity chewed holes in him. He called Richie up and mumbled an apology. Perhaps, he suggested, they could steal albums at another East Meadow store, a large discount house named Modell's.

"Can't," said Richie. "I'm just leaving for Roosevelt Field."

"You gonna rip something off there?" asked Mark, anxious to be invited along.

"Nah. My mother gave me money to buy a shirt."

"Why don't you just rip off the shirt and keep the money? I could help you."

"I may. I may not. I can manage."

Mark swallowed all the humble pie. "Can I come with you?" he almost begged.

"My mother's dropping me off. You'll have to meet me there."

Mark agreed, gratefully.

Making their way across the store, something caught Mark's attention and he told Richie he would meet him at the shirt counter. A few minutes later, Mark appeared there with cream on his whiskers. Richie held a package in his hands.

"You *bought* the shirt?" Mark asked incredulously.

"I bought one," said Richie, "and I borrowed one." He patted the package. "What'd you do?"

Smiling enigmatically, Mark started walking out. Richie kept pace with him. "It's very difficult for me to get through this store without ripping something off," said Mark quietly.

Richie glanced at his friend. He had no bulges of betrayal. "What'd you take?" he asked.

Mark fingered the cut of his blue pilot's jacket.

"You already had that on when you came here," scoffed Richie.

"Wrong," said Mark proudly. "I had one just like it—only cheaper and with no lining." Mark opened his stolen coat to flash a bright orange interior. "I saw a big rack of these and I just sort of switched," he said. "Then I put my cigarettes and some tobacco crumbs in the pocket of this one so it would look like I already had it on."

Richie nodded. He was impressed.

At a counter of watches and pendants, Richie stopped to look. Mark nudged him with a worried elbow. "There're two guys in suits following us," he whispered. "Every time we stop, *they* stop." He gestured with his eyes to a pair of obvious store detectives some fifty feet away.

"Walk out casually," said Richie, suddenly in command. "Whatever you do, don't look back."

But Mark could not resist a glance to the rear. The two detectives were but a few feet behind, within earshot.

Richie, keeping his eyes straight ahead, spoke in a strong voice that carried well behind him. "I'm sick and tired of being hassled by fuzz for things I didn't do," he said. Richie reached into his jacket and pulled out a small piece of rubber hose—probably the one George had cut as a weapon of discipline. Thumping it with one hand into the palm of the other, Richie went on, loudly, "If any motherfuckin' dicks try to hassle me, I'm gonna hit 'em with this. I'm fed up with taking the blame for what other kids do."

Whether Richie's remarks frightened the detectives, or

whether they merely sought to avoid a nasty scene in the crowded store, the two men took an abrupt right turn and permitted the two boys to leave the store.

As the two youngsters waited beside Carol's car for her return from shopping, Mark thanked Richie. "I'm on probation," he said, "and I'd kill before I'd go back to the Children's Shelter."

Richie accepted his friend's due bill.

This escapade quickly went the rounds of the group. All who heard it nodded in admiration of Richie's show of strength. Mark told Peanuts, "Diener's weird sometimes, he has a fucked-up attitude, but when it counts he gets his head together good."

Carol read Richie's next-to-last report card toward the end of the school year in spring, 1971, and put her head in her hands. In his junior year, Richie was failing algebra, failing typing, barely passing history and English, making a very low 72 in Earth science.

When George came in she showed him the dismal list.

"How can he make grades like these," she said, "when he did so well on his college boards?" On that test, Richie had scored 480 verbal, 520 math, "enough," the counselor at school said "for Richie to get in most colleges anywhere, any one except the Ivy League."

"I don't find it surprising at all," said George. "He doesn't study, he won't even stay home when I tell him to. Might be the best thing that could happen to him if he got kicked out of school."

Carol shook her head. This was not what she wanted. "Why don't you talk to him?" she said.

George snorted at her idea. "We don't speak. Haven't you noticed? If I don't talk to him, he doesn't yell at me, and if he doesn't yell at me, then there's quiet around the house."

With a sigh, Carol wondered if she ever did anything right. More and more she found herself not as buffer, but as victim, damned if she did, damned if she didn't. "You act like you've given up on him," said Carol.

George measured his response. Now seemed as good a time as any to let his wife know exactly how he felt. "I've been thinking," he said candidly, "that if we can just raise him up to eighteen, then maybe he'll leave, or go into the army, or get out on his own."

"You mean *put* him out, don't you?" said Carol, alarmed.

"I didn't say that," answered George. But Carol worried that what he said and what he meant were two different things.

Chapter Fifteen

On a fine early spring day in 1971, two years after Richie became a user of first pot, then pills, George Diener stole three hours from his grocery route. He was sitting instead on a bench in a crowded hallway of despair in the Family Court building of Nassau County. When his name was finally called, he told the harried young woman at the information desk, "My name is George Diener, and I want to file a wayward conduct petition against my son, Richard." He pronounced the ominous legal term with authority. He had learned of its existence from his policeman neighbor.

Even though Richie was almost seventeen, and liable under the law to be judged as an adult for any crimes that he might commit, the boy could still be brought under the arm of Family Court as a delinquent juvenile until he was twenty-one.

Told he would have to wait his turn for a caseworker,

George obediently returned to the bench and tried to keep from responding to the sad and solemn faces about him. He did not fit here, he reassured himself, not alongside the black women rocking tearful children whose fathers had run away, not with the Puerto Rican men who sat with stoic dignity and steel backs while their mustachioed sons slumped beside them, surly and impatient and, thought George, probably dangerous. Occasionally one of the black or brown people looked at George as if he were a member of their fraternity of domestic grief and pain.

It had taken an enormous act of will and a night of quarreling with Carol to bring himself to this place. And now that he was here, George wanted nothing more than to flee, to bolt down the stairs and out into the spring morning and be about his business of selling pepper flakes and bay leaves. No immediate cause had brought him to the court, no new straw had broken his resolution to handle his son at home by his own means. George acted only out of a feeling of despair. Deep within him, unspoken even to Carol, was the hope that the authority of the law could reinforce his waning role as father. Richie's truculence and insubordination were more than troublesome; they were a stinging slap across George's image of himself. The one thing he had done well in life, or so he imagined until Richie's irksome adolescence began, was sire and rear this son. He could not accept failure now—at forty-two —in *that* corner of his being. There were so many others.

But he was acting without Carol's support. Until past midnight he had tried to win her over, but she went to bed with tears, and although she rose as she always did at six and made coffee and got the boys off to school, she was noticeably chilly with her husband.

All this means, George had told her when he initiated the subject of a "wayward conduct petition," is that the juvenile authorities would keep an eye on Richie, and if he really went off the deep end, then he would have to answer to the law.

Carol would have none of it. It was a terrible idea, she said. She pleaded with George not to do it. Call it shame, call it admission of failure on her part, call it fear of her family and the neighbors finding out, call it anything you want, said Carol. But let's wait before we take our son and throw him into Family Court.

George was adamant. "His name is already on file there," he reminded Carol. "It's not like he was a lily-white angel and about to be blackened for the first time. And besides, it isn't the police. He won't get a criminal record. I'm trying to *keep* him from getting a criminal record. Everything's strictly confidential in Family Court."

Well, we might as well take an ad out in the newspaper and tell everybody, said Carol. And she left the room. All of this came back to George as he sat on the bench and listened to the crying babies. Just when he was about to weaken and find the steps, his name was called.

In a small office he shook hands with a serious-looking caseworker named Morton Ozur. George blurted out his business. "I have reason to believe my son Richard is using marijuana, LSD, mescaline, and possibly other drugs," he said. "The situation is terrible around our house. I can't control him anymore. I can't even talk to him. In other words, we don't speak."

Caseworker Ozur, who specialized in drug matters, listened impassively. He questioned George briefly, then made an appointment for the father to bring his son in for a joint meeting two weeks hence. There are many avenues open in a matter like this, said Ozur. "But the best beginning is to start talking with each other."

That night, Richie received the news from his father with a blank expression. He spoke not a word when George revealed that he was filing a "wayward conduct petition" against him. Probably Richie did not understand

its weight. He left the dinner table and hurriedly telephoned his circle of friends to reveal the news.

"My old man just filed a delinquency charge against
me," he told Mark, trying to sound as if the development
was no more serious than a fly on his arm to be shooed
away.

"Jesus," said Mark. "You better hope they don't send
you to the shelter." Mark often talked of his stay in the
county juvenile facility. A year before, he had given a
thirteen-year-old girl an LSD wafer, and she suffered violent reaction. Her boyfriend went after Mark with a
shotgun, and with good cause Mark elected to run away
with a friend to Pennsylvania.

The two boys stole food from supermarkets and blankets
from discount houses to survive during the freezing winter
flight. Once, Mark said, they used up two boxes of stolen
kitchen matches to heat up bricks for warmth in a farm-
er's field. After a few days in Pennsylvania, the pair returned to East Meadow, whereupon Mark was hauled
before Family Court. The prodigal son was furious. He
thought he would be praised for coming home.

"They're not gonna send *me* to any shelter," said Richie,
his voice not quite as steady.

"The judge said to me, 'I have to remand you,' and I
stayed there a month," said Mark. "Anything I am now,
the shelter made me. It's hell. It made me develop 'attitudes' against everybody." *Attitudes* was one of Mark's
favorite words. He summed up people as having good
attitudes, or bad attitudes. Richie, he decided shortly after
they met, had the most unpredictable "attitudes" of anyone he had ever met.

"What makes 'em decide to send you there?" questioned
Richie.

"Whatever they fuckin' well want to do against kids,
they fuckin' well can do," said Mark. "I had hair down
to my shoulders and they told me I'd have to get a

'baldie' every Wednesday. I fought 'em when they came for me, I fought 'em every day. I bet they fuckin' well remember old Mark at that fuckin' shelter. They used to lock me in my room a week at a time to punish me."

"I'd run away first," said Richie. "I'd join the marines."

"They'd find you," said Mark. "Everybody's hooked into a computer and they can find you no matter where you run to."

To her frank surprise, Carol noticed immediate improvement in Richie's behavior. He stayed home weeknights, he came to dinner on time and even conversed a little, he listened attentively when Carol suggested he go to the Drug Abuse Council—voluntarily—and talk about drugs. Only at that did he balk. Mark and Brick had both been in long attendance there, he told his mother, and it did not seem to be working for either of them. Besides, insisted Richie, smoking a little grass now and then is hardly reason to go to a shrink.

"If every kid in East Meadow who smokes grass had to go to Drug Abuse," said Richie, "they'd have to hold the meetings in Shea Stadium."

Soon afterward Carol read in a local newspaper that Burger King was opening a new hamburger restaurant in nearby Bethpage. She suggested that Richie put in an application for work. He readily agreed and came back with the happy news that he had been accepted. He would start work in early May. This meant that Carol would have to drive her son to work and pick him up, but she held hope that he could be transferred to the East Meadow store if his work was satisfactory.

In late April, George took his son to Family Court for the preliminary talks. There Richie was informed that, in the opinion of his father, he was "so deporting himself to willfully injure or endanger the morals or health of himself." Caseworker Ozur talked first to Richie alone, then with George. He suggested, not decreed, that both parents and son should go to the Nassau County Drug Abuse Council for counseling before the court took further action.

A full hearing was set for May 17, 1971, before a Family Court judge who would, said the caseworker, be interested to know if the family was indeed going to the Drug Abuse Council.

At home that evening, Richie once again refused. "I'm starting work after school and nights," he said. "I won't have time to go to any meetings, and besides, I don't think I need it."

George bided his time. He did not relish attending meetings with a psychologist any more than his son. But, of course, he did not say so.

On the day of the hearing, George went alone to Family Court and found himself standing in front of a formidable woman judge named Beatrice Burstein. A woman in her late fifties with several children of her own, with a deeply tanned face and dark pouches of overwork beneath her eyes, she spoke with a husky voice. Judge Burstein had a weary air about her, as if she had heard every tale of human despair to be told—she took the waters at Vichy, France, each summer to cleanse her head—but there remained a deep compassion for children. She was known as a judge who took any possible step to avoid sending a child to a state institution. For most of them, she charged openly, were "horrors." Often she would dip into her purse and find ten dollars for a boy who needed a bed for the night, or interrupt court to go to her chambers and make furious telephone calls trying to find a job for some youthful defendant.

Judge Burstein called George's name, and he appeared before her with erect military posture. He had rehearsed his speech.

"I wish to withdraw the charge I filed against my son," he said. "Richie is working at Burger King and things are going better at home."

Noting that the complaint had been filed less than a month before, Judge Burstein quickly read over the case-worker's information. She peered at George and spoke sharply.

"You mean that your son has made a miraculous recovery?"

"Yes, Your Honor."

"Then you want to give him another chance?"

"If he had acted like this before, I would never have brought charges against him."

"I accept the withdrawal," said Judge Burstein, scribbling something rapidly on the case file. "The court is pleased when problems can be worked out at home."

As George left the chambers, anxious to be in his old Chevrolet and about his sales work, anxious to be gone from the haunting faces in the corridors of the court, Judge Burstein called after him, "I still think it would be beneficial for you and your son to go to the Drug Abuse Council."

George nodded, but he did not obey the judge. Nor did Richie. It is a fair question to wonder why George Diener would wash his family linen in public waters, even though the proceedings were confidential, yet would not seek the professional counseling recommended over and over again for himself and his son. Money could not have been the issue here, because therapy at Drug Abuse was free to residents of Nassau County. Even had George decided that a private psychiatrist could best sort out the problems, Carol could have borrowed the money from her parents. Certainly she did not want them to know what was going on in her house, but there was no doubt in her mind that any sum she asked, they would grant. For that matter, if a man can borrow $800 to pay for summer camp, he can find money for a doctor.

Once again, there were two levels to George's action. On the surface, on the level of conversation with Carol, George pronounced psychiatry to be of a slightly liberal taint, a spoiled fruit not to be partaken of by a good conservative. "I just don't have much faith in that sort of thing," he told Carol, his tone indicating he placed psychiatry on a level with voodoo. "And besides, the only time those shrinks can accomplish anything is when the person in question *wants* help—and Richie doesn't want help. Every time I mention it, he is vehemently against it." But on that deeper plane, where the truth lodged in private recesses, George did not want anyone tampering with *his* head, violating *his* privacy, questioning *his* way of life. I am forty-two years old, George was saying to himself, and I am halfway through my life. I do not need a left-wing psychiatrist to tell me what's wrong with me. My ego is as fragile as one of Carol's china cups, anyway.

The job at Burger King lasted little more than two months. At first Richie had enjoyed counter work, stuffing hamburgers into slip sacks, filling cups with root beer, serving them to customers with a quip or a flip remark. With his bright red hair and cheery face, he was a good man to have in front of the public. He took his first paycheck, for $32.78, showed it to his mother, and opened a savings account, proudly vowing that he was going to hoard every available dollar to buy a car.

From mid-May to mid-July, 1971, Carol basked in one of the most pleasant periods in her home and family for two years. She did not say to George, "I told you so," but this nonetheless was how she felt. She knew, she always knew that one day Richie would get a job and dress overnight in the garment of maturity. Work was giving her son responsibility. He was certainly learning about the value of money. Every time he showed his mother his growing passbook, she exulted in his thrift. The Brick-Mark-Peanuts clique seemed less important to Richie, for they were rarely around anymore. Brick had telephoned a couple of times, but Carol recognized his deep, dark voice and hung up on him, even when he used a code name.

George was not yet ready to proclaim a miracle, but even he was impressed. It was obvious to him that the reason Richie was so improved could be found in his dash to Family Court.

But one night in July Richie came home from work early. The first thing Carol noticed was that he walked a little unsteadily. The second was that his eyes were a vivid red. Richie explained it all by saying that he was tired. Moreover, he was depressed. He had quit his job, he said, just a jump ahead of being laid off. There were several reasons, the principal one being that he had been unfairly given "all the dirty work." His assignment was to clean up after closing, which meant carrying out dozen of sacks of garbage and mopping floors. Moreover, the store had hired too many people for the grand opening weeks, and several would be let go. He decided to beat his boss to it.

Carol was disappointed, but she comforted her son. Perhaps with his experience he could find another job. Now that he had gone through the trauma of a job interview, he could certainly do so again with ease.

Richie did not tell his mother the real story. He was fired, not for any of the reasons he mentioned, but because the restaurant manager found him "sneaky, often late for work, undependable, usually cutting up with some other kids, and talking about pot." Except for the reference to marijuana, it could have been the remarks of his elementary school teacher.

Nor did Richie tell his mother that there had been no barbiturates around East Meadow for several weeks. Brick speculated that the feds were cracking down. But on this night he had bought a dozen, and three were working with him and coloring his eyes and shaking his steps as he entered his home.

There were signs, some clearly visible to George and Carol, others known only to himself, that Richie wrestled with his soul in the remaining summer months of 1971. The evidence was that he was not entirely happy with the direction of his life and with the friends he had chosen. On his wall, amid the vivid displays of rock and psychedelia, near a game he had stapled up called "Feds 'n Heads" (sample instructions: "The judge has been paid off, move three steps"), Richie pasted up a strip poster reading: ᴍᴀʀɪᴊᴜᴀɴᴀ ᴋɪʟʟs. By itself, the legend would have been facetious. But next to this he placed another warning: ʟsᴅ ɪs ᴀ ʙᴀᴅ ᴛʀɪᴘ, and next to this, almost in exclamation point, he pinned up the red cover logo from the magazine *Life*.

While cleaning the room one day, Carol discovered a card from Topic House, a drug therapy clinic in Nassau County. Was he saving it for future reference, wondered Carol? Or was he actually going there? She wanted to ask her son, but she was afraid of interrupting a private mission, or of tampering with an idea that was rolling around in his head. Now and then Richie pulled down one of the forgotten nature books and fell asleep reading. This excited Carol most of all. She elected not to mention this either, for fear she might extinguish the rekindled flame, if one was burning at all.

Always careful about his appearance, Richie became fastidious, dressing only in neatly ironed shirts and pants —thereby increasing Carol's work load—and in highly polished shoes, with such overall care that he seemed to be rebelling against the celebrated slovenliness of the blue-jean generation. He spent hours in front of the bathroom mirror, attacking the tight red curls of his hair and trying to shape them into the smooth length of young fashion. Finally he went to Carol and asked for fifteen dollars, necessary to have his hair professionally straightened. The passion seemed so important that Carol agreed, but when the work was done, Richie professed even greater unhappiness. "Now," he said morosely, "it looks like a Brillo soap pad."

His room and his closet were kept militarily neat, unlike the rooms of the other teen-age boys he knew. Had Richie gone to that psychiatrist, it might have been learned that because he so cluttered one corner of his psyche with drug-taking, it was important that he keep the place in which he lived as orderly as possible.

He did things, "square" things, "lame" things that his head friends found puzzling. The retarded children's charity of which Carol was president scheduled a gala dinner dance at the New York Hilton in New York. Members were asked to sell raffle tickets for an automobile—five chances for a dollar—and if a hundred dollars' worth was sold, the seller would get a free admission to the ball. Carol mentioned the plan to Richie, and much to her surprise, he wanted to go. Father and eldest son spent weekends at shopping centers, pushing raffle tickets, until enough were sold to grant Richie and Sheila free entrance to the Hilton ball.

The accomplishment and Richie's interest so elated Carol that she let him buy a new suit for the occasion. Richie selected a gray, conservatively cut Edwardian model, hardly the kind worn to Fillmore East. On the gala evening, Carol's eyes grew misty as she watched her son dance across the glittering ballroom with Sheila in his arms. Everyone complimented Carol on having such a handsome, well-mannered son. She held tightly to George as they danced, seeing in his eyes a glow of pride as well. If there can be laughter and music and warmth on this special night, thought Carol, surely there can be more.

The fact of the matter was that Richie impressed most adults with whom he came in contact. Brick Pavall's mother often called her son's best friend "that redheaded angel with the halo that tilts a little now and then." Your only problem, Mrs. Pavall told Richie when he sat in her living room waiting for Brick to come down the stairs, is that "you talk too much."

"Whatta you mean?" asked Richie, the first time she made the charge, knowing full well her answer.

"Because you've always got to have the last word," said Mrs. Pavall. "Usually it's funny, sometimes it's fresh mouth."

Richie's aunt, June Marck, made the mistake of commenting on Richie's heft when he was plump. Years later, as if he had stored up the grievance and was waiting for an opportunity to get back, he began calling her "Aunt Totie," after the corpulent comedienne. Aunt June had put on a few pounds. "Nobody ever scores one on you, do they, Richie?" she said. "Touché."

Another neighborhood woman, Mrs. O'Hara, whose son Sean maintained an on-again, off-again friendship with Richie, found him to be "the most personable kid ever to come to my house." During the late-summer months of 1971, Richie almost clung to Sean O'Hara and Bob Simmons, both "straight," both good students, both dedicated to eventual college, both tolerant of the drug culture but participants only as occasional pot smokers. Both worked delicately on Richie to turn him away from downs.

Mrs. O'Hara knew nothing of her son's missionary work

in this field, only that Richie was a polite and cheerful guest in her house. "His personality was vibrant," she would later say. "I was always glad to have him come to family parties—we have six children and our house is a stomping ground. I don't know what I'd do if there weren't at least twenty kids here on a summer weekend.

"Richie never came in my house without first going out to the den and saying hello to my husband and my eighty-year-old uncle. He usually had a joke or something funny to tell them. Then he'd help cook and serve drinks and clean the dining-room table—without being asked. That's unusual to say the least for a teen-age boy. Usually they're so worried about people looking at them and judging them and thinking bad of them. I always thought Richie seemed hungry for family life."

On one of the last summer weekends, Richie called around one Saturday morning looking for a way to pass the afternoon. Bob Simmons was working, Sean O'Hara was out on errands. George had taken Russell to baseball practice at the Little League field, Carol was visiting her sister, June. The yellow house was quiet, wrapped in summer languor. Bridget, the poodle, was asleep in a living-room chair as she usually was. Then Brick's call broke the loneliness.

"Whatta you doin', Diener?"

"Nothin'."

"Wanna drive around? Maybe go to the beach?"

Richie quickly agreed. He had not seen Brick for more than two weeks, having been in one of his "straight periods" in which he preferred the company of Sean or Bob. But he had no desire to hang around an empty house all day.

"Meet me on the corner," said Brick routinely, for he always picked up Richie there, realizing he was not welcome in the Diener house.

Richie slipped into a pair of bathing trunks and pulled his jeans over them.

On the way to the beach, Brick drove unsteadily. "You off on something?" asked Richie.

"From last night," answered Brick. "I did four downs."

"How much'd you pay?"

"Two for a dollar. Pharmaceuticals. Fantastic stuff. Mark got 'em from Cantrell."

They picked up two of Brick's friends, boys that Richie knew only slightly. Both were already high on grass. They also had bottles of strawberry wine, which, at eighty-nine cents, was fast growing in popularity among pot smokers. They are always thirsty.

At Jones Beach, Brick and his two friends ran immediately to the surf and watched the cold waves break about their bare feet. Richie held back. When the others settled down on a blanket and turned up the radio to WABC, Richie moved to join them. But suddenly he heard his name being called.

Looking down the beach a hundred yards, he saw a gang of straight kids, including one student leader at East Meadow, and a girl named Melissa, a redhead like him, whom he had met at Ryan's bar. With a smile and a wave, he headed toward them. But halfway there he stopped, as if he had reached the end of the rope that restrained him. He looked back at Brick and his entourage, who were paying no attention. He looked ahead at the others. For several moments he stood suspended between the two sets of his friends that he so carefully kept apart. He seemed unable to commit to either side. Finally he sat down on a sand dune almost equidistant between the two walls of his life. Alone, the sun reddening his fair shoulders, he looked out at the sea.

Finally, a decision apparently made, he walked back to Brick. A joint had been freshly lit and he accepted it. There was a quarter bottle of the sweet wine left, which he drained in one swallow. Then he stretched out and listened to the music and did not look down the beach again.

On the way home, Brick's car went dead at a traffic light several blocks from Richie's neighborhood. In the back seat, his belly warm from the sun, from the strawberry wine and the marijuana, Richie grew impatient. He jumped out and left Brick, in a similar condition, trying to get the belligerent machine started.

Richie found it difficult to walk. At first the pavement felt like marshmallows under his feet, springing him softly along his way. Then, as he told Brick later that night, the texture turned coarse and hard, pricking his feet through the soles of his tennis shoes as if he were an Indian fakir walking on a bed of nails. He said the journey felt like "a thousand miles across East Meadow."

He saw a bunch of little boys ahead, gathered around something. He entered the gathering and saw a mongrel dog lying near the curb. Blood dribbled from the black and white spotted animal. He had been crushed by a hit-run car. A child of six or seven was loudly crying. Somebody had gone to a nearby house to call a veterinarian, but neither the messenger nor the doctor had returned. Richie knelt beside the dog and touched it gently, the dying creature breathing in gasps and rattles. In a gentle voice, Richie comforted it. One of the little kids cautioned, "Better watch out, kid, he'll bite you." Richie shook his head. With tender hands, he lifted the dog and held it in his lap. A neighbor woman came upon the scene and saw the older, red-haired boy softly crying. She assumed it was his dog that was hurt.

In a few moments, the dog shuddered and, still in Richie's lap, died. Richie put the animal down on the grass, ran his hand across it one last time, and ran away, running to his home without stopping, running up the stairs and into George.

Seeing that Richie was upset, disheveled, and with blood on his shirt, George wanted to know what had happened.

Richie ignored the question. He continued to his room.

"What happened?" insisted George. "Were you in a fight?"

Richie slammed the door to his room. He screamed through the wood, "Leave me the fuck alone!"

Neither George nor Carol knew why their son returned home with blood on his shirt that day, or why, once more, he turned profane and truculent, or why he began missing meals, or why his eyes were on fire again and again, or why he lay around his room so often sleeping, sometimes as if in a trance. The dog dying in Richie's arms perhaps meant nothing in the progress of his life. Perhaps more important was the fact that school would begin in a few days, and just as notebooks and pens and sweaters and jeans and laminated book covers filled the shops of East Meadow, there also turned up a fresh supply of barbiturates. Richie had $375 in his savings account with which to buy all his supplies.

Two weeks into the new school year, Brick had a date to meet Richie at an amusement parlor favored by youngsters who played pinball machines and automatic baseball. Heads liked the place as well, for the flashing lights of the machines and the clanging of bells entranced those on a drug trip.

When Brick arrived, a few minutes late, Richie was leaning against the outside wall, his body sagging like an accordion. The manager came out and told Brick, "Get this kid out of here or I'm calling the police." With some difficulty, Brick threw his arms around his friend and half pulled, half pushed him down the street.

"What are you doin'?" asked Brick, meaning what kind of drugs had Richie taken.

"Downs," murmured Richie.

There had been a fight at the Diener home, Brick learned, between Richie and his father. Richie had run out of the house into the night with George crying after him, "Now don't come home high on anything!"

"How many'd you do?" asked Brick.

Richie held up several fingers. It took Eddie an astonished moment to count them. Nine!

"You're crazy, Diener. You're really flipped out. Nobody takes nine Seconals at once." Now Richie had a stranglehold on Brick, an old drunk of seventeen trying to pull his Good Samaritan down to the curb so he could sit awhile.

Brick looked at Richie in a new light. It was suddenly apparent that Richie deliberately set out to get as bombed as he possibly could, for little reason other than defiance of his father. Brick was frightened. He had never seen Richie this way before. He was comfortable with the Richie who did downs and glided across patches of winter ice in hilarious imitation of Charlie Chaplin, he knew and liked the Richie who could impersonate any rock star, he relished the Richie who usually had a fast, sardonic comeback in the voice of W. C. Fields while the pills were rushing over them all.

But now it occurred to Brick that Richie might die, here, on the street, in his arms. With a violent shudder, Richie vomited, on his shoes, on Brick's jacket. With spasms that shook his body, Richie threw up another half-dozen times.

"Jesus, Diener," said Brick worried, angry, frightened. "You're absolutely crazy."

Richie retched one more time before he was able to stagger with Brick's arm about him, toward his home.

They had not gone very far before Richie stopped and said, in what Brick took to be a sob, "I don't give a shit, really."

Chapter Sixteen

But what of the school where Richie Diener passed seven hours of every weekday under what should be, next to home and family, the most formative of adolescent experience? Was East Meadow High a blackboard jungle, with shattered windows and instructors walking in pairs through the gauntlet of student menace?

In fact, homes are overpriced in East Meadow because the public school system is considered so excellent. East Meadow High, where Richie became a senior in September, 1971, was known for its academic excellence, the small size of its classes—an average of twenty-three students per room—its lovely campus with playing fields and expansive grounds that resembled a small college, and its extracurricular achievements—powerful lacrosse teams, a celebrated marching band called The Jets, a jazz ensemble that won the New England Festival two years in a row, a drama department that put on Broadway plays and musicals such as *The Miracle Worker* and *South Pacific* with near-professional style.

By coincidence, or the hand of irony, the almost three years that Richie was in attendance there were also marked by massive change at East Meadow High, transformation from a rigidly conservative institution to one of bold and —to some people's way of thinking—confusing liberties. George Diener, for example, found it not at all unusual that college students at New York City's Columbia University should seize command of the dean's office, or that a protest march at Kent State should be bloodied with bullets from the state guard. The blame for student rebellion, George reasoned, rested heavily on the shoulders of high schools that relaxed discipline and encouraged students to assume voluntary responsibilities.

Nor did George have enthusiasm for the newfangled education, such as the learning centers at East Meadow's elementary schools, where walls were knocked out of classrooms to make large areas, where teachers did not instruct so much as act as "guides" to the resources of the center, where students chose a "learning contract" and fulfilled it by utilizing film strips, audio aids, books, and research materials.

Both George and Carol believed the swift changes in their sons' schools were due to the liberal politics of the East Meadow school board, the only elected public officials of the town. Carol often attended board meetings as a spectator—"I like to see what they're doing with our money," she told George—and came home annoyed at what liberal notions were doing to old-fashioned education, paid for with conservative tax dollars.

The 2,800 students who poured daily into the low-slung, buff-colored East Meadow High School were participants in a learning process radically different from that of the nuns and hard-line educators who molded both George and Carol in Brooklyn. Had he so desired, Richie could have selected from a dazzling array of courses—Russian, or black history, or communism, or contemporary music, or film-making, or a humanities series called "Man Is a Creative Being."

In Richie's senior year, the computer that kept watch over everything from daily attendance to student elections to each child's scholastic progress decreed that he needed but four required courses to graduate—social studies, mathematics, science, and English. In a school day of eight periods, this left four other periods open. Richie filled two of these with "pass-fail" subjects. When Carol wondered what *that* new term meant, Richie told her. "All you have to do to pass," he said, "is show up for class. You don't get a grade."

"Must be marvelous," muttered George. "Really makes a fellow want to put his nose to the grindstone."

The two remaining periods a day Richie chose to use as study halls. Here was an opportunity for abuse, if a youngster wanted to test the new freedoms at East Meadow High. The school set up four separate study hall areas, each of different character. One was held in the library, which, according to Richie, was "where the lames went." Another was in the cafeteria, where students could drink hot chocolate and munch sweet rolls. A third was called Quiet Study Hall, where no talking was allowed. This was the only one that George could identify with. The fourth was called Social Study Hall and was held in a refurbished area in the basement, with students permitted to "rap and move around socially."

At the beginning of each school year, a student chose his study hall periods and was given a color-coded pass valuable for access to any of the four areas during a given hour—a red pass for period 4, for example. Theoretically, the pass system would prohibit youngsters from being in the wrong place at the wrong time. But there was also the danger of youngsters not being *anywhere* they were supposed to be. It did not take Richie long to discover that only cursory attendance checks were made of study halls. It was easy to claim that he was in the cafeteria throng, say, when in reality he had left the campus altogether to meet Brick and smoke pot. Brick's jobs did not last very long, a few weeks at best.

The dean of students, Frank Saracino, was a vigorous supporter of the new student freedoms, even though he recognized the abuse factor. "A lot of parents would like for us to go back to the mid-sixties," he said in explaining the modern turn his school had taken. "They would like for the school to have a tighter rein, a more structured program, less emphasis on student rights. In the old days, the school was a dependable surrogate parent. Since then there has been a transferral from *in loco parentis* to application of the Fourteenth Amendment for the pupil. But let's face it, the child from fifteen to eighteen years old has a much different position in life today than he had a decade ago."

A major reason for the student liberation was to prepare East Meadow's youngsters for college, since at least 70 percent of them traditionally pursued higher education—well above national average. "We attempt to combat the mortality rate among college freshmen by giving high school seniors more freedom, more responsibility, more permissions," says Dean Saracino. "We hope this will prepare our kids better for the permissive atmosphere in college."

Theoretically, a child could leave the East Meadow High campus only during lunch period, and only with a *notarized* slip from his parent giving permission—the notary seal requirement being to eliminate forgeries of parents' names. But, as Dean Saracino candidly admits, "There are 2,800 students, and we can't keep track of all of them all the time."

Thus it happened that Richie Diener at seventeen began

his senior year in a school that invited him to act with maturity and enjoy its rewards. But if George Diener was right about anything, he was right in complaining that his son was not yet ready for such delights. The school became, in George's eyes, a factor in his son's decay.

By 1971 drug use at East Meadow High was alarming —but authorities took refuge in the fact that it seemed no more so than at other suburban schools near big cities around the nation. John Barbour, the principal, commented, "Our school has the same problems as any school in Nassau County. We're not lily-white, but we're not the worst, either, and we're working on it." Barbour embraced the "cyclical" theory of drug-taking and had a "gut feeling," with nothing tangible to support it, that the problem was easing by the start of school in 1972. He estimated that the number of regular users of drugs —including marijuana—was less than 500 out of a student population of 2,800. Dean Saracino refused to be that specific, saying instead that there were "a few hundred with serious drug problems."

"Quite frankly," said Saracino, "who knows? There are groupies who hang together to take drugs and talk about them, but there are countless unknown 'loners' who self-medicate themselves. Somebody's hassling you? You just pop a pill or two and drop out of the world that day."

To its credit, the school provided extensive drug information to students and enforced state laws against drug use as best as it could. "If a student is caught with drugs," warned Principal Barbour at orientation lectures each September, "we call the police immediately."

During the school year, students were also exposed to drug education lectures in health classes. Social workers from drug clinics in the area held voluntary rap sessions for students after school. Teachers were encouraged by the administration to be on the alert for suspected drug users. This had not always been the case.

Until 1971 teachers were reluctant to accuse a child as a drug user for fear of retaliation: a civil suit for slander could be filed if the youngster turned out to be ill from a virus or taking prescribed medication. The New York State legislature, however, passed a new law in 1971 that held teachers "safe harmless" from civil suits. A teacher who reported a youngster for possible drug use would be in the same protected situation as a football coach who, while demonstrating how to block, broke a youngster's leg.

For its faculty the East Meadow school administration established a course on drug abuse and how to spot users. But only some three hundred out of eight hundred high school teachers (East Meadow has two high schools) voluntarily took the course. "We are in a new era of teacher militancy," says Dean Saracino. "We cannot force teachers to take such courses. It's voluntary under their contracts."

If a student was suspected of using drugs at school, technically no law was violated. It is not a crime to be under the influence of drugs, only to possess or sell them. The teacher who spotted a stoned youngster nodding in class, or acting erratically, was instructed to *ask* the suspect to go to the school nurse. If the student refused, the assistant principal was summoned. If the student was ambulatory, and stoned, the parent was called to take him home. If the student was grossly incoherent, he was taken —forcibly if necessary, with the aid of police—to emergency room facilities directly across the street at Meadowbrook Hospital.

During the first three days of school in September, 1970, there was a severe drug case each day. Three students collapsed and were sent on stretchers across the street to Meadowbrook Hospital. When a child collapsed in the hallway from an overdose, or suddenly attacked a teacher, it was simple to suspect drug use. But many other youngsters were veteran enough at the game, and sophisticated enough in their dosage, to function at what would seem normal to any teacher. "If a kid is stoned every day," said Saracino, "then that's the way he is."

Even more difficult is catching students with drugs in their pocket. "Possession," said Saracino, "is very hard to prove. Especially with pills. When pot was *the* drug, it was not brought to school often. If you got caught, you couldn't get rid of it. If you threw it into your mouth, you were going to cough it right out. Pills, however, are a very convenient item. They are portable and very easy to dispose of in times of crisis. Just swallow the evidence. The worst you can do is become very drowsy if they're downs, or very skittish if they're ups."

George Diener picked up information around town that it was possible to buy or sell any type of drug in the corridors and playgrounds of East Meadow High, that pot-smoking was so routine in the boys' toilets that teachers were loath to enter. He said to Carol that he didn't understand why the school did not put a policeman in the hallway to at least inhibit the drug traffic.

Dean Saracino received that suggestion several times a year from parents. To them he replied, "Sure, drugs are available in our schools, they are available in society. If the problem exists in a kid's life, the problem that induces him to use drugs, then the problem will exist in his school as well. Youngsters spend a major portion of their lives here; it is their principal social contact. We have 2,800 students and there are an estimated one million interactions a day. If I see a group of kids waiting for someone in a certain area of the building on one day, and again the next, and my suspicion is aroused, then on the third day the seller has changed his rendezvous point. You cannot have a fascist, totalitarian system in a school. We cannot have policemen patrolling around. Not only would it intrude on the business of education, it would make kids even more uptight. They would feel they were being hassled."

George Diener felt a little hassling might not be out of line, for he once heard his son brag on the telephone to an unknown friend, "You can get anything you want at school. You want a hundred dollars' worth of dope? Give me a shopping list and one hundred dollars, and thirty minutes later I'll be back with whatever you want."

On October 19, 1971, Carol received a telephone call from the school office informing her that Richie was "extensively cutting" his pass-fail contemporary music course. This was the first disciplinary entry on his school record. Carol questioned him about it that night, but Richie answered, "The course is a snap, it doesn't mean anything." He was cutting it now and then to use extra time in study hall for more difficult subjects necessary to graduate. This seemed like a good explanation to Carol.

A few days later, Richie came down with a cold and a hacking cough. His mother suspected once again that the cough was aggravated by marijuana. To her there was no other sensible explanation for an otherwise robust seventeen-year-old who went around coughing and clearing his throat so much of the time. When the cold evolved into bronchitis and then pneumonia, Richie was ordered to bed by the family doctor for two weeks and put on antibiotics. On his second day at home, Carol received another call from the school to verify that Richie was really sick. During the conversation Carol further learned, to her astonishment, that Richie had been truant from school fourteen days since classes began two months earlier in September.

Carol demanded an explanation and Richie had a quick one. He often arrived at home room a few minutes late, he said, and was thus counted absent by an errant computer. "It's no big deal," he said, throwing in his favorite disclaimer. "Don't worry about it." Carol was so worried about her son's health that she did not seriously examine his story.

When Richie returned to school, Carol was summoned to the telephone on the morning of November 23, 1971, at the junior high school cafeteria where she worked preparing lunches. The assistant principal at East Meadow High was on the line, asking if Carol could hurry over to pick up Richie. That morning Richie had first threatened a woman teacher who was monitoring cafeteria study hall, then tried to attack the school nurse who was trying to question him, finally behaving "abusively" to the assistant principal.

Carol hung up and, never good at lying, mumbled to her superior that Richie had been "taken ill at school" and that she would have to take him home.

At the high school, Carol discovered Richie slumped arrogantly in the nurse's office. His half-mast eyes, a deep red, welcomed her. He smiled, lopsidedly, sullenly. When he stood up, he swayed gently. While Richie waited outside, the assistant principal took Carol behind closed doors and related in detail the morning's chain of trouble. The nurse said she had asked Richie if he was "taking medication" and he replied affirmatively.

"He said he was still taking antibiotics for his pneumonia," said the nurse. "He said he took two on the school bus this morning and they made him sleepy and made him act strangely." But the nurse's tone indicated that she did not believe him.

Carol summoned her courage. Somehow she had always suspected this day would come, and it would do no good to hide from the revelation any longer. "Do you think he was taking something else?" she asked. The nurse nodded.

"Drugs?" The nurse nodded once more. Probably barbiturates, she guessed.

It was the first hard information that either Carol or George had received from an adult authority that Richie was using drugs other than marijuana, even though he had been on them for more than eighteen months. The land where Carol lived, bounded by Naïveté on one side and Not Wanting to Know on the other, was suddenly under invasion, by an enemy she could no longer ignore.

One last embarrassment awaited Carol. When she left the assistant principal's office and walked over to her waiting son, Richie refused to leave the school. Proclaiming loudly that he had been falsely accused, that he had been but briefly discombobulated by the antibiotics, he threatened and cursed anyone who dared touch him. Despair filled Carol. She did not know how to handle this. Gently she tried to persuade him that he was "tired," that he should rest at home for the remainder of the day. In answer, Richie glared at his mother with the reddened eyes. But in *her* eyes, he saw the tears he did not have.

After she took Richie home and put him to bed, Carol drove back to the cafeteria and en route she made a decision: I'm going back there and tell them the truth; I'm going to make a clean breast of it. They are my friends. They'll understand.

Desperately, at this moment, Carol needed a confidant. She yearned for another pair of ears besides her husband's to accept the turmoil churning within her. From the day two years earlier when the summer camp owner telephoned the Diener home and said Richie was being expelled, throughout the roller coaster that their lives had become, Carol had never told another person of the trouble. Nor had George, save for the caseworker at Family Court and Judge Burstein, but their attention was coolly official and of no comfort to Carol. Neither she nor George ever asked their family doctor what to do, or their minister, or their friends (some of whom were trying to cope with similar difficulties in their own homes), or their families. Carol could no longer count the nights when she sat down at the dining-room table after the house was asleep and began a letter to her parents in North Carolina, fully intending to bare her soul and plead for help. But always she lifted her pen after a sentence or two and crumpled the paper and threw it deep into the trash. It would take a fifty-page letter to tell everything, she rationalized, and it would shatter the peace of their retirement, and even then, no one could understand, no one who is not living through this hell.

But as she walked into the lunchroom she lost her courage and decided once more not to tell anyone what tormented her. She put on her white apron and began serving the meat loaf she had prepared an hour or two before. "I looked at them all," she told George that night, "and I just couldn't get the words out of my mouth. So I made up a story of Richie being sick with the flu."

The next morning, Richie was ordered to the principal's office where he met for the first time John Barbour, a medium-sized man with precise military-cut hair. Barbour had an air of tenseness about him not unlike George Diener's (curiously the men resembled one another) that manifested itself in his forming and re-forming a fist with his right hand as he spoke. He also prided himself on being an educator accommodating to change. When the student government of East Meadow had petitioned him a few years earlier for more liberties, the notion was "alien" to him. "I'm from the old school," he told people. "I used to make girls kneel, and if their skirts did not touch the floor, I sent them home. Or I told boys to take two steps back from my desk, bend over, and take their licks from my paddle—like a man."

But the principal considered himself a man of reason and one who could tolerate change even if he did not believe strongly in it. No longer was there a hair or dress code at his school, other than a notation in the student handbook that taps on shoes seriously mar and scuff the floor; therefore they may not be worn in the building at any time; offenders would have the taps immediately removed. No longer was corporal punishment used. Barbour was also growing familiar with the dismaying sight of a young person sitting across from his desk in suspicion of using or selling drugs in the school. Most disciplinary matters were handled routinely by the dean and assistant principal. "But when youngsters become involved with drugs," he told parent groups, "then I become involved with the youngsters."

Barbour elected to move firmly but tactfully with Richie. He did not make a direct accusation of drug use. Instead he warned that Richie's graduation in June was in jeopardy. Picking up Richie's academic record, he ticked off the disappointing entries. With the ten-week marking period just completed, Richie was failing *every* subject. Barbour repeated himself. "*Every* subject!" His attendance at the pass-fail contemporary music course was so rare that the teacher could not affix a grade other than "incomplete." He was cutting twice-a-week gym class regularly. Out of fifty class days since school began, he had been absent twenty-two, including his illness. "You have cut some classes more than 50 percent of the time," said Barbour, "and your citizenship grade is poor."

Richie listened to the warning attentively. Barbour noted that throughout the conference the boy's attitude was "good." The principal said he was as of that morning dropping Richie from contemporary music altogether and assigning him to a gym class every day, no doubt in the belief that a little sweat, calisthenics, and discipline under a coach would improve any errant young person.

"Do you want to graduate?" asked Barbour in conclusion.

"Yes, sir."

"Then your effort and your attendance must improve —fast."

Things began to disappear around the Diener house. George had bought a ten-speed bicycle for himself, and Richie had asked to borrow it. When he brought it back, the bike was damaged from a spill. Annoyed, George put it in the tool shed until he could find time to repair it. When that day came, he opened the shed and the bike was gone. "Where did the bike go?" George asked his older son.

"I dunno."

"I think you do. Where did it go?"

Richie turned to walk away. "I sold it," he said.

Anger flooded George. "What makes you think you have the right to take other people's property and sell it?"

Richie shrugged. That night, George told Carol that their son had "no guilt" whatsoever. "He just gave me his standard look," said George, "the look that says I am an old fart butting into something that is simply not my business."

An Italian knife that a friend had given George suddenly vanished. Then small sums of money were discovered missing from George's wallet and Carol's purse. She began hiding her purse, thinking as she performed the act, "This is incredible, I have to hide my purse from my own son."

One afternoon in late 1971 a burglary was committed at the Diener house. One of George's two guns, a .25 Colt automatic pistol, was taken, along with a small sum of money. Although the intruder(s) rummaged through Richie's room as well, George could not put it out of his mind that perhaps his own son had been the thief. Other homes in the neighborhood were suffering daytime break-ins. Neighbors stood in their yards, leaning on rakes, discussing crime. The peaceable lanes were, to George's thinking, as imperiled as the ghettos of New York City. Police had arrested some young people near the Blackstone corner on suspicion of selling narcotics. And, though Richie was not among them, George was irate. "Nothing whatsoever will happen to them," he predicted. "They'll be back on the streets in one day pushing their poisons."

By late November, 1971, the atmosphere in the Diener house had never been so critical. Carol discovered a small box filled with empty transparent pill capsules on Richie's desk. She questioned her son.

"What are these?" she asked.

"Capsules. You buy 'em at a drugstore."

"What do you do with them?"

"I suppose people put medicine in them."

"How do kids buy them?" Carol demanded.

"They're hard," Richie admitted. "But if you tell the druggist you need them for a school project, you can get them. I told him I was making a map and needed them to fill with cotton to show industry in the South."

Carol weighed the explanation. She decided she did not believe her son.

"What else do you do with them?" she asked.

Richie smiled. He seemed to take pleasure in telling his mother exactly what he did with them. "I fill them with sugar and sell them to dumb kids," he said.

"That's wrong," said Carol. "That's illegal."

Richie began his answer, and Carol could join him in silent unison. "Don't worry about it," he said.

"But I *do* worry about it," said Carol. "I worry so much that it seems I have nothing else to do."

When Carol told George of the incident, he nodded, as if putting one more piece into a jigsaw puzzle. The same expression had crossed his face when Carol had seen her husband in the kitchen lately eavesdropping on Richie's telephone conversations.

One evening Carol prepared dinner and watched in discomfort as her husband and her elder son ate in hurried silence. After the episode at school and the series of thefts in the house, George and Richie were refusing again to speak to one another, passing mutely in the house, heads down, eyes averted as if two ancient enemies were forced to occupy the same living space. If George had anything to say to his son he used Carol as go-between, a role so wearying that she was growing thin from lack of appetite, and wrinkles started to surround her eyes.

When the meal was done, Carol washed dishes and called out that she was going to the school board meeting. "You're staying home tonight and studying," she told Richie. Because a week had passed with no yelling in the house, Carol sensed Richie's attitude was at least no worse. Moreover, she held one trump card—the boy's passionate desire to get a driver's license and use of the family car. Unless his grades rose, unless the atmosphere in her home warmed, Carol made it clear, she would not sign his application and he would have to wait until he was eighteen the following June.

When Carol drove away, George settled into his easy chair to read the newspaper. Immediately the rock music from Richie's room annoyed him. Since Carol was not present to act as his advocate, George strode into the kitchen and shouted down himself. "Would you turn that music down a little?"

No response. George cried out again, this time sharply. "Richie!"

Nothing. Furious, George stormed into his son's room and brusquely snapped off the tape deck. It had been a Christmas gift from Mr. and Mrs. Ring, and Richie treasured it more than the animals of his childhood. With the room suddenly quiet, George took his leave. Richie screamed after him, "If you broke that tape deck, I'll take care of you. And if I can't, my friends will."

The threat burned into George and he considered whirling and discussing the challenge. But he checked his temper and, with nothing more than a glare, returned to the living room and his newspaper.

A few minutes later, Richie appeared in a jacket, prepared to go out. Breaking his rule of silence a second time, George said tersely, "You're not going anywhere. You heard your mother." Ignoring his father, Richie continued toward the door.

George stood up and touched his son's arm. "Did you hear me?" he said.

Wrenching his arm free, Richie bestowed upon his father an expression that George had never seen. It was not only disobedience, it was hate. Obviously, thought George, he has taken something. The chemicals he put in his mouth make him look at me this way. He could not try to destroy me with his eyes—I gave him his life!—if it were not so.

George softened his voice. "We've got to talk, Richie," he said. "I know we've been over this ground a hundred times before, but . . ." George stopped. His words were locked inside a vacuum. His son gave no sign that he heard them. Richie was at the door, opening it, stepping onto the threshold.

"If you leave now," shot out George, "then don't bother to come back."

The door slammed. And Richie was gone.

When Carol returned from her meeting, George said that Richie had gone out against his will. In his anger, he went around to all the doors, locking them from the inside so that keys would not open them. When they went to bed, George held Carol tightly, as if her body could draw all the ill from within him.

At two in the morning, when both were at last fitfully asleep, there came a pounding at the door. It would not go away. George lay in the warmth of his bed and listened to it. Carol started to get up, but George threw out his hand to restrain her.

When the knocking had gone on for a quarter of an hour, when Richie began to cry out, when the neighbors would surely hear, George finally rose and went to the front door. Carol followed him.

Richie entered in anger. He began to rage at his father's cruelty.

George cut into the harangue. "Richie," he said, "your mother and I love you."

Richie considered the extraordinary response from his father, standing before him in pajamas, in the middle of the night. The boy threw it back. "No you don't!" he said. "The only reason I'm even here is that you had hot pants about seventeen years ago. I'm a mistake. A mistake! I'm the mistake that happened when you and Mama started fooling around."

George blew up. He slapped his son hard across the mouth. Richie felt the blood trickle onto his chin. He took his hand, wiped it away, and flung the blood against the living room wall. Dazed, George watched the few drops slip down the wall of the house that had been his dream. Richie ran wordlessly into the kitchen and down the steps to his room. The last door of the long night slammed.

Lying awake until almost dawn, Carol and George spoke in terse sentences.

"What are we going to do?" Carol asked, not so much of her husband, but of herself.

"I don't know," said George. "I honestly don't know."

After a time, Carol spoke again. "We've got to get Richard some help."

George nodded.

There was an idea gestating in his head, and as soon as it formed, as soon as he had thought it out, as soon as he could concoct the proper way to let Carol in on it, he would put it into being. Carol would not like it, but it had to be done. George was positive it had to be done.

Chapter Seventeen

At seventeen years plus a few months, Richie remained
relentlessly boyish-looking. Despite the serious expressions
he screwed onto his face, despite the mature swagger he
tried to affect, he looked even younger than his years.
Some of his friends teased him mildly with a nickname,
"the Kid," which enraged the red-haired boy who wanted
to be much bigger than five feet seven and much more
important than 140 pounds. His size was a handicap in
gaining entrance to Ryan's, a bar in neighboring Hempstead that was usually crowded with college students from
Hofstra University across the road and those of high
school age who could slip past the ID check at the door
with a forged credential or an adult aura.

More often than not, Richie was turned away at the
door by a bouncer who did not believe he was eighteen,
the legal drinking age in New York. But now and then,
usually on a weekend when a mob overspilled the popu-

lar gathering place, Richie managed to gain entrance. Inside the pseudo-English pub with a Union Jack behind the bar, dark tables carved with initials of lovers from years past, and a jukebox that offered the latest and loudest rock, Richie rendezvoused one early September night in 1971 with a kid named Fritz. Through Brick, Richie learned that Fritz often had large quantities of drugs for sale and specialized in filling orders for whatever a buyer desired.

On this night, Richie came to the point quickly. "I wanna buy a pound of grass," he said.

Fritz looked surprised. A full pound? Richie was known to Fritz as an avid user of grass and downs, but his purchases had always been on a small scale—a nickel or dime of pot at the most.

Richie saw the suspicion in Fritz's eyes. "I have the bread," Richie hurriedly said. "I worked most of the summer at Burger King."

Fritz nodded. Then it so happened, he said, that he had a good pound of Colombian grass for sale at only $100.

Richie quickly calculated the economics of the sale. The going price in his community for a full pound was normally between $180 and $250, depending upon market fluctuations. If he broke the pound down into nickel bags —$5 worth, enough to fill a whiskey shot glass—he could make up to $480. Even if he kept a half pound for his own use, and even after deducting the original $100 purchase price, he could anticipate around $100 profit.

Richie went to the savings bank the next day and withdrew $100. He bought the pound from Fritz, who expressed confidence that his customer would enjoy it, and excitedly took his investment home. But after the would-be entrepreneur rolled the first joint and lit up, when ten minutes passed and there was no rush, no sensation whatsoever, Richie grew alarmed. He finished the joint and rolled a second. Sometimes one joint hits and another does not, he knew. Sometimes your mind is not receptive to turning on.

But when the second cigarette produced nothing within him, Richie stormed to the telephone and dialed Fritz. No answer. He called Brick and complained. "It's worthless," shouted Richie. "Old and weak and totally useless. I couldn't sell a nickel of this shit to anybody if they asked to try it out first." It was customary for buyers to sample pot before buying it. Richie had trusted Fritz and now regretted it.

"I'd say you've been ripped off pretty good," said Brick.

"I'll beat his ass!" cried Richie.

"You'll have to find him first," suggested Brick. "I imagine he'll be hiding out for a while."

Several weeks passed before Richie's rage eased. Nor did he receive much consolation from Brick or Mark or Peanuts, because all had been ripped off by Richie at one time or another, and vice versa. There is companionship and need among drug users, but the honesty of deep friendship is not a part of it. Mark pointed out that once a sandwich bag of pot had been missing from his room after Richie had been present. Brick openly accused Richie of lifting a vial of Seconals once when the foursome was lying about his room, heavily stoned. Peanuts had bought a small amount of marijuana from Richie, only to discover that it had been generously laced with parsley and oregano. Richie admitted it cheerfully, saying he had raided his father's supply of spices in his basement. But Richie had grievances against his friends, as well. He could match every one of their complaints with one of his own.

Petty crimes among them were part of the drug culture. None of the quartet was guiltless enough to throw a very sizable stone. Each subscribed to the youthful philosophy that ripping off was neither illegal nor immoral, only necessary. "How can it be wrong to steal something that is illegal to have in the first place?" Peanuts always said, he being clever at stealing drugs from other people. And Mark, returning from a highly successful rip-off tour of a department store record shop, told Richie, "If you don't have anything, and you need it bad—and somebody else has something, then it's all right to take it. Every man has a basic greediness and it just has to come out."

Still smarting from the $100 loss, Richie picked up a rumor in school that a boy named Beaver had opium for sale. Opium! This was the first time Richie had heard of the rare drug being available in East Meadow, even though he had heard Mark and Brick brag ecstatically of its mystery and power upon encountering it in New York.

Beaver showed Richie a tiny chunk of the black, soft, tarlike material at their meeting place in the boys' toilet. Richie asked the price. One gram, said Beaver, cost $20. One pound, said Beaver, cost $10,000! Richie whistled in disbelief. He bought a chip for $20 and watched as the small boy with two oversized front teeth methodically whittled it off from the mother lode. "If this isn't opium," warned Richie, raising a clenched fist. Beaver shot up his right hand as if swearing in court.

After school, in Peanuts' room, first locking the door to keep his junkie sister away in case she tried to come in, Richie put the opium in his hashish pipe and inhaled. Quickly he pronounced his verdict. "Sensational! Fantastic! A new high!"

The next day Richie found Beaver again in school. He said the opium was everything Beaver had promised. Now he wanted to buy a quarter ounce. Beaver rapidly calculated in his head. The price would be $200. Richie nodded in approval.

Beaver knew that Richie's reputation in drug transactions was not exactly impeccable. He said the terms would be cash, in advance.

Richie reached into his notebook and pulled out his

savings passbook. It showed approximately $180, what was left from his $375 nest egg after several weeks of buying grass and downs. "And I'll get the other twenty from somebody who's going in with me on this," promised Richie.

On the day of the sale, Richie turned up at Beaver's house and the seller, with a voice like Mark's that refused to change, demanded his $200. Richie counter-demanded to see the quarter ounce. He inspected it at length. "I'm not satisfied with the weight," Richie finally said. "I think it's a short count." Beaver said he had weighed it that afternoon at school, on a gram scale in the chemistry lab. "You got a gram scale here?" asked Richie, knowing full well Beaver did not.

When Beaver shook his head negatively, Richie snapped his fingers in inspiration. Could he use the phone? Dialing a number, Richie spoke confidentially.

"This kid I know will let us use his scale," said Richie, hanging up. "We've gotta meet him in fifteen minutes behind Waldbaum's."

His suspicion perking, Beaver demanded first to see the money. Richie pulled a fat white envelope from his jacket. "It's all here," he said. "It's yours as soon as I weigh the stuff."

Richie led Beaver to a deserted parking lot behind the supermarket. Twilight was darkening the area, a chill wind scooped up the last leaves and threw them about. Beaver was both worried and frightened.

"Give me the money," he pleaded.

"Give me the dope," ordered Richie.

Suddenly Peanuts stepped out from a shadowy place of stacked-up boxes and approached Beaver. The little boy sagged. His mouth flew open. The normal solemnity of Peanuts was now alarming. Calmly Richie snatched the opium from Beaver's hand and said, "Thanks very much."

Richie and Peanuts, laughing, skipped successfully away.

As they rounded the corner, they heard Beaver moaning, "I can't believe this is happening. I can't believe I got ripped off for $200." Beaver sat down on an apple box and wept for several minutes before he began the long walk home.

As they smoked the opium together, Richie speculated on what Beaver might do in revenge. "Nothing," said Peanuts. "He's a little jerk, and besides, he's in business. Businessmen have problems. You know, like strikes."

Although the two boys relished the big opium rip-off, and the telling of it for weeks thereafter, it paled beside the Solly Greene caper, a blustering drama of violence in two acts.

One winter afternoon Richie assembled his foursome and asked if everyone knew Solly Greene, a boy of twenty-one who lived in East Meadow with his well-to-do parents. "He's a creep," proclaimed Peanuts. Mark nodded. "A real schmuck, he's that skinny lame with fuzz coming out of his face."

Satisfied, Richie laid out his plan. "He's a cheap cocksucker and we're gonna rip him off tonight." A small grievance was held by Richie against Greene, because in their last transaction, during which Richie bought forty-five dollars' worth of hashish, he idly picked up a book of matches on Solly's desk. Solly wanted an extra penny for them.

Now, weeks later, Richie went to the telephone and made an arrangement to buy thirty-five dollars' worth of marijuana.

At 8:30 that night, Richie rang Solly's doorbell. The older youth opened it instantly and seemed surprised to find Richie accompanied by Brick, Mark, and Peanuts. He did not know the other boys well, but he knew they were Richie's running mates, so he let them all in. An enormous black dog growled behind Solly's legs. Mark, fearful of animals from his burglary days, asked if Solly

could put the monster away. Mark, at 110, weighed perhaps less than the dog. Later that night he would brag
that this had been expert thinking on his part. "That dog
could have gotten rough on us," said Mark, because that
was the only thing he contributed all night. His mouth
surpassed his muscle at all times.

Solly shut the dog up in a room off the hallway and
brought out a medium-sized plastic garbage bag. He led
his customers into the living room, available for drug
transaction because his parents were on the last day of a
winter Florida vacation. He turned to Richie. "Two
ounces, right? It's twenty dollars per ounce, but you're
getting a discount for two."

Brick interrupted. "I also want a quarter ounce of
hash," he said, "if it's good stuff." To emphasize that he
was "quick with the bread," Brick whipped out his wallet.
At the same time, Richie was peering into the open garbage
sack. More drugs than he could estimate lay in its recesses.

"What all have you got in there?" asked Richie casually.

Solly replied with some pride. "Couple ounces blond
hash, best that's been around here for months. Four ounces
Nigerian grass. A few ups. About fifty downs. Pharmaceuticals. It's all worth around $380, I guess."

Brick made a different calculation. On the spot he
figured mentally the bag's contents would bring at least
one thousand dollars.

Mark's eyes shifted from the bag to Richie. His red-
haired friend obviously had the same thought: We have
no money, nothing to smoke, and all that is going to be
ours.

With no grace, no cunning, Richie simply shot his hand
out and seized the bag from a startled Solly Greene. Even
as Solly formed a protest, Richie was out of the living
room and through the front door, his trio of adventurers
a split second behind him. Crashing out, Richie broke a

window pane on the door and cut his hand. Blood ran onto the thousand-dollar garbage sack.

Shrieking hysterically, with long piercing screams that reminded Mark of "a woman getting raped," Solly raced after his goods. He made a flying tackle at Richie, but just as the antagonists fell to the grass, Richie made a dazzling forward pass to Brick, yelling "Grab the bag!" Brick had rushed to his car, flinging open its doors to receive his friends. It was left to Peanuts, who made a balletic leap high into the air to catch the bag. Richie disentangled himself and ran toward the open car door. Brick bulled into the pursuing Solly and pinned him to the ground. With the aid of Peanuts, they pummeled the skinny dealer. Brick even yanked out a clump of his hair.

Fearful that neighbors would soon materialize, drawn by Solly's terrible screams, Mark yelled for Brick to get into the car. As the elderly Plymouth hurried away, Solly hurled rocks and threats in its wake. "Bastards!" he bellowed. But his words were lost on Richie and Peanuts and Brick and Mark. All four were doubled up with laughter and pride in their accomplishment.

Now the problem was where to go to examine the haul and partake of its promise. Each boy said his parents were at home that night. It was decided to visit a friend named Turk whose parents, Mark always said, "were lame, like the Beverly Hillbillies." Mark bragged of once stealing a car, driving it into Turk's garage, stripping it there, and at the same time eating a sandwich brought to him by Turk's mother, who allowed that the child must be hungry from all that mechanical work. "You can blow grass smoke in Turk's old man's face and he'd think it was corn silk," agreed Richie. He had found a piece of cloth on the floor of Brick's car to wrap around his bleeding hand.

The four were warmly received by Turk and his parents. True to form, the father noticed Richie's bleeding hand and began to bandage it. "I fell on the playground

after school and cut it on a bottle," explained Richie. The
mother bustled into the kitchen to bring cookies and milk.

After the social amenities, the boys went to Turk's
room, where they divided the bag's contents, tested the
hash, proclaimed it indeed excellent, and awarded their
host a small sample for his hospitality.

Not trusting Brick's ability to drive, for his body was
jiggling from his high, Richie and Mark and Peanuts
elected to walk home together, creeping through back-
yards and across fences to avoid the streets. "Solly'll be
out looking for us," predicted Richie. Mark was more
worried about a cop stopping them and discovering the
forbidden riches in their pockets.

When he reached his home, Richie noticed that his
parents' car was missing, and he invited his friends in for
a few minutes. Carol no longer informed her son in advance when she and George planned a rare evening away,
even when they were visiting her sister, as they were doing
this evening. She was afraid Richie would fill their home
with his pot-smoking friends. The last time she had asked
Richie to baby-sit with Russell, she returned home at
midnight to find a dozen boys and girls, and a house ripe
with the odor that she was now sophisticated enough to
recognize. The next day, a neighbor complained not only
of the noise, but of one of the revelers swinging on his
tree branch and breaking it. George ordered Richie to
saw the limb off, apply tree medicine, and apologize to
the neighbor.

Only Russell, then eleven years old, was in the Diener
house when the three boys returned from the Solly Greene
rip-off. Sitting down at the dining-room table, they rolled
joints and began to smoke. Mark noticed Russell watching
them. "Wanna try it?" he said. Russell shook his head. He
was watching a comedy on television. Mark walked over
to the child sprawled on his stomach on the green carpet.
"It won't hurt you. Come on and try a puff." Russell put

the cigarette into his mouth and blew smoke out inexpertly. Instantly he began to cough.

Richie moved over and snatched the joint from his brother's hands. "Don't make him do it if he doesn't want to," said Richie to Mark. And he warned the child, "If you tell Daddy, I'll bust you." Then he knelt down and looked the little boy squarely in the face. His voice was oddly tender. "If you turn into a head, I'll break your bones."

The next day Richie stayed at school only long enough to hear that Solly Greene had vowed to kill him. The victim had even sent an emissary to East Meadow High to spread the warning. On hearing it between first and second periods, Richie professed scorn. But he cut out before noon and went home. Telephone calls flew back and forth between the foursome the rest of the afternoon. It was decided the best defense was a good offense. "We'd better get him before he gets us," said Mark, ominously, although his soprano voice never sounded so incongruous as when making dark threats.

At 7 P.M. Brick collected everyone, and the four smoked grass and hash for a half hour to boost their courage before pulling up in front of Solly's home. Each was prepared for battle. Richie had two short pieces of rubber hose, one of which he gave to Brick. Hose is limp in the summer, but in winter, Richie pointed out, it is cold and hard. "It can rip your skin off," he said. Peanuts had a pair of homemade brass knuckles that he had fashioned from an old sword handle. Mark juggled a rock in his small, girlish hands.

Richie rang the doorbell. To his surprise, Solly's father, returned from vacation, answered it. The four boys stared at him. Mark, with his gift for imagery, described the man later as "a gray, sad-looking old poop. He looked like Silly Putty, like he was ready for the coffin."

"Yes?"

"Is Solly home?" asked Richie.

At once the giant dog began to bark from within. Mark tensed, trying to keep the smirk on his face that the others had.

Solly appeared at the door. "Did you pricks come to pay me, or give me back my stuff?" he said.

Richie broke out laughing, his comrades following suit. Solly quickly sensed he was in danger. He saw the rubber hoses, the brass knuckles on Peanuts' clenched right fist, the rock in Mark's hand.

He let out another of his eerie screams. Mr. Greene rushed back to the door. "What's the matter, son?" he asked. He saw his boy dive at Richie, yelling, "I just wanna get this one motherfucker!"

Like two objects that had been glued together and resisted all attempts to unstick them, Solly and Richie rolled across the lawn, both screaming, both enraged. Mr. Greene ran to the aid of his son, only to see Brick hurrying to help Richie. The father intercepted Brick, grabbed him by the shoulders, and pushed him against the family car. Shaking Brick's shoulders so hard that his long hair and scraggly beard bounced, Mr. Greene shouted, "Had enough? Had enough?"

He stepped back for his answer, whereupon Brick made a fist and slammed it into the gray old man, square in the stomach. Across the yard, Richie had now freed one hand enough to crack Solly over the head with his hose.

Mrs. Greene, hearing the commotion, rushed to her front door and began screaming, "I'm calling the police!" Behind her, the giant dog yelped and begged to be turned loose into the fray. Mr. Greene staggered about his yard with his hands at his stomach, doubled over in pain. Solly managed to rise, blood streaming from somewhere on his head.

Mark, more valuable as lookout and warning siren than

combatant, shouted that it was time to leave. The four piled rapidly into the car and Brick slammed his foot against the accelerator, throwing up a shower of dirt and gravel.

Mr. Greene ran after the car until his breath gave out. He cried in triumph, "I've got your license number." But the number he called out, which Brick heard, was not correct. "He's not only old, he's blind," whooped Peanuts.

As soon as the Plymouth careened around the next corner, out the window and into a clump of brush flew the pieces of rubber hose and Peanuts' brass knuckles. Tires screeching, the car sped away, its occupants merry and proud. "Just like in the movies," cried Mark. "We're the fucking late show."

George Diener answered his telephone later that night and spoke with Solly Greene, who demanded that Richie's father do something about the assault.

"I'm deeply sorry," said George. "But the only thing I can do is suggest you call the police and let them handle it. I'll back you all the way."

But Solly never notified the police. He was between a rock and a hard place. How could he seek help from the law when the cause of the fight was a thousand-dollar garbage bag of drugs, when the law said it was illegal—and worthy of prison—to possess them?

For weeks the postmortems went on among the four boys. The episode, though it lasted only five minutes, stretched into an epic drama of heroism and high danger. Mr. Greene turned from a gray old man into a giant, his son from a schmuck into a mean potential killer. Richie spent hours on the telephone telling and retelling the great Solly Greene adventure. He spoke in low tones on the kitchen phone so that his father would not overhear.

But George did not need to overhear. He knew it all. For several weeks now he had been tape-recording every word his son spoke on the telephone. For more midnights than he could count, he had listened with sorrow, anger, and total bewilderment as cassette after cassette revealed the story of the son who was becoming his enemy.

Chapter Eighteen

A few weeks before the Solly Greene incident, George chose an evening when there was quiet in the house, with Richie away and Russell asleep. He sat down next to Carol on the burnt-orange sofa. Almost casually he brought up an idea, one that, if successful, would allow them to find out exactly what Richie was doing in the drug world.

But, as George had predicted to himself, Carol was immediately opposed to the plan. In fact, she was shocked.

"How can you even think of bugging your own son?" she said.

George grew impatient. He was spending as much time bickering with his wife these days as he did with his boy.

"Because I think Richie has graduated from just using drugs himself," answered George. "I think he's buying and selling them to other kids. I think he's a pusher."

The charge brought alarm to Carol's thin face. She shook her head in disbelief.

"If he is," George went on quickly, "then I want to stop it before it gets any further. And unless I get some proof, some concrete proof, he wouldn't listen to me. You know that."

Carol considered what her husband was saying. The scheme was beyond her imagination. "I still think it's wrong," she said sadly.

"Of course it's wrong," said George. "But it's not as wrong as what Richie's doing. I can't think of any other way to stop it."

In an outdoor magazine, George had spotted an ad for "surveillance devices." He drove to a store on Queens Boulevard in New York City. There, with no more trouble than in buying ammunition for his target pistols, he purchased a bug for his home telephone. It consisted of four special wires. It cost only fifty dollars.

Two of the wires hooked into the telephone wire, anywhere on the line. The other two went, said the instructions, into any home tape recorder. George borrowed Russell's inexpensive machine and told him that he was taking it to the shop for repairs. He placed the recorder in the basement, inserted a cassette for one hour's playing time, and tested the apparatus. Everything worked. The instant someone upstairs picked up the telephone receiver, either to answer an incoming call or to make an outgoing one, the recorder snapped on automatically and taped every word. When the telephone receiver was placed back on its cradle, the recorder automatically shut off.

The next morning George went to work with the impatience of a man who has set out a trotline. He could not wait to see if he had snared the big fish. When he reached home that night, he went immediately to the basement. To his dismay, the tape had run out, so that the machine was inoperative. As he rewound the cassette, he thought that there would be nothing recorded. But the moment he pushed the Play button, he heard what he wanted to hear—and what he did not.

No matter where George stopped or started, there was talk of drugs. Ninety percent of Richie's telephone conversations seemed to deal with pot or hash or downs.

At the beginning, for example, Richie was speaking with a boy whose name was Carlos:

RICHIE: I had two joints on me the other night, you know? And my father started pulling his usual shit on me. I figured he was gonna call the cops or something to check my room. But instead he goes, "Richard, would you please empty out your pockets?" So I got a little nervous, you know? I say, "No." He says, "Richard, I told you to please empty your pockets." I don't even answer him. I just walk out. So he dropped it. He couldn't do anything about it.

CARLOS: So what'd you do with 'em?

RICHIE: I smoked 'em in school today. There was a nark—I think they got narks in school now, guys who watch to see that you don't smoke in the parking lot. They seen me doing it. I saw 'em fuckin' starin' at me. So I ran out in the football field where I could eat 'em.

CARLOS: You ATE 'em?

RICHIE: Yeah. I'm gettin' good at it. I used to throw up.

Several minutes later on the tape, Mark telephoned Richie. Richie sounded heavily stoned, his speech slurred. Gaps appeared not only between sentences, but between words in sentences. Apparently Peanuts had asked Mark earlier in the day to buy ten dollars' worth of hash. Mark inquired of Richie if the sale was legitimate—or a rip-off.

MARK: Where'd Peanuts get the ten bucks?

RICHIE: Don't worry about it. He's here now. He doesn't have it right this minute, but someone's buying some grass from him in about ten minutes.

MARK: Who?

RICHIE: I said . . . don't worry about it.
(Peanuts' muffled voice is heard in the background.)
He says he has five so far. He'll have the other five as soon as this kid gets here and pays him.

MARK: Put him on for a second?

RICHIE: *(Irritated)* What for? What difference does it make where and when he gets the money?

MARK: I don't wanna walk all the way over there and then he doesn't want it.

RICHIE: Don' be lame, Mark. If you got something to sell, then Peanuts's got something to buy with.

An unidentified young voice calls Richie. He does not introduce himself, but Richie seems to know him well.

RICHIE: Brick got some really good grass.

VOICE: I was there when he bought it.

RICHIE: You get it for him?

VOICE: No.

RICHIE: But you think it's good?

VOICE: He paid $130 for a half pound.

RICHIE: *(Incredulously)* What? You serious?

VOICE: Swear to God. And listen to this. There's about five ounces of twigs in it.

RICHIE: Five ounces of twigs!

VOICE: You couldn't even see green. All you could see was lumber.

RICHIE: I knew he'd get took. Brick's so lame. I bought fine stuff. That Colombian grass. Dusted with mescaline, you know? I bought four ounces and had four more fronted to me. They'll be linin' up to buy that.

VOICE: I may ask you to front some for me sometime. Sometimes I haven't got time to sell it as fast as I need to. You know anybody who wants acid?

RICHIE: Nah. Not me. It flips me out.

VOICE: Well, I got like five hundred tabs.

RICHIE: I'll ask around.

Just before they hang up, Richie and the caller make an appointment to meet the next afternoon in the teachers' parking lot at East Meadow High to discuss the sale of a quarter pound of hashish.

George played the tape twice, before and after dinner. He made several pages of notes, then took them to bed to read them. Carol said that she had no interest in either the tape or the notes.

The next day George sat Richie down in the living room, brought out the tape recorder, and played a portion of the tape for him. When it was done, when Richie was still sputtering and professing profane outrage that his father would do such a thing, George issued an icy directive. "Assemble those friends of yours," he said. "Get them over here fast."

Brick, Mark, and Peanuts, warned by Richie of what they were about to hear, entered the Diener house with none of the bravado of the street and the school corridor. Suddenly they were three extremely worried boys, one only fourteen, one fifteen, one nineteen, none over five feet eight, all with faces the color of ash. George had earlier told Richie that the bug had been on the family telephone for an entire week, that he now possessed numerous cassettes of damning conversation.

In reality, George had but one. He would have to play his bluff carefully. He did not relish the coming scene, but then, on the other hand, neither did he dread it. Into an ordinary life a splash of color and excitement had fallen. The heroics he had pursued in vain across the seas of the world were in, of all places, his living room. There was a moral purpose to the coming confrontation, but there was more. In George's fantasy, he was no longer just a salesman and part-time moonlighting security guard. He was a crack detective. He had the evidence. The enemy was in his grasp.

Draining his voice of color and passion, trying to keep it as crisp and professional as a plainclothesman would, George made a brief accusatory speech in which he charged that his own son and three accomplices were actively engaged not only in using illegal drugs, but in buying and selling them to others.

"Let's hear the proof," challenged Mark. George found him to be the "snottiest" one of the four.

As he spoke, George held several cassettes in his hand. He selected one, seemingly at random. The others were fresh and blank. He placed the tape on the machine and pushed the button to let the hour of incriminating talk spin its course. When it was done, an uncomfortable silence enveloped the room. Carol, sitting at the dining-room table, rose and went to the kitchen on an imaginary errand.

Suddenly Peanuts spoke up. "What are you gonna do with them?"

"I *should* give them to the police and stop this business right away," said George, pausing for effect. Brick shifted uncomfortably on the sofa. He was on probation for drug possession already—and George knew it.

"But . . ." George hesitated. "I've decided to call your parents instead and play them these interesting little dramas."

Peanuts stood up in alarm. "Oh, Jesus, don't tell my parents. They have enough problems already."

Carol, standing in the doorway to the kitchen, spoke for the first time. "If they have enough problems," she said, "what are you doing this for?" She pointed toward the tape recorder.

Peanuts and Mark and Brick now focused on Richie, who had remained silent for the painful hour. They ex pected him to come to their defense, to disabuse his father of the plan. But Richie appeared almost amused by the situation, as if—for the moment at least—he rather enjoyed the whole affair, as if he relished being found out, like a man who carries around a painful secret that finally is revealed.

Not Mark, however. He elected to challenge George's invasion of his privacy. "Go ahead," he said. "My parents know already. They let me smoke pot in front of them."

Carol shook her head in disbelief. "I doubt if that's true," she said.

"Is it, Mark?" demanded George.

Mark dropped his eyes, backing off.

Brick cleared his throat. It was difficult for him to speak, not only because he was slightly stoned from a pre-dinner joint, but because he pictured himself being sent that very night to the Nassau County jail.

"What if we all promised to stop doing . . . that," said Brick.

"I would," put in Peanuts, eagerly.

Mark bounced his head in affirmation.

George balanced the taped evidence gingerly in his open hand. He stretched the suspense for all it was worth. Finally he spoke. "I don't believe you," he said, "and it's against my better judgment. But I'm going to give you a chance. For the time being, I won't call the police. And . . . I won't call your parents."

His side of the bargain, George said, was his decision not to tape any more telephone calls.

Once more a fragile peace settled on the Diener household. It held, however, only a few days. Richie skipped dinner a week later and emerged from his room obviously stoned, on his way out the front door. George remarked that the vow Richie had presumably taken with his compatriots had not lasted long.

Richie responded that it was none of his father's business.

Then it could become police business, or court business, shot back George. He rose to intercept his son. Richie raised his fist.

"All right, son," said George. "You believe in the law of the streets. You believe strong is best. Put up your dukes." George raised his fists and crouched as if in the ring.

Richie, seemingly prepared for an encounter, patted a noticeable bulge in his jacket pocket. It was a razor, he said, and if his father pushed him too far, he was ready to use it. George, his temper once again full out, seized a piece of bicycle chain to defend himself. In an earlier quarrel, Richie had produced the chain as a weapon. George had taken it away from him. Now, for a few moments of paralysis, father and son glared at one another; then they circled slowly in the living room while the television set delivered canned laughter in accompaniment.

Carol came into the room and broke the spell. "Stop it!" she cried to George. And, to Richie: "If you hate us so much, if you don't like our way of life, the things we believe, then why don't you just leave? Why don't you go away and . . ." She faltered. She wanted to swallow the words that had come rushing out at the sight of her husband and her son.

George put down the chain. "I'm sorry," he muttered, to Carol, not to Richie. Richie looked first at his mother, then at his father. With eyes reddened from grass, or pills, or possibly even tears, he ran out of the house.

George found a new place that night, under his desk, to hide the tape recorder. He also called the police department and, when an officer appeared at the yellow house, told him of the razor incident. George gave him the cassette containing the drug talk. The officer promised to listen to it, but, in the meantime, he suggested that George seek the counsel of Family Court.

"Your honor," wrote George in a letter to Judge Burstein of Family Court, "we need help. It seems my son hates me and I don't know why, because I can't talk to him, every time I try he gets nasty and we get into a fight and I end up calling the police. He says he loves his mother but he is killing her with the crazy things he is doing to get even with me, like having my wife called to pick him up at school because he was high on some drug and causing trouble in class. If I try to exert any parental authority, he threatens me with retaliation, he has threatened to have a bunch of his friends beat me to a pulp, he has threatened to take my possessions while I am at work and destroy or sell them, in fact he *has* taken some of my things and sold them. We have not had much trouble since the last time I called the police because I haven't been talking to him, I let him go where and when and with whom he pleases, because this is the only way there can be any peace in my house. This is the way he likes it, he has since returned to hanging around with the group I told him to stay away from and with whom he was involved with drugs. I must admit I am at the end of my rope, I just do not know what to do and I sincerely hope you can help us."

The letter, which took George the better part of an evening first to wrench from himself, then to translate to paper in his hunt-and-peck method of typing, was presented to the same caseworker, Morton Ozur, who had dealt with the Dieners six months earlier. George declared that he wished to file a "family offense" charge against his son. He also asked for an "order of protection" against the boy.

Caseworker Ozur read the letter and questioned George. Did Mr. Diener realize that an "order of protection" was an extremely rare tool, decreed by a judge only in the most drastic of domestic circumstances? Judges are very loath to issue such an order because it is a powerful weapon for a parent. It lays down a bill of particulars for the youngster: no drugs, for example, rigid curfew, no confrontations with a parent. "If a kid breaks such an order," pointed out Ozur, "the police make an automatic arrest and the kid usually goes to jail for six months."

George nodded. This was what he wanted. He had done a little homework on juvenile law, and it seemed to him that this was the only way to solve the problem of Richie. "I've tried to work things out with him," said George, "but nothing I try seems to last very long. If he starts up another one of these awful fights, then I want to be able to call the police and have him arrested and let them cool him off."

George ticked off his reasons. Most immediate was the chilling scene with Richie patting the razor in his pocket and George picking up the chain to defend himself. But there had been other evenings as forbidding as this one, he hastened to add. George also told of putting the tap on the family telephone for one twenty-four-hour period, of removing it, and of putting it back on secretly. It was still there, George said, whirring away every time the phone rang. George had full particulars of the opium rip-off from Beaver, the Solly Greene violence, the daily and nightly conversational wanderings through the puzzling world of drugs.

Ozur noted that several months earlier George had haled Richie before the court, only to withdraw the charge because the boy had made a "miraculous recovery." He further pointed out that at the time, the court had strongly recommended family counseling at the Drug Abuse Clinic.

Had this been done?

George shook his head.

Why not?

George shrugged. "He refuses to go," he said.

The caseworker cautioned George that the possibility existed of doing Richie more harm than good by bringing him before the court again and again, only to withdraw the charges.

But George persisted. He did not consider himself a man who owned a balky animal and, in an attempt to make it behave, ran it by the rendering plant now and then.

A hearing was set for December 16, 1971, and George brought Richie to court. They drove there in silence. Once more they stood before Judge Burstein. She advised Richie of his right to counsel and explained what that meant. He waived the right and said he could speak for himself.

Immediately the judge asked for an explanation of the

razor incident. Richie said that he did not threaten or intimidate his father. George attempted to interrupt, but the judge shushed him, saying he would have his turn.

Judge Burstein steered the conversation, for it was only an informal hearing at this point, to drugs. Here she instructed the court stenographer to go off the record and told Richie he could speak candidly, without fear of his words finding their way into a permanent file.

Riche admitted smoking pot and taking barbiturates. Judge Burstein nodded gently. As a lawyer, she had represented her first drug client in Nassau County in 1952, before suburbia had such problems. "I have a particular empathy for any child who comes into my court on a drug charge," she said. "I am going to recommend immediate family counseling before this court does anything."

She turned to George and addressed him firmly. "It is very, very rare for a parent to bring such serious charges against his child. We get a lot of people like you who come to this court and say, 'Do something!' Well, we can't do anything unless we have *your* cooperation. I am recommending family counseling, because you say you and your son cannot talk to each other. You *have* to talk to each other. If you don't, the problems will never be resolved. Certainly not by this court."

When George and Richie left the court, Judge Burstein sensed a "tremendous antagonism" of the father toward his son. She did not like the idea of a father using her court to punish his child.

On December 6, an East Meadow High art teacher named Vartanian reported to the assistant principal's office that Richie Diener had suddenly showed up in crafts class, for the first time since early September. Assistant Principal Castelli called Richie in and said he could not return to class, that he would be given an extra study hall.

When Carol learned of this much later, she wondered how her son had managed to cut crafts class each day for more than two months before the school discovered it. Why didn't the art teacher report Richie's absences earlier? The explanation was that the teacher was a new one, who worked only two days a week, and who was not fully familiar with "the ropes."

As the holidays neared, and Carol began planning the clever decorations for which she was known and the large Christmas Eve feast at which the entire clan would gather to open gifts, George was not infused with the spirit of the season.

Instead he would come home after work and go immediately to the tape recorder, which he moved regularly about the house to new hiding places so Richie would not discover it. Then he would sit down and play the day's telephone conversations. Like any telephone tap, they contained considerable extraneous material, which George had to sit through patiently before Richie's husky young voice came on again and again. The tapes were, in fact, a panorama of family life, a daily chronicle of George and Carol and Richie and Russell. As George sat in his locked bedroom listening, he heard himself talking to a superior about a supermarket running out of gravy mix, or a Boy Scout official wanting the names of two youngsters George had signed up for Russell's neighborhood troop. Or Carol talking almost curtly to her sister, who was calling to borrow a department store charge plate. (June Marck, the sister, did not know of the telephone tap's existence for several weeks and she complained to her husband, Joe, "What's the matter with my sister? She won't talk to me anymore on the telephone!" When Joe found out the truth, he told June, and only then did she realize why

Carol spoke so economically and hesitantly on the telephone.) Or Russell talking to a playmate about Saturday's game. And, finally, Richie, speculating on the possibilities of ripping off someone who claimed to have fifty pounds of marijuana, or of going into partnership with someone who can get a thousand Seconals.

As the tapes spun, George made notes, a daily chronicle of what went in and out on his family telephone. Then he painstakingly transferred a synopsis to a typewritten log, using the blank back side of his salesman's Daily Performance Sheet. The sheets began to grow.

Often George would shut off the machine and go in search of Carol, asking her to come hear something particularly informative—or damning.

Carol hated the tape recorder. She found herself wishing it would break, or that the tape would run out before Richie could finish a conversation, or that the telephone system in East Meadow would cease so that people could retain their own secrets.

"Listen to this," George would say.

Carol would shake her head sadly. "I don't want to," she would answer. "I might hear something I don't want to hear. I might learn something I don't want to know."

On December 19, 1971, George made the following entry in his chronicle:

Richard called a boy named Timmy J. and bragged about ripping off Solly Greene. He also told him the gang was planning a New Year's Eve party at some motel and Richie expects everyone to bring at least a half ounce of "STUFF." Richard made a date with some kid named Peter to go to a rock concert at Queens College, and Richie would bring some other people to Peter's house on the way in and have a "Pot Party" before the show. Richard said he would bring the "stuff." I then contacted Patrolman Moran of the Nassau County narcotics squad to follow them when they left here and raid their little "Pot Party" and arrest them all, but Richard did not go to the concert and the whole plan fell through.

On December 20, the entry read:

Mark Epstein called and told Richard to meet him and another boy at Peanuts' house and Mark would provide stuff to smoke. Richard told Mark that a boy named Ozzie had "turned on" ten or twelve kids in the boys' room at school today. Peanuts went out Christmas shopping so Richard went to Mark's house instead to "turn on." Richard called Sheila, his girl friend, and during conversation told of the night his friends tried to "turn on" his little brother, Russell, while we were out to a friend's house for coffee.

December 21:

Richie had conversations with Peanuts and Mark about getting a driver's license and a car. Richie said he had promised his mother he would give up marijuana if he could get his license and use her car. He said he didn't really mean this, of course. They talked about some pot they ripped off another kid, but Richard was afraid they would have to pay for it, after all, because the victim had a partner who is a friend of Richard's and he didn't know it at the time. Honor among thieves? They also talked about a quarter pound of "hash" that they are bringing to the New Year's Eve party. Richie is getting a bunch of kids together to rent a motel room and smoke so much grass and pot that everybody will pass out.

December 23:

Richard was on the phone quite a few times today talking "pot" and "hash" and planning the New Year's Eve party. Mark Epstein came over, and while he was here, Richard got a call from someone offering to sell him as much hash as he could afford. Richard didn't have the money, but Mark did, so Mark made arrangements to meet the seller at twelve tomorrow in the teachers' parking lot at Woodland School to buy one quarter ounce for $25.

In carving twenty-four hours each day down to a few stark lines, George was like an artist drawing a stick figure of a man, leaving out the flesh and bones and texture and emotion. True, he received daily reinforcement of his suspicions of his son until they were no longer suspicions but sorrowful facts. But perhaps he overlooked more poignant information available from Richie's words. Behind the tough talk and the moments when the sentences were slurred and punctuated by long, drugged silences, there stood revealed a bewildering child-man, insecure, desperate for affection/attention, and very, very lonely.

Three days before Christmas, Richie telephoned Sheila and caught her in the midst of wrapping packages. Sheila reminded Richie that this was the fourth Christmas they had known each other, their fourth anniversary "so to speak"—even though their relationship was more "brother and sister" than anything else—and that she expected an appropriate gift.

RICHIE: (Embarrassed) I didn't go Christmas shopping yet.
SHEILA: Christmas is Saturday, darling.
RICHIE: I know. (*A fit of coughing*)

SHEILA: What are you stoned on?
RICHIE: Whatta you think?
SHEILA: Knowing you, downs.
RICHIE: No.
SHEILA: Pot?
RICHIE: Yeah.

There is a long pause that stretches for almost a minute. Richie cannot think of anything to say. Even with the courage of grass, he is not comfortable talking to girls. (One of the most discouraging factors of drug use among the young, Dr. Victoria Sears, the Drug Abuse psychiatrist, has often noted, is that it robs them of sexual experiences and prohibits their maturity in that area. "Kids who are afraid of sex often substitute drugs instead," she said. "At the most crucial period of their lives, they get stoned and opt out." At seventeen and a half, though he would have bloodied anyone's nose who even hinted at it, Richie remained a virgin. As did many of his friends who spoke with veteran sophistication of sexual triumphs.)

RICHIE: So . . . what are you doing?
SHEILA: Wrapping Christmas presents.
RICHIE: I know that. Besides that.
SHEILA: Listening to the *Concert for Bangladesh* album. Twelve dollars. But it's worth it.
RICHIE: (*Another pause*) I got a whole three Christmas cards.
SHEILA: What?
RICHIE: I only got three Christmas cards this year.
SHEILA: Well, how many were you expecting, fifty?
RICHIE: (*Rather sadly*) I don't know. At least a few more than three . . . a few.
SHEILA: Who sent you Christmas cards?
RICHIE: You. Grandma. (*A rueful laugh*) My aunt.

SHEILA: You didn't get one from Kathy [a girl whom Richie briefly dated and of whom Sheila professed jealousy]?

RICHIE: No, but she sent me a message. She hopes I OD.

A few days later, Richie was called by a girl named Anne Marie, who attempted to invite him to a party. But Richie declined. There would be a number of people there he did not know, and he indicated he would be uncomfortable.

ANNE MARIE: But why can't you come? We *want* you. It's good to feel wanted, you know?

RICHIE: What?

ANNE MARIE: Did you ever feel wanted?

RICHIE: Who, me? Never heard the word.

And, in discussing an LSD trip with a friend named Peter, Richie delved, unknowingly, deep into his reasons for drug-taking:

PETER: I'm telling you, man, this new acid is unbelievable.

RICHIE: How so?

PETER: It's like taking sixty-eight Seconals, something like that.

RICHIE: How so? Explain it. Nobody's home at your house.

PETER: It's hard to explain. It's weird. Like I'd move my hand in front of my face and my hand seemed so far away. Like it was somebody else's hand, disconnected. Everytime I'd lie down I'd lose touch with reality, you know?

RICHIE: Well, that's the point, isn't it?

PETER: What did *you* feel like, that night you took three tabs, before you puked?

RICHIE: I dunno, man. It was like . . . it was like the room was shrinking, and I was all alone, and nobody would listen to me. I kept crying, and nobody would do anything. I remember thinking, "Well, Richie, you've killed yourself. Finally." The others were laughing at me, huh?

PETER: No, that girl thought you were stupid for taking three tabs—that's all. One would have been enough.

RICHIE: They were laughing at Richie cracking up, huh?

PETER: They always laugh.

RICHIE: I know. . . . Did you see the way I was walking? Those lumps on the floor flipped me out. They were like mountains. . . . God, I was scared. But it was worth it.

PETER: You only get that way on acid and stuff.

RICHIE: Brick's cousin flipped out on us the other night. On real strong pot. He was having "horrors." He's like twenty-three.

PETER: (*Surprised*) He flipped out? Really?

RICHIE: You *can* flip out on pot.

PETER: (*Scoffing*) I never do.

RICHIE: You can. I'm telling you. . . . I got scared a couple of times. Paranoid. I thought people were coming in the windows. . . . You ever read those drug books, "Pot can cause temporary insanity," stuff like that? . . . It could. It definitely could. But when your parents read something like that, they say, "Oh, Richie, you're going to go insane smoking that." It could . . . but it usually

very rarely does. . . . I mean, you'd really
have to smoke powerful pot every day to
flip out, wouldn't you?

PETER: You just about do, Rich.

RICHIE: (*A long pause*) I know. . . .

On Christmas Eve the Diener living room was crowded
with a gracefully decorated tree, a small mountain of gifts,
an array of laughing uncles, aunts, cousins, and grandfathers and grandmothers. Carol drew warmth and protection from the gathering in her home, even though she
went about preparing the traditional meal with less than
her normal zeal. Her mother, up from North Carolina,
commented that Carol "looked tired." Her father suggested that she was trying to do too much, with work,
charity endeavor, and family duties. Fortunately my parents do not know what is the reason for the pouches under
my eyes and the tremors of my hands, thought Carol. She
envied George, who was a better actor than she, who
could celebrate the rite with what seemed his dependable
good humor, telling jokes, flattering the women, dispens-
ing wine and eggnog, remembering fragments of holidays
past and the strength of them that binds families. No one
else in the living room knows the secret of my house,
thought Carol. No one here has witnessed the terrible
scenes. No one gathered around my tree would even have
a frame of reference for what happens between my husband and my son and me. They must never know.

Richie did not appear for the early part of the evening,
and when his relatives inquired about him, Carol tried to
make light of his absence. "He's down in his room listening
to music," she said. "You know teen-agers." The remark
was accepted. Youngsters are difficult these days. And
Richie *was* known to his tribe as an independent kid who
had a fight now and then.

When it was time for dinner, Carol went to her son's

room and opened the door without knocking. Smoke and odor of burning marijuana assaulted her. Quickly she shut the door so it would not creep through her house.

"Put that out immediately," she ordered, pointing to Richie's cigarette. "And come to dinner. Everybody's waiting for you."

With wonder, with a curious smile that seemed disconnected from his face, Richie looked at his mother. Oh, God, screamed Carol inside herself. He's stoned. "Not tonight," she pleaded. "Oh, please not tonight. It's Christmas Eve."

Richie did not move from his bed. He only smiled.

Carol made her voice as firm as she could. She would have fallen to her knees and begged if it would have done any good. "Please get up and come to dinner," she said. "They have presents for you."

Slowly Richie shook his head. "I can't . . ." he said. "I just can't."

And then Carol knew. He cannot face the decent people in my living room, she realized. He cannot bear to let those who love him see him this way. With enormous sadness, she nodded and left her son alone on Christmas Eve.

She made up a clumsy lie that Richie had taken ill with a virus and had gone to sleep early. Later, when the family began singing carols, she slipped into the bathroom and began to cry.

Chapter Nineteen

"Richard's New Year's Eve 'Pot Party' fell through," wrote George in his December 30, 1971, entry of the log. In celebration of Christmas, perhaps, he had taken the tap off the telephone on December 23, but he put it back on after the unpleasant episode when the family was gathered about the tree. "Richie found out that I knew about the 'Pot Party' and that I planned to have it raided, so he called it off. He called up Sheila and asked if she wanted any THC (a powerful synthetic marijuana) and she said NO. Richie said he and two others were pooling three ounces of marijuana for New Year's Eve. The other 'two' are apparently Mark and Peanuts. I do not know where they will do their 'turning on.'"

On the first night of the New Year, 1972, George listened to a crowded tape. Richie had been busy on the telephone most of the day, rehashing the party of the night before, which was transferred from the planned

motel room to an apartment owned by a relative of Brick
Pavall. As Richie had predicted, most of those who attended eventually passed out after liberal intake of sangría,
apple wine, Seconals, amphetamines, marijuana cigarettes,
and hashish in pipes. One novice youngster at the party
was turned on by Richie to pot for the very first time,
only he embarrassed himself by throwing up violently on
his girl friend's new party dress. "Richie, of course,
thought this was very funny," wrote George in his
transcription.

He was becoming fairly immune to such talk, hearing
it from his son's unknowing lips for weeks now, even as
he was growing sophisticated in the jargon of drug chatter.
But one piece of news startled George as he heard the
latest tape. Richie, in speaking with a friend named Nick,
said he was furious at Sean O'Hara for telling people he
was an addict "just because I shot up a few times."

George played this portion of the tape twice, then shut
it off. In one sense, he was not surprised. This was the
logical progression, he told himself. Now Richie is a
junkie. But on the other hand, he felt revulsion. He felt
total loss. He felt as he had when he attended the funeral
not long before of a neighborhood youngster who died
tragically of a blood disease. The boy had been bright,
handsome, athletic, full of promise. How much better it
would have been, George thought to himself in a confession so dark that it haunted him, if Richie were dead and
this other boy alive.

Brick Pavall began "chipping" heroin sometime in 1971
and soon moved from snorting the narcotic up his nose to
injecting it in his veins. Immediately he told Richie how
"good" it was, but Richie seemed totally uninterested.
"There's no way I'm gonna stick a needle in my arm,"
said Richie with finality.

But Brick persisted, even after he was stopped by East
Meadow police, discovered to have a small amount of

heroin in his car, kept in jail a week, and put on a year's probation. He never developed what might be called a New York City habit, perhaps because the drug was so scarce in his community. "We never had much of a heroin problem in East Meadow," said one drug clinic therapist. "Probably because there's so much other stuff around."

Brick maanged to satisfy his drug needs by using pot and pills, heroin only when it turned up and he had enough money to buy some. By late 1971, most New York area heroin was so diluted with sugar, so undependable a high, often as little as 3 percent pure, that many addicts turned to barbiturates instead.

One evening during the Christmas holidays, Brick and Richie were lounging around Peanuts' room listening to new albums he had received as gifts. Brick casually produced the paraphernalia of heroin—a cooking spoon, a rubber tube, a syringe, and a packet of white powder.

"You wanna get off on dope?" he asked Richie.

Richie shook his head vigorously. "I told you before," he said. "No way."

Brick persisted. "Just try it once. Satisfy your curiosity. You won't get addicted."

Richie glanced at the hypodermic. "I'm scared of needles," he said. "I wouldn't even know where to stick it."

"I'll do it for you," said Brick. "You really ought to try something just once, and if you don't like it, well, you've at least had the experience. You might never like ice cream if you never even try it."

Richie did not respond, but Brick walked over to him and took his left arm, which was suddenly trembling. Expertly he attached the rubber tube just below the biceps. Veins stood out like cord on a package. "You got good veins," said Brick.

Richie flinched.

"Don't worry," continued Brick. "I know what I'm doing. I'm gonna 'boot' it a couple of times." Richie turned his face away so as not to see the needle. Brick injected carefully, pulling blood in and out of the syringe as he had been taught.

Almost immediately, Richie said he felt the "hit." He began pulling at his nose, scratching his face, which itched all over. He touched his body almost wonderingly. The experience lasted for two hours. Richie stretched out on Peanuts' bed and nodded on and off. Occasionally he would say, "This is good, man."

"Enjoy your head," said Brick, who was right there with him.

Twice more in succeeding days Richie shot up with Brick. Then Brick explained the facts of heroin life to his friend. "It costs $5 a bag in East Meadow, when you can get it, and that's not often," said Brick. "That's enough for one fairly weak hit. But if you go into Harlem, you can buy the same bag for $2.50."

Richie had never been to Harlem. That scene, he said, was heavy.

But a few nights later, when Brick suggested at least driving around Harlem and seeing if anything could be bought, Richie agreed.

As Brick piloted his decaying Plymouth on the Long Island Expressway, cutting off to the Triborough Bridge, and into Harlem, he explained what would be done. "There's a place called the Edgecombe Rehabilitation Center, and I'm gonna drive around there until I see a likely colored dude. Then I pull up easy and I roll down the window and say, 'You got anything to sell, man?' And if he's cool, he'll have some on him. And if he doesn't, he'll know where to send us."

After fifteen minutes of circling the crowded streets, of exploring the ghetto world a million miles away from East Meadow, Brick spotted someone he knew.

"That's Butch," he said. "He's cool. He deals dope."

Brick pulled up beside Butch, who was strolling with a friend. He called out his name. Butch came to the car, opened the door, and got in. Richie moved over quickly, nervously, to make room.

"We wanna cop. You got anything to sell?" asked Brick.

"Well, how much you want, baby?"

"Half a load." Brick had previously instructed Richie that "half a load" meant fifteen glassine bags, at $2.50 each. But by buying fifteen, the street price was only $30, instead of $37.50.

Butch hesitated a moment. He knew Brick, but he had never seen the red-haired boy beside him. Richie was looking straight ahead, through the windshield, as if he were not a part of this scene. Brick saw Butch's apprehension. He put his arm around Richie's shoulders. "He's cool," said Brick, brotherly.

"Let's see the bread," said Butch. Brick produced $30 in worn bills. Butch seized them, pocketed them, produced fifteen small bags, handed them to Brick, and was quickly out of the car. The entire transaction took only two minutes.

As Brick drove away, exultant, he told Richie how lucky they had been. "It's a scary place up here," he said. "Lot of strange shit going on. I know one kid who bought some dope, kept walking down the street, met another guy who ripped him off, stuck a gun to his head, took his dope and all his money."

Richie's body began to tremble. He could no longer conceal his fright. "Let's get out of here," he said, his voice shaking. He did not speak for the rest of the trip home.

When Brick offered him one of the glassine bags a few nights later, Richie refused. "I don't need it," he said. And he told Brick that never again would he go to Harlem. "I did it once," he said, "but I ain't gonna do it again."

A probation officer, Moira Kosmynka, investigating George's action against his son, asked Carol and Richie to come to the Family Court Building in early January for a conference. Interviewing Carol first, the woman asked her to summarize the problem at home.

"There's no communication between the two of them," answered Carol. "No matter what George says, Richard gets on his high horse and won't listen and won't answer."

Did Carol feel George was in any way to blame?

Carol hesitated. But she answered candidly. "I feel that on some occasions George has been unduly harsh and critical and that this provokes Richard," she said. But, she quickly pointed out, this had been only in the deterioration of recent months. Before that, she felt George was a loving and devoted father who "never tried to force his will on Richie."

When it was Richie's turn, he sat in a slouched position, arms folded, immensely bothered and bored by the entire session. The probation officer touched but lightly on the drug question, asking if Richie had considered going to Topic House, a voluntary drug therapy clinic.

"I don't want to," said Richie. "I know too many kids who went there and other places like it and it didn't help them at all."

Mrs. Kosmynka suggested family counseling for Mr. and Mrs. Diener and Richie, individually and as a parent-child unit. Carol was surprised to see Richie suddenly sit up and agree. "He seemed to welcome it," said Mrs. Kosmynka in making a report on the meeting.

Carol asked, in private, if Richie could not immediately

start therapy with a court-appointed psychologist or psychiatrist. She was told that family counseling should be tried first.

On January 6, 1972, all three Dieners went to the Family Court Building for their first meeting with the family counselor, a young man named Malone. George went in first and said, behind locked doors, that there had been another "violent confrontation" in his home. "When Richie is eighteen," George said, "I'm going to put him out."

Richie went in next and complained that his father made no attempt to understand him, accept his point of view, or communicate with him. Rather than fight with him, Richie said, he chose the silences that enraged George.

Carol waited outside for her turn. Suddenly her husband and her son and Mr. Malone came into the waiting room after a session that had lasted less than twenty minutes. Malone announced that he would be in touch with the family for another appointment.

"You can't see *me* now?" asked Carol, annoyed. Malone looked at his watch. "All right," he said, "if you really want to."

Carol felt her words and feelings were being endured by the counselor, not particularly welcomed. Malone asked a few perfunctory questions: Did Carol love George? Did they fight? Did they have other children? Then he said he was going on vacation, and when he returned, he would resume counseling with the troubled Dieners.

Carol expected more than this. Her fantasy had been that the family counselor would wrap his arms about them and comfort them and bind their wounds. Didn't this man realize there was danger in her house? Didn't this man hear a time bomb when it was ticking?

But she did not complain. She did not complain even when Malone returned from his vacation and telephoned her to say that he had been transferred to another position and that a new family counselor would take over the Diener case. She did not complain when days and weeks went by and there was never a call from the new family counselor, whoever he was. "I'm a person who respects authority," she would later say in bitterness. "I'm not pushy, I do what people tell me. When George and I used to go out driving on Sunday afternoons and he would turn around in a driveway that said 'Private Driveway: Do Not Enter,' I would tell him, 'We're not supposed to do this.' "

That one brief thirty-minute session was the only time that George and Carol and Richie would have any kind of family counseling. A Nassau County probation officer would one day not long after tell an associate that "everybody around our office felt George Diener was a very angry man," and that "George Diener seemed a fellow who was running . . . running . . . running all over the place . . . running mainly from himself."

But somehow the case of George Diener v. Richard Diener fell in a crack.

The entries in George's daily log, which had begun as terse paragraphs, began to lengthen, even as George began to spend longer hours listening and writing down what he heard. He became so consumed with the tape recorder that Carol's worry for her family deepened. It occurred to her that George seemed actually to enjoy what he was hearing, that he was participating vicariously in the world of his son. He had seemed absolutely zestful when on the track of Richie's motel pot party, crestfallen when it fell through. Was he a hunter stalking elusive game? Of course not. Why then did he set the trap night after night and listen hour after hour? Carol could not put away one feeling that pressed down on her, the feeling that kept her awake until it was dawn and time to rise and make coffee and call Richie to get ready for school, a feeling that George had abandoned any hope of solution. He has given up on Richie, thought Carol. He is just marking time, playing policeman, until June, when Richie becomes eighteen. And then I am going to lose my son.

On February 2, George wrote:

Richard took off from school today, supposedly sick. He called Mark about 10 A.M. and they made plans for Mark to come over here at 12 with some "STUFF" because nobody else would be here until 3 when Carol gets home. Richie now calls his mother "that scumbag," which is about what he thinks of me. Mark called his mother from our house to tell her he was going to his appointment with the psychiatrist at the mental health clinic of Family Court, but he came here to smoke pot instead. Richard called Fritz, the boy who sells drugs. Fritz said he hated Brick, that he told Brick never to call his house again, that he was worried because Brick had his phone number written on his wall. Richard said for Fritz not to worry, that he had erased it. Richard warned Fritz that Brick planned to kick him in the ass. Fritz said, "Let him try, I'll blow his fucking head off." Richard said that was cool. Richard said Brick was in trouble already for selling Dick somebody a nickel's worth of parsley, that Dick wasn't so tough but he has a few friends in the "BREED" and they are going to kick the shit out of Brick if he doesn't give them Dick's money back by Friday. Richard said Cameron, another dealer, has some good "blond hash," at least two ounces, which he has been carrying around in his pocket. "Cameron's crazy," said Richard. "He drove Mark and me to Roosevelt Field to steal albums and waited out front with the hash in his pocket. He even lit up a bowl of hash and smoked it in broad daylight while walking down Merrick Avenue. Cameron told Richard, "Don't worry, if the fuzz come by, I'll eat it." Fritz said if he ever ate as much as two ounces, Cameron would go to sleep forever. Richard said "Yeah, a couple of times I had to eat some and it fucked me up good." Fritz was stopped by the police outside his house about eleven o'clock last night; he had eleven ounces of hash in a package under his arm, but the policeman just said, "Good evening, son," and didn't bother him about it.

February 4:

Richard called Mark. His mother answered and said Mark was in school where he was supposed to be and why wasn't Richard for the past several days? (Evidently Richard is cutting out early every day and calling Mark's home before either of them are supposed to be there.) Richard next called Fritz and asked him if he wanted to buy another gram scale; he stole two more today from school. Fritz said he knew somebody who needed one. Richard is apparently out of money altogether, even his savings from last summer, because he offered Fritz his prize tape deck for one quarter pound of pot, the brown pot that Fritz has been selling for seventy-five dollars a quarter pound. Fritz said his parents found out he is dealing and won't let the people he is dealing with in the house, so kids have to throw stones at his window. Somebody named Splatte used too big a stone and broke their big window. Richard said a dealer named Milligan has his girl friend make up nickel bags for his high school customers, and if she makes a mistake, he beats her; he seems to get his kicks that way. Richard bought Seconals from Arthur K. today. Arthur has a thousand caps and is selling them at two for one dollar. Richard complains that this price is "outrageous" except for genuine pharmaceuticals with "Lilly" written on them. Fritz says Arthur K. is crazy; he has seen him smoke three bowls and grab a girl by the throat. He thought Arthur was going to kill her, but he threw her out the front door instead. Fritz says he is not going to do any dealing for about three months; things are hot for him at home. Richard offered to take the one quarter pound of hash Fritz has now and sell it for him. Richard says he can get rid of it easy because he has his driver's license now and can take his mother's car anytime he wants it and get around. It seems that Richard is going to buy a large quantity of Seconals tonight, if he can find the money. He is well fixed for drugs. He brags he has some "nice red hash." Late today he called David and says he has sold one of the scales he ripped off from school for "a terrific dime of hash" and he somehow got an extra nickel of blond hash for getting this dealer a big buyer. (Finder's fee?) Richard finally got through to Mark, who has been at somebody's house smoking all day. Mark is so stoned he can hardly speak. Richard says he is coming over to join him and that he has just ripped off some kid named Rob for five dollars. Mark says he is going to connect for twenty Seconals "at least" tonight, and Richard says to save some for him. Richard says he usually takes two Seconals before home room and, aside from being a little sleepy, he is OK the rest of the day.

George summoned Carol to hear a portion of the tape in which Richie referred to her as "that scumbag." Carol clasped her hands over her ears and refused. The next day, when George was at work, Carol went to the hiding place of the hated tape recorder and thought about sabotaging it.

She had the idea of picking up the telephone and screaming into it—screaming for an hour, or until the tape ran out. The machine was becoming part of their lives, a new member of the household.

Chapter Twenty

Early one Sunday morning in February, Richie called up Brick and suggested driving over to the Roosevelt Field shopping center.

"You gonna rip off something?" said Brick, who was still unsteady from the drugs he had taken the night before. He was not sure he would make a good accomplice so early.

"No. Let's just walk around. Shit, there isn't anything else to do."

Richie's complaint was a common one in the homes of East Meadow. George and Carol had heard it for years, and even though it was tempting to list the assets of their quiet village, they realized that the town was not accommodating to youngsters. Dean Saracino of East Meadow High believed that the restlessness of the young, indeed, the drug explosion of the young could be blamed in large part on East Meadow's lack of "things to do."

There were movies, of course, but they cost $2.50 to enter, and often the same feature stayed for several weeks, and if it was rated R or X, a youngster could not even go. There was a roller-skating rink, but the conservative-minded owner refused to admit "longhairs," thus eliminating a large segment of the town's under-eighteen population. Richie once went there on a Sunday afternoon with a group of his "straight" friends and all were denied admission. "This is really ridiculous," said Richie. "You've gotta have a crew cut to roller-skate." East Meadow High experimented with a weekend recreational program, opening the gym to jocks and the cafeteria for dancing, but after a brief spurt of heavy attendance, the idea expired. "Kids want to be away from school on weekends," said Saracino.

More generally, East Meadow had no community identity, no Main Street, no mayor, no sense of belonging to a special place. No central, cohesive factor, either political or structural, united its citizens. Three divisive geographical elements—Eisenhower Park, Nassau County Medical Center, and Nassau County's Jail Farm—split the town and made social contact between youngsters difficult. Because no boundaries marked the town's limits, it was eminently possible to go from one village to another without realizing it. By 1972 East Meadow had become a place where more than 60,000 slept—the classic bedroom community. The residential lanes were about as quiet and beautiful as they had been the day when George and Carol emigrated from Brooklyn. But the broad boulevards, as wide as those of Paris, had become infested with the landmarks of urban blight—massive shopping centers with acres of asphalt parking, parades of franchise restaurants, rows of shops festooned with so much paint and neon that one could imagine giant strips of Southern California being ripped up and transplanted in the alien soil of faraway Long Island. The smell of plastic fouled the air.

Richie and Brick wandered aimlessly through the giant Walgreens drugstore in the shopping center, looking over the record albums, checking out the magazine rack. On their way out, passing through the prescription department, Richie stopped at a counter of toothpaste. For the moment there was no pharmacist in sight. Casually edging his way behind the drug counter, Richie spotted a bottle of pills that he instantly recognized as Amytals, a barbiturate.

Brick, seeing Richie's eyes "light up," cautioned, "Hey, man, don't."

"I see Amytals," said Richie. He snatched the bottle and began putting it under his jacket. Suddenly a druggist materialized and noticed Richie.

"Can I help you?" asked the man.

Richie tried to ease the stolen bottle onto a counter, but the manager noticed him. "I'm calling the police, and you'll have to wait until they get here," said the manager.

Protesting his innocence, Richie lunged at the manager's throat, seizing his necktie, twisting it. The two went at one another for several moments while Brick watched, at first in fascination, then in fear of being accused of participation. Brick fled quickly, giving testimony to the loyalty of friends in the drug culture. When police arrived, the store manager accused Richie of throwing a display basket and a wooden table at him, of trying to choke him, and of suspicion of shoplifting and drug theft.

Shortly after noon, George was telephoned at home by Nassau County police who informed him that Richie was being held on a charge of simple assault. "Is it a juvenile offense?" asked George. "He's almost eighteen," said the officer on the phone. "He's a big boy now."

George went to the police station, engaged an attorney, and arranged for Richie's release pending a hearing. Upon seeing his father, Richie insisted he was innocent. "I didn't do anything," he said. "That guy at the drugstore accused me of stealing something I didn't steal, then *he* jumped me."

At the hearing the next day in District Court, Richie fell asleep in his chair while waiting for his case to be called. George nudged his son awake, but he drifted off again, still groggy from the barbiturates he ate the night before in apprehension of the morning's court appearance. Not knowing this, George assumed his son was merely bored, indifferent to the serious charge. He looked at the slumbering youngster. Richie was now letting his hair grow into a semi-Afro; his sideburns were well below his ears. The beginnings of a wispy red beard and mustache further offended George. Disgusted at the way Richie looked, and at the way he was acting in a court of the land, George walked out on him, leaving the boy to speak for himself.

Richie's attorney arranged for him to be released until the trial, set for the last day of February at 10 A.M. "I think congratulations are in order," said George to Richie that night as they passed one another in the house. "You now have a grown-up police record. To go with that lovely beard and hairdo."

Carol, always looking for a fragment of hope, something to get her through the next few days, told George that she hoped the trouble would shock Richie out of his troublesome ways. George nodded. "I hope you're right," he said. "But I doubt it."

The tape recorder had not been snooping for a few days because George had run out of cassettes. His do-it-yourself detective work was an expensive habit to support, and now there would be an attorney's fee for Richie's assault charge. Carol so hated the bug that she took Richie aside one afternoon before George came home and warned her son that, unless he behaved better, his father would start listening in again.

For a few days, things were relatively quiet in the

Diener home. Carol's morale rose, as if her child had been long ill with a fever that was suddenly breaking. But within a week, Richie left the house against his father's orders, and as soon as he was out the door, George went to the tape recorder to bait it once more. His reason, he told Carol, was that more tapes were needed in support of his petition to Family Court, still presumably under investigation.

"I'm so sick of these confrontations, I'm ready to do anything to avoid them," he said. "As far as I'm concerned, Richie can come into the house and shoot up heroin at our dining-room table if it will avoid these terrible confrontations."

When a day had passed, George sat down at the machine to hear what had transpired on his telephone. It was as if he had put down a book for a time, and a strong wind blew the pages forward, yet when he picked it up to begin reading again, he could follow the plot without losing the thread.

Richie telephoned Fritz, the dealer, and began telling the story of a rip-off in school that day.

RICHIE: Guess who I ripped off? Stegler. The little one. Wanna hear what happened?

FRITZ: Really?

RICHIE: You know that shit green hash he's had around? Smells like hamster food? You know, it's hash all right, but . . . it's not *good* hash. I figured I might as well take it, right? So that little scumbag, I set him up yesterday and told him to bring it to school today. So I went into the cafeteria, and he's sittin' there with these girls, and I take a look at his stuff. So when he turns his head away, I just casually put it into my pocket. And when he turns around, I go, "Whoops, it's nice doin' business with you." And he says, "It'll be nicer when you give me my hash back." He pulls out this motherfuckin' knife. So I stood up and I yell, "Stab me, Stegler," and he fuckin' didn't do nothin', so I grab him by the fuckin' hair and I say, "Come on, Stegler, stab me!" And he wouldn't do it, so I fuckin' cracked him in the fuckin' face and he started crying. And he ran out of the cafeteria.

FRITZ: No shit? Then what happened?

RICHIE: So I take the hash. . . .

FRITZ: So how much was there?

RICHIE: Nice quarter ounce.

FRITZ: Real hash?

RICHIE: Yeah. All right. Probably compressed pot, like what you had. I should have ripped Stegler off for that knife as well. Looked like a stiletto.

FRITZ: I hear Brick has a switchblade, the kind where the knife pops out of the handle.

RICHIE: So he says. It makes me feel so good, you know! Then fuckin' Stegler pulls a knife on me. A lot of people saw it. 'Cause I'm yellin', "Come on, Stegler, stab me!" And then I go upstairs and this kid Kapper catches up with me and he says, "Let's see what you got?" He keeps hassling me, so I was gonna show him in the boys' room, but this teacher sees me and says, "Whatta you got in your pockets, son? You a student, son?" I shoulda said, "No," but instead, I go, "Yes," and the teacher says, "Then come with me." So I said, "Fuck this," and I started walking faster and faster and I run outside. He could never catch me.

FRITZ: How can anybody even speak to a freak like Kapper?

RICHIE: For one reason, he has about a thousand Quaaludes. And I ain't got a one. . . . (*An idea comes to him.*) Remember that kid in Hempstead, that connection you had? Remember those pharmaceuticals we got last year? Seconals and Tuinals? Is he still dealing?

FRITZ: He's a pain in the ass. Like Brick, you fuckin' curse at him, and he still thinks you're friends with him. That's the way most down freaks are. . . . (*Fritz hesitates, seemingly pondering whether to tell Richie something.*) . . . But I know somebody who might be getting like ten thousand tonight.

RICHIE: (*Excited*) Wow. What kind?

FRITZ: Seconals. The real thing, baby.

RICHIE: If you don't wanna deal, just do me the favor.

FRITZ: If I get 'em, you can't tell nobody.

RICHIE: I could sell them so fast . . .

FRITZ: I mean, like don't even call me up to ask about 'em. (*He lowers his voice.*) Your phone, I mean, it's OK, isn't it?

RICHIE: No sweat. I found the fuckin' wires where my old man was tapin' me, and I ripped 'em out.

FRITZ: The price may be, like, really heavy. Like I've already fed this guy $600 the past two nights.

RICHIE: Wow!

FRITZ: As a matter of fact, if I don't get 'em
         tonight, I'm gonna demand my money
         back. But this guy is a reputable down
         dealer. He doesn't deal smack or anything.
         Sometimes it takes him a week, but he gets
         'em. He's like the only person in Nassau
         County who can get 'em.
RICHIE: How much would I have to go in for?
FRITZ: It depends. Maybe a couple hundred. Could
         you raise it?
RICHIE: I dunno. My parents hide their money. I
         could sell my tape deck for maybe seventy-
         five dollars.
FRITZ: I'll see you at Ryan's then. Tonight.
RICHIE: There's methadone going on at Ryan's.
FRITZ: Methadone! Can you get that?
RICHIE: Yeah. I know the guy. Like ten bucks a
         bottle. I got some. I don't know how many
         milligrams, but it's a pretty big bottle.
FRITZ: Maybe you could work out a trade or
         something.
RICHIE: Maybe.

On the morning of February 15, George was late in
leaving for his food route, staying home to fill out sales
records and to arrange his sample cases. At midmorning
the telephone rang. Castelli, the assistant principal at East
Meadow High, was on the line.

"We had a little trouble with Richie this morning," said
Castelli.

George gripped the receiver.

"One of the teachers in the hall brought him in to me
for being abusive. He saw Richie in the hall and asked for
his pass and he didn't have one. He said he was coming
from the cafeteria so the teacher told him to go back to
the cafeteria. Instead he ran up the stairs in the other

direction. His mouth was a little fresh in talking to the teacher. He practically invited the teacher to strike him. I found out he hasn't brought his report card home this quarter. In case you don't know, he's failing everything. I've suspended him."

"Yes," said George. His voice was pained. He chose his words carefully. "I've got him now in Family Court. He's involved with a bunch of drug nuts and . . . he seems to like this, and there's no way I can talk him out of it. He has to go to court now. He attacked the manager of the Walgreens drugstore in the Roosevelt Field shopping center. There'll be a hearing on this. We are . . . we are at our wits' end trying to find something that might stop him . . . and we can . . . he's just . . . he's just . . ."

"You'll follow up on that, I suppose. Let me know," said the assistant principal. "I hope you can keep his nose clean here. At school. If we let him back in."

George hesitated once more. He seemed ashamed to make his next admission. "Well, there's nothing really I can do. If he doesn't shape up . . . then I would suggest you throw him out permanently."

"I'll discuss it with Mr. Barbour, the principal."

"He's determined, my son. He's got a suicide complex. He's determined he's going to ruin himself and his mother and me, and there's nothing we can say that's going to change his mind. He thinks this drug stuff is swell. . . ."

Then George ran out of words. Both men hung up awkwardly.

A few minutes later, as George prepared to leave, he saw Richie and a carload of young people drive slowly past the house. They're coming here to smoke pot, guessed George. But they'll never come in as long as my car is in the driveway. George left the house, drove away, killed ten minutes, and returned home. As he expected, the car belonging to Richie's friends was parked in his driveway.

His first idea was to enter the house and break up the

party. But then another thought took its place. George drove to a nearby police call station and rang the local precinct house. He had reason to believe that a marijuana party was going on in his son's room, and could officers come and break it up?

With two uniformed patrolmen as escort, George entered his home. He directed them to where the rock music was playing, down the steps, into the chamber of colored balls and psychedelic hues. Richie looked up in anger. There were four young people with him—two girls and two boys. George recognized only one of them—Sean O'Hara, and he was disappointed to see what he thought was a "straight kid" in with the others.

But, to George's further disappointment, there was no familiar odor of marijuana. The group did seem a little giggly, but Richie said they had used nothing stronger than a little wine. "Go ahead, pigs, search the room," said Richie.

While the police looked about his room, Richie taunted them—and impressed his friends. To one of the cops he chanted, "You should become a dick. You think like a dick, you look like a dick, you get out of a dick car, you've got a dick set of handcuffs. Put a zipper on you and you're solid dick."

The officer stopped his search. "Someday you'll lose that smile on your face," he said.

Richie toughened his voice. "Yeah, when it's me in handcuffs and there's about ten pigs in the pig room somewhere at the back of the pig house."

Nothing was found and George took the police to the door. He apologized for his son's behavior. Suddenly another idea came to him. Asking the police to wait, he telephoned headquarters and asked for the narcotics squad. In the basement of George's home, the tape recorder whirred and took down the conversation, as well as others on what would soon become a remarkable day:

GEORGE: Is Patrolman Moran there, please?

MORAN: Speaking.

GEORGE: This is Mr. Diener. Remember me?

MORAN: Yes, sir. Right.

GEORGE: Well, I just had another problem with my son, and I was wondering if we could have him arrested on the strength of anything I've given you so far. . . .

MORAN: Well . . .

GEORGE: The police are here now.

MORAN: There? In your house?

GEORGE: Yes. Could there be an arrest from the information in those tape recordings?

MORAN: Well, I did talk it over with the supervisors. Some people have been listening to the tapes and writing down different bits of information. . . . But as far as having him locked up for what he said on the tapes, we can't do it because we don't have any evidence . . . you know, as far as physical evidence.

GEORGE: (*Sadly*) Right.

MORAN: If he had the hash, you know, it's gone, it's not there now. It could have been catnip and so we might be locking him up for something that wasn't even a dangerous drug. Even though you thought it was. So we do have a problem right there, and we won't be able to lock him up.

GEORGE: I see. . . .

MORAN: OK. . . . I'm sorry about that. Does he have anything on him now?

GEORGE: No. He expected me back.

MORAN: He assaulted you?

GEORGE: No. I brought the police in with me. But there was nothing around, so—

MORAN: I'm sorry you—
GEORGE: So right now he's very cocky. See. He's got his father beat, he's got the police beat, and nobody can touch him. However, as they say, if it's not today it'll be tomorrow.
MORAN: I see. OK, we're still going through the tapes and pulling off bits of information. We have to get another tape recorder to transfer your tapes. Somebody's working on it but they're off today. They'll be in tomorrow. . . . I am sorry about that. 'Cause there is a lot of information on there and we thank you for that. We'll see what we can do later on. OK? Thanks very much.

Now the police were gone, and the young people went away, and Richie and his father were alone. George prepared to leave the house, but Richie began to taunt him. He draped himself against the kitchen door and stopped George from passing.

"Someday," said Richie, "I'm really gonna kick the shit out of you."

George lowered his head and attempted to go through the door. Richie shot out a hand to stop him. "You hear me? Someday you're gonna get it."

Seizing his son's hand, George pushed it away, his face white. He backed up and took a stand. "OK," snapped George. "Let's get it on right now. Man to man. Come on." George raised his fists.

Richie was not sure how to react. He seemed stunned. George flattened the palm of his hand and slapped his son. "Now you've got a reason to fight back," said George.

On the end table next to the couch rested a pair of Carol's mending scissors. Richie seized them and held them up. They were golden scissors that Carol had once used to create the masquerades for Richie when he was young.

George felt fear. Richie came at him, grabbed his arms, pinned one behind him, put the scissors to his father's throat. "Motherfucker, when you and me fight," he hissed, "it ain't gonna be fair. Some night when you least expect it, these scissors'll come at your throat. Only next time . . ."

George broke free. He dropped his hands to indicate he wanted no more fight. "Richie! Sit down! We've got to talk."

"I'm fuckin'-A tired of talking! I've had enough of this shit. I'm tired of everything!" Richie threw the scissors onto the end table. George watched as they gouged out a small chunk of wood and fell clattering to the floor.

"Please, son. We're killing each other."

Richie glanced at the fallen scissors. "I don't know if I should do you in now, or let my friends do it later."

This time George fled the house. Richie sank to the floor and began to cry as he heard his father drive away.

George drove blindly through the streets of his town, playing the scene over and over again in his mind. He drove past the precinct police station, almost stopping, then pressing the accelerator. Finally he saw a candy store and stopped and dialed his home. He wanted to try, once more, to talk to Richie. But the number was busy. He stayed in the telephone booth fifteen minutes, trying to get through.

Hanging up in frustration, he began to drive to the junior high where Carol was working. Maybe she would know what to do. He glanced at his speedometer. He was doing seventy in a thirty-mile-per-hour zone.

Richie first called Fritz and began to brag of the incident. "My old man was scared shitless. He thought he was dead. . . ." Then his words began to tumble out, dipping and diving like a radio fading in and out. When George heard them late that night, Richie seemed incoherent on the tape: "I kicked the shit out of some kid in the cafeteria today . . . because I heard he gave my name to the cops.

. . . I said something to him. . . . I wouldn't hurt him . . . but I grabbed him by the neck. . . . He wouldn't answer me! They've got to listen to me, man! . . . I said, 'Hey, motherfucker, you gonna answer me?' He was like scared, man. I popped him in the eye to make him look at me . . . and he didn't do nothing so I popped him again. And he started fighting and a bunch of people broke it up . . . some fuckin' Jews. . . . I was holding my coat over my shoulders and one of them knocked it off and I said, 'Can't you say you're sorry, you little cocksucker?' and he said, 'I *am* sorry, Richie.' And I said, 'Watch it,' and . . . Did you ever pull a knife on your old lady? That's the same thing as what I did. . . ."

Fritz was trying to interrupt the rambling monologue, but Richie gave him no entry.

"I know you wouldn't hurt your old lady," plunged on Richie. "But that's what I did today. I swear I couldn't help it, man." Richie paused briefly; his voice broke and his words were sobs. "He called me names in front of my friends. He called me a dope addict. . . . I couldn't help it. . . . I was stoned on Amytals. . . . I only took one, but I was stoned from last night. . . . All of a sudden he smacked me in the face. . . . I can't take that from him . . . so I picked up those scissors. . . . 'If we're gonna fight,' I say, 'it ain't gonna be clean. . . .' O God, O Godgodgod-godgodgod. . . ."

The line went dead. Richie kept holding the phone in his hand. He sobbed for several moments—on the tape—before he dialed another number.

Still sniffling, he waited for Carol to dry her hands and come to his aid.

"Ma?"

"Yes. Who is this?"

"Ma. This is RICHARD." His voice was full out, like a man shouting across an overseas cable from East Meadow to Moscow. "Ma . . . I got KICKED out of school today."

"Yes? How come?" Carol's voice tensed.

"'Cause I wised off to a teacher. They can't do that . . . just because I'm failing. Ma, I'm a senior. I'm supposed to graduate." Richie could not keep his voice in check; it began to crawl sideways. "Then Daddy came home with two cops."

"Why, Richard?"

"'Cause he thought we were having a POT party. And they came bustin' in, and . . .

"And?"

"And we were just drinking. I'm at home now, and he smacked me in the face and I pulled the scissors on him. I didn't . . . I didn't *touch* him with it. . . . I just punched him in the face."

"*Where* are you?" The line crackled with static. Carol wanted to ask her son to hang up and get a new connection, but she feared she would lose him. She strained to hear his voice.

"I'm right here. At home. This is where it happened. This is where it started. Two girls and two other guys. Daddy started getting loud, calling me names in front of these people. So I told him to shut up. . . ."

"Richard . . . are you . . . *on* anything?"

"What?" It took him a moment to absorb his mother's meaning. "No. . . ." Once more his voice went out of control. It cracked. A sob caught in his throat and dragged its way into the phone. "I think I'm crazy, Ma. . . ."

"Who's crazy?"

"I'm crazy!"

"No, you're not." Carol's voice trembled even as she denied her son's diagnosis of himself. But she feared it was true. Richie was going mad on the telephone, and Carol was having to listen to it.

"I pulled a scissor on Daddy. Twice!"

"All right," said Carol, soothing as she had tried to be when the boy had come home teased and weeping a dozen years ago. "Now calm down. Just calm down. Go to sleep. You want me to come home?"

"Stay at work. If you can work, stay there. Ma, I pulled the scissors!"

"All right, please. Try and take a nap. I'll get home as fast as I can."

The line went dead. Carol replaced her receiver. She thought fast. June would know. Her sister was working now as a secretary at Meadowbrook Hospital, or by its more formal name, Nassau County Medical Center. She called June and gave her a capsule version. June reached another secretary named Elsie Molinelli, who worked for the medical examiner.

Carol rushed out the back door of the junior high school cafeteria toward her car. George was running at her. She flew into his arms. "I know," she said. "Richie just called me. He's ashamed. He's crying. He's got to have some help."

George hurried to the huge medical center. By the time he reached Mrs. Molinelli, she had already made an appointment for Richie with a psychiatrist, for the next afternoon at two. So distraught, so ashen was the man she knew from Carol's charity functions as a "happy-go-lucky guy," Mrs. Molinelli told George to sit down for a minute.

"I've had trouble with a child in my family, too," she said. "Don't blame yourself for everything."

George nodded. "At this point, I can't blame myself. It would be wrong to blame myself. I've done everything I know, everything I can for my son."

Late that afternoon, Joe Marck, Carol's brother-in-law, dropped by the Diener home to see if he was needed. To his surprise, the storm seemed subsided. Richie was in the kitchen. He called out cheerily, "Hi, Uncle Joe." Carol was preparing dinner.

Still tense, George was reading the newspaper. He did

not let on there had been trouble, nor did Joe reveal what his wife had told him.

When he reached his own home, Joe told June, "Something's wrong with that boy. He pulls a pair of scissors on his father and a few hours later he acts like nothing happened. He should be down in his room ashamed of himself. Something's going to happen in that house. A catastrophe. Mark my words."

Carol prepared a special dinner—lasagna, spaghetti—the things Richie liked, and called her family to the table. Richie appeared promptly, his face and hands sparkling from a long shower, his hair arranged as best he could, his clothes neat and crisp. He ate with enthusiasm. He praised his mother's cooking. Later that night George typed a next-to-last entry in his log:

> This evening everything went well. Richard sat down with us and talked with us and spent the whole evening with us for the first time in about three years without blowing up and walking away from us.

Chapter Twenty-one

The next morning Richie rose, showered, and took two secobarbitals to prepare for the session with the psychiatrist. When he felt them working within him, he called Mark.

"I've gotta go to the hospital today to see if I'm . . . craaaaaaaaaaazy." He stretched out the word and decorated it with a strained laugh.

"Why?" asked Mark. He had not heard the story of the attack with the scissors.

"I don't know. . . . My father . . . I'm goin' to this place. . . . They want to see if . . . if I'm *gone.* . . . Some ree-taard place."

"Well, call me when you get home." Mark accepted the news with little more interest than had he heard Richie was going to his grandmother's house.

"Why?" said Richie. "You gonna smoke?"

"Yeah. . . . Hey! I gotta get off the phone. My mother's

coming. Call me back in ten minutes. I can't call out today."

When the conversation resumed, Mark suddenly began painting dark pictures of what might happen to Richie at the "ree-taard place."

"Who's driving you there? Your old man?" asked Mark.

"No. He's the reason I'm going. My old lady's taking me. I don't *have* to go, you know. . . ." But Richie's show of strength trailed off.

"They could commit you, you know," suggested Mark with an air of experience.

"What? Commit me to where?"

"To some mental institution."

"Fuck that. I'm leavin' the country before that."

"You know what you're getting into? Everybody running around in sheets? You'll be in there for life." Mark found his remark funny and laughed until Richie's serious voice stopped him.

"I'd kill 'em."

"They could put you in there for surveillance."

"What's that? For how long?"

"For a couple of months. They have the power, man. They can do anything they want. They can say, 'Old Rich takes narcotics . . . and narcotics cause brain damage.' They can make that up—and they can lock you up for two months and shave your head bald."

Richie made a gagging sound. "Fuck that," he said. "I'll kick the shit out of all of 'em. I'll kill 'em. Why can't everybody just leave me alone? . . ."

On the drive to the psychiatrist, Richie told Carol he was glad to be seeing a doctor. During recent weeks, his health had worried him. Every time a small cut or sore did not heal promptly, Richie showed it to his mother and wondered if he had diabetes. He felt his heart was pounding irregularly. Carol jested with him over becoming "something of a hypochondriac," but she realized he was perhaps concerned over what drugs were doing to his system.

"Only one thing, Ma," he said as the hospital came into sight, "I don't mind seeing the shrink today—but if he wants me to come back once a week, I couldn't stand it."

"We'll cross that bridge when we come to it," said Carol.

At the psychiatric clinic, Richie was handed a questionnaire and asked to circle statements that he felt pertained to his problem. Out of sixty-five questions, he put "yes" circles after the following:

—Do you often suffer from an upset stomach?

—Are you often sick to your stomach?

—Do you bite your nails?

—Do you wear yourself out worrying about your health?

—Do you feel alone and sad at a party?

—Do you have to be on your guard even with friends?

—Are you easily upset or irritated?

—Do little annoyances get on your nerves and make you angry?

—Does it make you angry to have anyone tell you what to do?

—Do you often get into a violent rage?

When Richie was called into the psychiatrist's office for a private talk, he gripped his mother's hand tightly. Carol smiled gently and patted his arm and let him know silently that she would be waiting for him.

A third-year psychiatrist resident from India, a Dr. Kuruvilla, conducted a brief clinical examination of Richie, consisting of little more than questions and conversation. The doctor made the following notes:

Patient has court hearing coming up on assault charge. . . . Smokes pot, uses LSD, heroin and down pills. . . . Patient spends time with friends, boys and girls, smoking pot, going to bars and drinking. Usually he is not interested in studies. Mother tried to find him a job, but boy did not stay wtih it. . . . Patient feels angry, aggressive and confused toward others, especially his father, who criticizes him. Patient says he likes pot and down pills very much. Uses them more or less regularly, especially when he is with groups of boys and girls, and before going to bars. Patient says he has no sexual problems with girls. He goes out with different girls to have fun with them, but he has no close relationship with girls. . . . Patient has a buddy named "Bob" * whom he trusts. No homosexual tendencies. . . . Does not like school, does not want to study, unable to get interested, likes history and science. . . . Complains about his health all the time. Weighs 140 pounds, is 5′ 7″ tall, thinks there is something wrong with his heart, not sure what. Sleep is often disturbed. Wakes up in early morning, but has no nightmares or disturbing dreams. . . .

Next Dr. Kuruvilla spoke privately with Carol for a few minutes. He asked if she was strict or lenient, if she and George had a "good" marriage, if she approved or disapproved of marijuana. Carol responded that she was lenient, that her marriage was good, that she firmly disapproved of marijuana. The psychiatrist excused himself to consult with a senior psychiatrist. When he returned, Dr. Kuruvilla announced that Richie would be accepted as an outpatient, but that nothing could be done until the assault charge from the Walgreens incident was cleared away.

"You call us for an appointment as soon as that is taken

---

* *Richie did not mention Mark, Peanuts, or Brick as friends.*

care of," said the psychiatrist in his crisp, faraway accent. He handed Carol a card.

Numbly she looked at it. Had Richie mentioned the scissors attack on his father, she asked? Yes, said the psychiatrist. Well, then didn't the doctor feel treatment was needed immediately? No, the best thing to do was wait until Richie was not entangled in a court action.

Nodding, silent in a moment of helpless disappointment, once more doing as she was told, once more unwilling to go against the voice of authority, Carol thanked the doctor for his time and went outside to take her son home. Richie was pleased that his treatment would not begin until an indefinite future time.

Later that day Dr. Kuruvilla made three alternative provisional diagnoses of Richie's condition: (1) Sociopathic with drug abuse; (2) latent schizophrenia with drug abuse; (3) passive aggressive personality with drug abuse.

Within two weeks, questions would be asked of a Dr. Pasternak, the senior psychiatrist at Nassau County Medical Center, questions that wondered why Richie was not accepted immediately, that very afternoon, and treatment begun.

"Whenever we're faced with a court situation," Dr. Pasternak would answer, "we usually wait. We get more than enough people who need immediate care. If a patient isn't climbing the walls when we see him, we usually let the court take precedent. Besides, you get to the point where you say, who is the boss? The court? Or the doctor? The court usually wins.

"There weren't any flagrant psychotic disorders here. I reviewed Dr. Kuruvilla's report and okayed the delay. If I had personally seen the boy, I might have recommended a detoxification program to get him free of drugs, or I might have recommended a separation of the boy and his father, sending Richie to a relative's house to live for a while."

Dr. Pasternak would respond to one further question. Was any attempt made to find out how serious was Richie's drug use, the amount of his daily barbiturate intake?

"This was a clinical examination. A preliminary talk. In other words, no."

Strike three, thought George, when Carol told him of the psychiatrist's decision. The court lets me down, the police can't do anything, the psychiatrist says wait. I am a man falling from the top of the Empire State Building, but I am not close enough to the pavement for somebody to stick out a net.

There was but one particle of hope in George's day. While Carol and Richie were at the clinic, he had gone to East Meadow High for a conference with Barbour, the principal. That night, when his house was quiet, George played the last tape and made the last entry in his journal:

Today I went to see the principal of Richard's school and told him that Richard felt so bad about being thrown out of school that he went off the deep end and threatened me. The principal said he had to worry about the safety of the rest of his students, but that if Richard promised to stop acting the way he has been, and start working and making an effort, he would take him back on a trial basis.

The principal also told me that Richard has been reported as being one of the top pill pushers in school and that he was the one who sold pills to a girl who overdosed on them in the school a couple of weeks ago. This girl became violent and had to be carried out of school on a stretcher to the hospital across the street. They had to tie her down with straps to keep her from running out screaming into the street. Richard admitted that he was the one who sold her the pills, and he said he has talked to the girl since then and apologized and that she doesn't blame him.

Richard was glad he was taken back into school and promised to stop with the drugs and to apply himself in school. But one thing makes me wonder. He got on the phone this afternoon after going to the psychiatrist and called all of his friends—Mark, Peanuts, Brick, etc.—and bragged about calling the police PIGS yesterday and of making his father turn white and shit in his pants by holding a scissor to his throat. He also called Fritz to buy some pot. It doesn't appear as though Richie is as sorry as he says he is.

Chapter Twenty-two

Richie was readmitted to class on Tuesday morning, February 22. The week stretched to its very end without trouble. Richie did not cut class, nor did he go out at night. He stayed home, he studied, he ate dinner with his family, he called up Sheila and said he was through with drugs and determined to pick up his grades so he could graduate, he even engaged his mother in a long, tender conversation about the enduring comedy of Jimmy Durante. It seemed to impress him that a man at whom his mother had laughed twenty-five years ago was still funny, that there could be a continuity to life.

Carol had not felt so close to her son in months. During one of their talks, she brought up the subject of college. "Why don't you put your application in for Nassau County Junior College?" she suggested. "You could take a two-year physical therapy course, and then, if you liked it, maybe you could transfer somewhere else. Maybe NYU."

Richie nodded hesitantly. "They *have* to take you," said Carol. "Even if your grades aren't too good right now, you're a citizen of the county. And we're certainly tax-payers."

Realizing that the suggestion and the need for commit-ment bothered her son, Carol put the idea away. The truce was too delicate to molest. She would bring college up later.

On Friday afternoon, February 25, in the very last hour of the school day, a lunchroom lady at East Meadow High noticed a group of boys suspiciously gathered around a cold-drink machine. She observed something small being handed from one boy to another, apparently some sort of transaction. She heard talk of drugs. She called out, "I see what you boys are doing. I know all of your names, too. I'm going to report you to the principal's office."

Richie was in the group. Upon hearing the accusation, he ran out of the cafeteria. But he must have known that the brief new world he had built in one week was tumbling down.

That night Richie went to Ryan's bar and gained ad-mission. Moving among the tables, greeting people he knew, he saw Fritz toward the back, sitting with a girl. Fritz beckoned, making room for him, sending the girl away. He had interesting news. He confirmed that if Richie could raise $200 by Monday, he could become full partner in the sale of ten thousand Seconals. Pharmaceu-ticals. The real thing. They were promised for delivery Monday night, in the parking lot of Roosevelt Field.

"Who's dealing?" asked Richie.

Fritz shook his head. "It's too big. Like, I can't even tell you anything. Only it's this absolutely dependable guy from Southampton. He's never let me down."

"I can't imagine how many ten thousand would be,"
said Richie.

"A lot."

"Enough to fill a grocery sack?"

"Enough to last somebody ten years."

Richie saw Brick across the room. Promising to keep
Fritz's offer confidential, he rose to confer with his friend.
At that moment, police entered Ryan's on an ID check.
"Cops," hissed Brick. "Tons of 'em." Brick wriggled
through the crowd and out the door without being
stopped, even though he was over eighteen and not the
subject of the law's attention this night. Richie tried to
follow, but an officer grabbed his arm and asked to see his
identification.

Awakened, George got up from his bed and drove to the
precinct house to retrieve his son. No charge was made
against Richie. The police intention on such raids was
usually to scare underage youngsters and warn them with
a lecture on staying out of bars until they were eighteen.
Because there was no suggestion of drugs being involved,
because Richie seemed thoroughly chastened by the experience, because George could think of nothing to add
to what the police had said, he did not scold his son.

The next night George and Carol went to a "Las Vegas
Night" party for the retarded children's charity. Russell
was sleeping over at his Aunt June's house. Richie found
himself alone in the house at 8:30. Normally he would
have found Mark or Peanuts or Brick, but instead he
dialed his friend Bob Simmons, the one whose name he
had mentioned to the psychiatrist. Bob was the type of
clean-cut "straight" whom Mark referred to as "totally
lame, a mama's boy, the dregs of society as far as we

heads are concerned." But on this night, Richie needed him.

Bob and his steady girl, Cindy, picked up Richie. The youngsters drove around East Meadow for a couple of hours. Fresh snow had fallen, and when Richie spotted a vacant lot crowded with snowmen and a fortress built by little children, he wanted to stop. For more than an hour, they played in the winter night, hurling snowballs at one another, throwing ferocious body blocks into the snowmen and falling, laughing, shoulders in brief pain, "defending" the fortress against Cindy's attacks, their merriment, their normalcy obvious to anyone, worried about the condition of America's young, who might have encountered the scene.

Bob drove Cindy home first and kissed her good-night. When he reached Richie's street, he parked in front of the yellow house. But Richie was reluctant to go inside. For more than an hour he sat with his friend, listening to music on the car radio, talking of rock stars he liked, impressing Bob with his far-reaching knowledge of various little-known groups, mentioning that perhaps he would become an electronics expert someday and work with musicians. Bob allowed his friend to rattle on and on, sensing that Richie needed someone to hear him. Just before midnight, Bob finally begged off, explaining that he had to get up early to go with Cindy to the Brooklyn Museum on an assignment for art class.

"You want to come with us?" invited Bob. "It's a great place."

Richie declined. But he would call Bob late in the afternoon and perhaps the three could do something together, again, on Saturday night. As Bob drove away, Richie threw a halfhearted snowball at the car. In the rearview mirror, Bob saw Richie laughing. And he laughed, too. Drugs had not been mentioned during the pleasant evening, but Bob understood that Richie was trying to show how he could pass a clean Saturday night. I think he wants out of the drug world, thought Bob, as he passed the Blackstone corner.

Carol rose first the next morning, at eleven, a late hour for her. She and George had not gotten home until 4 A.M. after the Las Vegas Night party for her charity. Not until the last guests had left the hall and the proceeds from the "gambling" games had been locked into a safe could the couple leave, declining an invitation to have scrambled eggs at an all-night diner.

Making coffee and glancing at the Sunday paper, Carol began answering the phone. People were calling to compliment her on the party. It was a successful evening and Carol basked in the aftermath. Several thousand dollars had been raised for the retarded children's shelter.

Around 11:30 A.M. George appeared and gratefully accepted a cup of coffee. He had worked hard the night before in twin roles as host and security guard, with his .38 at his waist. He told Carol he would spend most of the afternoon down in the basement, sorting out his sample cases and broken packages of spices and food mixes. That was fine with her, because she had a big load of washing and ironing to do.

Carol was in her bedroom gathering up clothes for the wash when Richie came in. His face looked well rested, his eyes clear. He was neatly dressed. Mother and son quietly discussed their Saturday nights. Richie's had been successful as well. He told of the hours he had spent with Bob and Cindy. "I was home in bed asleep by midnight," he said.

Carol nodded. "I looked in on you when we got home."

He came quickly to his business of the moment. "Can I borrow the car, Ma?" Carol glanced up from her clothes.

Her instinct was to refuse, quickly. Only a few weeks before, immediately after getting his driver's license, she had lent Richie her car and he had been in an accident. His story was that he swerved to avoid hitting a squirrel running across the street and sideswiped a station wagon parked at the curb. Carol had been inclined to believe him, since it bore echoes of her son's long-ago reverence for animals. But George suspected the boy had been stoned on drugs. He had been opposed to Carol giving in and signing Richie's license application in the first place. But he's the only kid his age around here without one, said Carol, and he needs it to get a job, and if he does, I don't want to chauffeur him back and forth every day.

"What do you need the car for today?" she asked.

"I need to go to this girl's house to study."

Carol weighed her decision carefully. Despite everything that had happened, she clung to the belief that the heart of Richie's trouble was his lack of confidence in himself, that he needed the burden of responsibility and the gift of trust. "All right," she finally said. "I'm doing this against my better judgment. But I'll give you this one more chance."

Happily Richie took the keys and went whistling on his way.

When George asked Carol where Richie had gone, she told him. "I believe in confidence and trust, too," he said. "But he wrecked another car just two weeks ago."

Shortly before 1 P.M., when George and Carol and Russell were having lunch, the telephone rang. A man was calling to report that Richie had backed his car into an automobile in the parking lot of Dave Shor's, a hamburger restaurant popular with youngsters. "I just want you to know the accident occurred," said the man. "Nobody was hurt. And damage is negligible."

George raised his eyebrows to Carol in an "I told you so" expression, but Carol urged him to wait until Richie could present himself in person and explain what happened.

When thirty minutes had passed, and Richie was not back, Carol went to the delicatessen to buy food for the evening meal. In her absence, the doorbell rang. George answered it. Sean O'Hara was standing there.

"Richie's had an accident," he said.

"I know," answered George. "The fellow he hit called us."

"No, Mr. Diener. I mean Richie had *another* accident, the second one today. He just hit a parked car and crashed into a fence."

"Jesus," said George. "Is anybody hurt?"

"No. But you'd better come. The police are there." George drove with Sean to the scene, only a few blocks from his house. The Dieners' 1966 Buick LeSabre was totally demolished. Another car parked at the curb was crumpled. George saw Richie standing several feet away from the crash. From the investigating officers, George learned that his son had been driving at high speed on the quiet, curving residential lane, had skidded on a patch of ice, had smacked into the parked car, had careened wildly, and had gone through a fence.

"He must have been going at least sixty to mess things up like this," said one of the officers.

George went over to talk to Richie, but it was as if the week of peace had never happened. It was as if their relationship had picked up exactly the way it left off at the moment of the golden scissors flashing in the living room.

Richie's eyes were red, and George knew the cause. He wore his mask of arrogance. He did not even nod as his father approached.

"Well, what are you on this morning?" said George sarcastically.

"Why don't you just shut the fuck up," said his boy.

George tensed. "Don't start up with me, son. You just wrecked two cars."

Richie walked away to join Sean. "If I want any of your lip," he said, "I'll scrape it off my zipper."

George called out that they would discuss things at home, but Richie gave no sign of hearing him.

In reconstructing the afternoon, several people gave testimony. Mark remembered that Richie pulled up beside him and Brick around noon, shortly after winning Carol's permission to borrow the car. "He leaned out his window at a stoplight," said Mark, "and he said, 'Happy days, I just took four Seconals.' He said he was going to this chick's house and try to score. But he must have flunked out because he went to Dave Shor's restaurant and had his first accident there."

Sean O'Hara's mother remembered Richie coming to her house about 1 P.M. Her son went outside to inspect the Diener car's right front tire. This was a few minutes after the first minor accident in the restaurant parking lot.

She watched the two boys shaking their heads and kicking at the tire. When Sean came inside, Mrs. O'Hara asked, "Is there a problem?"

"Yes," said Sean, slipping on a jacket.

"Are you going somewhere with Richie?"

Sean nodded. "I'm going to follow him home and . . ." He hesitated. "Mom, if there's trouble at Richie's house because of this . . . can I bring him back here?"

"Of course." Mrs. O'Hara liked the feisty redhead. And she knew, as did most of the parents of the youngsters in Richie's circle, of the trouble. Despite George and Carol's attempt to keep their lives out of neighborhood gossip, Richie had spread the war with his father far and wide.

At 3:45 P.M., Sean O'Hara returned home. His mother noticed that he was "visibly upset."

"What happened?" she asked quickly.

"Richie had another wreck. He was trying to get me

to race with him. He hit the curb . . . totaled his car. He wanted to take off and run away. I told him that wouldn't solve anything. Then I went to his house and got Mr. Diener."

"How was Mr. Diener?"

"Calm." Sean looked at his mother in puzzlement. "Too calm almost."

Sean said he had just dropped Richie off at his home, and that he was to pick his friend up again at six. Richie told Sean that once he explained to Carol what had happened, she would understand.

Carol and George sat in silence at their dining-room table, waiting for Richie to come home. There must be no raised voices, insisted Carol. We are lucky nobody was hurt. "I don't even want to talk to him," said George. "You do the talking. You're the one without a car now, and without collision insurance." Carol nodded. That seemed somehow less important to her than the tenuous bridge her son had walked on for a precious week.

When Richie came into the house near 4 P.M., he saw his parents waiting for him at the dining-room table. Pulling out a chair and lounging over its back, he waited silently for their first move. Carol examined his face before she spoke. In it was the flush of drugs, across his hands a tremor as they clenched the chairback.

"Do you realize what happened, Richard?" she began, in a voice so low and controlled it seemed to be speaking the opening line of a poem. "You could have killed somebody. You could have killed yourself."

Richie would not look at the woman speaking in the quiet voice. Instead he gazed out the glass patio door onto the redwood deck. Once he had played with the family of squirrels there. Once he had turned on there, on the spring night when thunder came from the sea. Several moments crept by before he found an answer for his mother.

"Maybe that would have been better," he said, his voice even lower than Carol's.

George would not have it. He shook his head in reproach.

Suddenly Richie came alive. "That's right," he said, his tone rising. "Shake your fucking head at me."

What do I do to set off his explosions? thought George. He's not at all sorry. He's standing there so stoned he doesn't even realize what he has done.

Carol could feel the electricity beginning to crackle between her two men. She jumped back in, continuing to point out the things Richie should consider. If he ever bought his own car, the insurance premium would be enormous because of these accidents. He could even lose his newly obtained license from negligent driving. As she spoke, keeping Richie's attention, Gorge left the table. It seemed the best thing he could do, for his presence was salt in the wound.

Richie accepted everything his mother told him. She was right. She was definitely right. He would drive more carefully. He was indeed lucky that no one had been hurt. Contritely, he said that he was tired, very tired, and wanted to rest. Could he go to his room? Carol took his hand and squeezed it tenderly to give her permission.

Now Russell, the eleven-year-old second son, bounded in. Carol had promised to take him and a friend to the bowling alley. Wearily she remembered her obligation. Thirty minutes later, when she returned, the house was quiet once more. George was in the basement working. She could hear him moving boxes around. The music from Richie's room meant he was there. She began preparing sandwiches and soup for a light supper.

Abruptly, Richie lurched out of his room and into the kitchen. He seized the telephone and dialed Brick. Carol turned from the stove because there was a new presence in the room. A stranger stood in her kitchen, a stranger with eyes burning, eyes drowning in a crimson sea, eyes little more than slits in a face suddenly puffy and worn and—Carol thought—oddly old. Richie began to talk at the top of his voice. Every other word seemed to be "fucker." He pronounced them vigorously, as if newly and proudly come to profanity. It was not that Carol had never overheard the words from her son before. But always in the past he had tried to hide his conversations. Now, for some terrible reason, Richie chose to fill his mother's kitchen with obscene talk. He is forcing me to see him as he really is, thought Carol.

Richie hung up. "I'm going out," he announced, his words sticking together like taffy.

Almost in pity, Carol gazed at her son. "You're in no condition to go anywhere," she said sadly. "You couldn't make it around the block."

Ignoring her, Richie bolted from the kitchen into the dining room, where he struck a chair and fell to the floor. The chair toppled beside him. Carol rushed to him, saw him sprawled in pain half on the tile of the dining room, half on the green carpet of the living room. My God, she thought. He's taken an overdose. He's dying.

But Richie staggered up, grabbing another chair to support himself. The twin crashes—boy and chair—brought George racing up from the basement.

"What happened?" he asked. Carol could not respond. She could only point. Words could not escape the ice in her throat.

Richie whirled and faced his father. "Did you tell the cops back there I was on drugs?" he yelled, jerking his thumb in the general direction of the second accident.

George was taken aback. Why was Richie suddenly angry over something he had not even mentioned at the table an hour ago? He did not answer.

"Goddammit," said Richie, raising his right arm as a trembling club, "I asked you a question. I want an answer."

So contorted was his face, so taut with rage, that George left the room. He had an idea. He walked to his bedside table. Outside, behind the slammed door, he could hear his son screaming, "Answer me!" George reached under the table to where he had hidden his .38 the night before when he returned from the charity party. It rested on a carefully placed wire, a secret nest George had built when his other gun had been stolen in the autumn burglary.

George seized the gun, checked to see that it was loaded, stuck it in his belt. The loose-fitting wool plaid shirt he wore covered the bulge at his middle. Wordlessly, he opened the door and passed his son and descended the steps to the basement. In his mind was the notion that he could terminate the quarrel by simply getting away from Richie. And if the boy persisted, then the gun would frighten him away, even as the golden mending scissors had sent George racing from the house the week before.

No sooner did George reach the eleventh and bottom step of the stairs than Richie burst onto the top landing. George spun around to face his son. The boy swayed in the half-light from the kitchen. George was illumined by a work light. Darkness fell between them.

"Did you tell those cops I use dope?" shrieked Richie. Is this the most important unanswered question in his life, wondered George, or is it just his reason to explode?

Unsteadily, Richie made his way down the steps. He never took his eyes from George, father and son locked in a painful visual embrace. When he reached the bottom, Richie looked for the first time about him. He saw an ice pick on a workbench and snatched it. He raised it in his hand and cried, "Answer me! I want an answer! Answer me!"

George's answer was to reach slowly inside his wool shirt and take the .38 from its hiding place and point it at

his firstborn son. This would frighten him. This would
send him away. In the movies of his Brooklyn youth, the
antagonist always dropped his weapon and backed away
at the sight of the gun.

But Richie would not cooperate. He flung out his arms
like a crucifix. "You've got your fucking gun," he shouted.
"Go ahead and use it!" As in a nightmare, one that an
awakening would never shatter, Richie began to walk
toward his father, arms outstretched, the ice pick glinting
in the naked work light.

When he was five feet away, George cocked the .38.
The noise was unmistakable. Carol, who had followed
Richie silently down the steps and who was now pressed
in terror against a wall near her washing machine, cried
out, "You two stop it! Please!"

Richie stopped. He thrust his chest forward as if to
make the target larger. And he shouted, once more, "Go
ahead. . . . Shoot!"

But when George did not fire, Richie dropped his arms
and the ice pick fell loudly to the floor. With that, George
lunged forward, grabbing his son by both shoulders and
shoving him out of the way. At the same time he kicked
the ice pick into a corner. Richie wrenched free from his
father and rushed upstairs, falling clumsily, crying as he
went, "I'm going to get the scissors!"

Carol threw her arms around George. "Oh, my God,"
she moaned. "What are we going to do?"

"I don't know," said George. "Maybe he won't come
back." He stroked her hair, but he kept his eyes locked
on the top stair.

While they waited fearfully in the cellar, George and
Carol could hear Richie rummaging wildly in the kitchen
directly above their heads. He pulled a drawer out too
far. It crashed to the floor, utensils rattling about like
hailstones on a roof.

Within seconds, Richie reappeared at the top of the stairs, this time with a steak knife in his raised right hand. Once more he began the ceremony of descent, crying, with each step, "Shoot! Use your fucking gun!" In insane counterpoint, the family poodle, Bridget, yelped and barked behind him.

George pushed Carol behind him and out of the way. She began to plead, desperately, hysterically, "Oh, my God, you two, please. Oh, please!"

George's finger trembled on the trigger he knew so well. He had fired this gun a thousand times at black and white circles on cardboard squares. He raised the gun in one last show of warning. But Richie refused to heed. He took another step.

Images and questions swam through George's mind. Before him were the frustrations of his life, telescoped, refusing to go away and let him be. Why had his world come to this? Why was this enemy loose in his house, an enemy he could not understand? His seed had produced a son, but where was the son? What stood before him was not the mirror image, not a son, not with his mouth a generator of hate, not with his hair tossed about by the new winds, not with his arm promising death. It did not occur to George that in this terrible moment was contained Richie's plea for help. Reason is not always present when the finger is on a trigger.

What God spared Abraham from committing on his son Isaac, what the makers of myth and literature could scarcely imagine, George Diener in the forty-fourth year of an unhappy life at last did.

He fired.

The bullet went directly into Richie's heart, a neat, precise bull's-eye. He slumped backward onto the stair in a sitting position. He brought his young hands to his chest and he saw his blood. He was puzzled. He stood straight up and raised the knife again. Now its handle was soaked with the life draining from him. As Carol screamed, she thought—how young he is.

George Diener was not yet done. He fired again. All of his furies had to be slain. This time the bullet went wide, tearing past his falling son and ripping a hole in the rear wall of the lemon-colored house that had been his dream.

Richie did not speak again. He sat down and toppled forward, down the stairs, down and down until the cold cement floor caught him.

Grabbing Carol, George pushed her up the stairs and into the living room. He went to the telephone. He dialed the police.

"Hello," he said, surprised that his voice was firm. "This is George Diener, at 1903 Longfellow Avenue in East Meadow. I want to report a shooting. I . . . I just shot my son."

"Was it accidental?"

George did not hesitate. "No. Deliberate."

He replaced the telephone and walked to the stair landing. In the dim light he could see his son crumpled at the foot of the stairs. Now it was his turn for the slow descent. At the bottom, he knelt beside Richie. He was not moving. George touched his throat. There was no pulse. He picked up his hand. It fell limply away.

Slowly he pulled himself up the stairs. Once he had wanted a mountain to climb and a life at its summit. But there would never be a mountain.

George went to Carol and dropped down beside her chair. "He's dead," he said. "I've killed our son. Can you ever forgive me?"

Then they sat and cried and waited until the police siren shattered the winter stillness of Longfellow Avenue.

Chapter Twenty-three

The first policeman to enter the house crept in like a hunter with his hand on his gun. George rose to meet him, putting on an expression to show there was no longer danger within.

"Where's the gun?" said the officer. It seemed to Carol that a more proper concern would have been, where is the victim?

"I put it away," answered George. "Would you go down and look at our son?"

Immediately the officer took out handcuffs, pulled George's arms behind him, and snapped them shut. George cooperated fully, even though the cuffs were tight and bit painfully into his wrists. I don't mind this, he kept reassuring himself. Criminals deserve it. But the police don't understand what happened here. They'll take off the cuffs as soon as they hear the truth.

Now another policeman rushed in. Then there were

ten. Soon there seemed, to Carol, that hundreds of men filled her living room. She heard the constant sound of doors slamming, of police radios crackling in her driveway. She saw the stark white light of spots bathing her house.

One officer decided that George was not manacled securely enough. He snapped a second pair of cuffs on the man who had shot his son.

Carol heard the sound of feet hurrying up and down the basement stairs. To one of the men who came up, she asked, "How is he?" For a few moments she had had the idea that perhaps Richie was not dead.

The young detective shrugged. "What can I tell you?" he said, but that was enough.

A deputy medical examiner named Dr. Benjamin Beck arrived and formally pronounced George Richard Diener, age seventeen years and eight months, dead at 6:30 P.M. on the evening of February 27, 1972. He wrote on his notepad:

> Young white male was discovered lying in supine position at foot of basement steps, clad in dark blue dungarees and dark blue turtleneck cotton shirt. Shirt was stained with blood over left chest. Blood smears over left upper arm. Upon lifting shirt, there was an oval penetrating wound in left chest representing entrance wound. An apparent exit wound on posterior chest below left scapula.

When the examiner was done, Richie's body was put into a canvas sack, a drawstring tightened at the neck, and carried out the kitchen door. Carol was spared the sight of her son leaving her home for the last time.

Outside, the crowd, gathering rapidly, could not tell who was in the sack. Rumors had it that Richie shot his father. As word spread across East Meadow that night, no one seemed sure exactly who shot whom. The first local radio report confused the matter further, since the victim was identified as "George Richard Diener," and no one knew Richie's first name was the same as his father's.

Brick Pavall had been waiting on the corner for his friend, but when Richie did not appear, and the commotion began, he went to the house. Upon seeing so many of his nemeses—cops—about, he did not stay long enough for information.

Sean O'Hara also went to pick up Richie at six, as they had arranged, but all he found were police and searchlights. He went to the front door and asked an officer, "Can I see Richard Diener?"

"No."

"What happened?"

"Everything's under control." The cop turned away.

Sean slipped back into the crowd across the street to elicit information, but all he could learn was that a body had been brought out in a sack. He spent the rest of the night searching East Meadow, fearful that Richie had shot his father, that Richie had run away, that Richie was hiding somewhere in bitterly cold flight. When Mrs. O'Hara heard the news, she rushed into her garage, thinking that Richie might be hiding in one of their three cars.

At the police station, George was mugged, printed, and searched. The procedure was brusque and humiliating. Told to strip, he stood naked before the police whose defense of law and order he so ardently supported. He had to bend over and spread the cheeks of his anus while someone saw to satisfaction that no weapon was concealed therein.

All of his property was taken from him, even a piece of paper towel he had been using to wipe his tears away. It would be returned, they said: his money, keys, the piece of paper towel.

Permitted at last to put on his trousers, minus the belt,

George was taken in handcuffs to a homicide officer where he was advised of his constitutional rights and told that he did not have to make a statement.

"But I want to give a statement," George said. "I always told Richie and those friends of his that if a person is innocent, he has nothing to hide. The law and the police will protect you."

In detail, George took the detectives over the story of his life, and of his years with Richie. He told everything he could remember leading up to the moment when Richie stood at the top of the stairs. He said he was certain that drugs had altered his son's personality and turned him mad.

Q. Was your son high today when he came down the stairs?

A. Today he was definitely high. He told his mother—when I came up the first time and heard the crash, he was high. He said he had been down into his room, where he took a few Seconals.

Q. Did he appear wobbly as he came down the stairs?

A. I guess, I would say slightly wobbly, swaying.

Q. Do you feel that you could have disarmed him?

A. I was scared to death of him.

Q. Well, wasn't he in such a condition when he had the ice pick that the ice pick flew out of his hand?

A. Yes.

Q. Then what about the knife? What did you feel?

A. I don't know. If I thought I could have disarmed him . . . I definitely didn't think I could disarm him, because if I thought I could have disarmed him, I would have tried without shooting him. But the thought of my dying and leaving him to be the head of my household and telling my wife and other son what to do was something I really couldn't—

Q. But when you fired, you fired right at his chest?

A. Yes. I didn't shoot to wound him. All these things went through my mind, such as, if you shoot to wound him, what happens if you cripple him? Then you've got a mad animal on your hands. I felt I had to do what I did.

Q. Is there anything else you want to put on the record?

A. If there was any way in the world around what I did, I would have taken it.

A. Okay. Thanks very much, Mr. Diener.

Carol was not permitted to see her husband until almost midnight, after the detective had finished questioning him. She had spent the hours at her home after George was taken away, making coffee for the investigating officers. Then she went to the police station and sat on a hard bench outside the homicide office. June Marck took a detective aside and warned that Carol had had a heart condition since childhood, that she must be treated gently or face the possibility of an attack.

When George was led out, Carol went to him. They embraced. George held her tightly. "I'm sorry," he said. "There was no other way."

Carol bit her lip. She wanted to be strong at this moment in support of her husband. "I know. . . . If I hadn't been home when it happened, I might have blamed you," she said. "I would have hated you. I would have taken Richard's side, like I usually did."

She had one piece of news for George. Her brother-in-law, Joe, was getting in touch with an attorney, the same one who had been engaged to handle Richie's assault charge from the Walgreens incident.

As they talked, policemen hovered near, watching them,

eyeing his reaction to her, and her reaction to him. George then realized he was still a prisoner, despite the story he had told, despite the apparently sympathetic attitude of the homicide officers. "I can't get out of here tonight?" he said.

Carol shook her head. The lawyer was trying to arrange bail the next morning.

The holding cell was at least private, one used for murder suspects. It consisted of a toilet bowl with no seat, a sink, and a slab of wood on which to sleep. There was no mattress or bedcovers. George lay on the board without closing his eyes through the hours that seemed like years. Sometime during the night black coffee and a hard doughnut were given to him, but his mouth was dry and he could not swallow. He wept, but his agony was not heard. In the next cell, a prisoner let out war whoops that did not stop. Down the row another prisoner chanted curses almost melodiously, and still another cleared his throat constantly, in a manner that sounded eerily like Richie's.

The next morning at five, perhaps earlier, perhaps later, for George's watch had been taken from him, another cup of coffee and a piece of store cake wrapped in cellophane were brought to his cell. At nine, guards came for him, snapped on the handcuffs, and moved him efficiently into a police wagon.

Unshaven and red-eyed, his heart pounding, George looked at his companions on the ride to the courthouse. They were mostly black, loud men who had taken this ride before and who insisted they were not afraid of what lay ahead. "I ain't scared," said one. "They can't do a thing to me." Some found merriment in the trip, one crying out, every time the driver made a turn or hit the brake, "Shit, man, can't you drive this mother?" One nudged George and started to speak, but he abruptly stopped when the white man's face showed that he felt no kinship. "I guess I looked too straight," said George to Carol when he told her of the ride.

Placed in another holding cell, George waited with fifteen prisoners. Their talk was of grand auto theft and burglary and felonious assault. Curiously, thought George, none mentioned murder.

A deputy at the barred door spoke to George routinely. "Who did you knock off?" he said, glancing at the clipboard and noticing "murder" beside the name.

"My son," said George.

The deputy turned his head away.

"I shouldn't have answered him," said George later. "But look what happens when I ignore somebody. I ignored Richie and he's dead."

The first judge refused to set bail, accepting only George's plea of not guilty of first-degree murder by reason of self-defense. He pronounced the crime of serious enough nature for George to remain incarcerated until the grand jury took action. Hearing this, George wanted to cry out that he could not endure another night in the tiny cell, but his lawyer raised his hand to silence him.

Later that afternoon, the lawyer, Martin Massell, took his plea for George's release to another court. More eloquent this time, he called the killing "a new American tragedy." He said the death was the final act of a tragedy that had been played for years. The judge set bail for $50,000.

One of George's fellow employees from the food company stepped forward immediately with the money. "This was not a sudden act," said George's friend. "George Diener is a decent and honorable man. His company thinks highly enough of him to write him a blank check, whatever it takes to bail him out."

Carol's brother-in-law, Joe Marck, the mortician, went to the Nassau County medical examiner's office to identify his nephew. He waited in the "Family Room" while a freight elevator groaned up from the basement autopsy area. Red drapes were parted and Joe glanced through the mesh glass window. He nodded.

The autopsy report would show that large amounts of pentobarbital and secobarbital were present in Richie's blood, brain, kidney, and liver, with a trace of secobarbital in the stomach. It was estimated that he had taken a walloping dose of the drugs a few hours before his death, a dose at least six times as large as that given for therapeutic purposes, perhaps as many as six to ten pills, enough, surely, to rip away the human brain's violence barrier.

Police found no pills in Richie's room, but they did discover a small amount of marijuana in a plastic bag. Several days later, when Carol had the strength to enter the room and dismantle its trappings, she found one of his nature encyclopedias with a two-inch-square hole cut into the pages, a secret place to hide whatever Richie wanted to hide.

At the funeral home in East Meadow, Richie's body was put into a poplar coffin with a mahogany finish and a white-satin lining. Joe Marck told George that Richie was eligible to be buried for free in Long Island National Cemetery, because George was a veteran. Had the death occurred four months later, after Richie's eighteenth birthday, he could not have lain in a military dependent's grave.

On the second night of Richie's wake, the coffin was open. Carol was both surprised and touched at the large number of East Meadow youngsters, seventy-five at least, who came to pay their respects. She had no idea that her son could count that many friends. As it had been in Richie's life, there were both "heads" and "straights" at his death. A few of the former, Carol noticed, were obviously stoned for the occasion.

Richie was dressed in the gray Edwardian suit he had worn to the dinner-dance at the New York Hilton. Neither Mark nor Peanuts had ever seen their friend dressed formally, and they muttered to one another that jeans and a polo shirt would have become him more.

One further change in Richie's appearance incensed his young friends.

Richie's wispy red beard was gone, his sideburns raised, his stubborn red hair neatly, forever cut. The undertaker's razor had accomplished what George could not do. It had, of course, been the father's idea. He conferred with Carol and she agreed. There was criticism of the barbering, but George dismissed it. "I didn't want him to go to his grave with that Charles Manson look," he said. "I wanted to remember my son the way I wanted him to look."

Sheila passed by the coffin and looked at Richie for a long time. Afterward she told Peanuts, "He looks exactly the way he did when I first met him, when he was fourteen, before the trouble with his father began."

"I guess that's the point," said Peanuts, bitterly.

Brick Pavall asked his mother to telephone Carol and ask if his presence at the wake would offend anyone. Carol said all were welcome. With a joint quickly smoked to fortify his courage, Brick entered the parlor and approached the coffin. Later he broke down and became hysterical, more so than anyone else.

When Peanuts passed by, George said pointedly, loud enough for the boy to hear, "I hope this will be a lesson to some of these kids."

Peanuts went outside and told his sister, "What is the lesson? Be good or your father will shoot you?"

Later that night, Mark and Brick met to share a bottle of apple wine and talk of Richie. Brick reminisced about their drug experiences. "The night before he died, he copped downs," said Brick. "I sold him the downs and the funny thing was, they weren't too good. I warned him they were bad. The next day—the day he died— he looks at me out his car window and his eyes are rolling around and he says, 'You think these downs aren't good?' He was reeling! Downs always hit him harder than anybody else."

Mark disagreed. The blame, he said, lay not with drugs but with George Diener.

"That old man is a fuckin' hard hat," he said. "He flat hates kids. Maybe he hates us because we have long hair and money and spirit. Mr. Diener is the winner now, you see. You don't even get to hear the loser's side, because the loser is dead. Richie's dead!"

Brick began to cry again. His grief was real. He had depended on Richie.

"I was in a fuckin' trance in that funeral parlor," went on Mark. "I was flippin' out seeing my best friend lying in his coffin. I kept saying to myself, 'Oh, shit, I am at Richie Diener's death wake.' How can a father kill something he's raised since he was an infant? It's like a puppy. You raise a dog up to five or six and if he goes crazy, you take him to a doctor.

"If it had been the other way around—Richie with the gun—you think Richie would have gotten off? He'd have been in jail for the rest of his life. I think Mr. Diener planned everything. He kept records, he made tapes, he looked like a conqueror in there tonight—standing there with his arms crossed. Just slidin' along. Practically accepting congratulations. No wonder Richie hated him."

Once, Brick remembered, Richie had run out of his house and to the Blackstone corner to meet his friends. "He was so fuckin' mad at his old man. He says to me, 'I'll give anybody a hundred dollars to kill him.' I didn't think he really meant it. Did you?"

Mark shrugged.

When it was time to close the coffin, Carol put an old photograph of Boots, Richie's first dog, beside her son, along with a poem two girls had written and left on the condolence book stand. She found it touching and appropriate, even though she did not know the authors:

> To us you will exist
> in the flowers
> in the trees
> and all things of nature
> God has given us.
> Richie, you are now in a world of peace
>   and happiness forever.
> Pray for us as we pray for you.
> And somewhere, sometime, we shall join.
> Love from all your friends.
>   Diane and Joan.

George asked Carol for one last minute alone with Richie. When he caught up with her, she asked what he had done.

"I asked Richie to forgive me," he said.

Mr. Barbour, principal of East Meadow High, was requested by a delegation of Richie's friends to comment on his death over the public-address system during the home room period.

He refused. "We've had other students who died and I made no such remarks," he said. "I don't want to establish a precedent."

Chapter Twenty-four

Although it was not required, George asked permission to testify personally before the grand jury investigating the charge of murder. Both he and Carol made appearances before the panel of respectable, middle-class Nassau County citizens—the kind of people George felt sure would understand.

So often had he told his story by now, to police, to his lawyer, to his and Carol's parents, that he felt he could get through it without weeping. But he began to cry at the moment when Richie faced him with the steak knife. Some of the jurors cried too.

Grand jury deliberations are secret, but it was learned that the decision was unanimous. They voted *not* to indict George Diener for the murder of his son. He was a free man.

The verdict was not altogether popular in the community. Judge Burstein of Family Court, for one, was openly annoyed that the case would never be heard in public trial. "As far as I'm concerned," she said, "it was a deliberate act. As far as I'm concerned, he murdered his kid."

Hundreds of letters from all over the world poured into the Diener house, most expressing sympathy for the loss, many expressing approval of what George had done. Carol answered every one, even the cruel notes that made her break down and weep and send Russell outside to play. On the day of his release from jail, George took his younger son aside and spoke to him quietly of what had happened. "Richie was very sick," said George to the little boy. Russell nodded, saying he understood and did not hold his father to blame. But both parents wondered what memories lodged within their second son and what the years would bring.

The Dieners found strength in the letters that told of other tragic households. One California man, the president of a large corporation, wrote on his letterhead to say that he and his wife propped a chair against their locked bedroom door each night, so fearful were they that their son, "also a down freak," would murder them as they slept.

Fritz the dealer had not attended the wake or the funeral of his friend and customer. It was not that he lacked grief over Richie's death, it was just that he was more upset over the loss of the $400 he had paid for ten thousand Seconal pills that were never delivered. On the two nights that Richie lay in the funeral parlor, Fritz waited in the bitterly cold parking lot of Roosevelt Field for the Southampton connection, who never showed up with the grocery sack full of barbiturates.

Two months later, around a table at Ryan's, talk turned —as it often did—to Richie's death. Suddenly Fritz grew morose. He revealed his shame in not going to the funeral and "paying his respects."

Another boy mentioned that he and his girl had visited Richie's grave the previous Sunday. This gave Fritz an idea. He would journey this very night to say good-bye to Richie! The second boy warned him that the grave was difficult to find, even in daylight hours, so enormous was the cemetery.

But Fritz, emboldened by some good hash he had elected to use himself rather than chip off and sell, was insistent. He received instructions from the friend on how to find Richie's grave.

The cemetery was closed and dark and cold. Fritz parked his car and climbed over the fence. He tried to follow the instructions, he looked for the grove of cedar trees, he tried to find the curving road with the bushes beside it, but suddenly all he could see were tens of thousands of white markers on graves, all alike, none of which contained the name or the body of Richie Diener.

He began to run, wildly, hysterically, in panic falling across the tombstones, fear rising in his throat. For a moment he could not even find the road on which he had parked his car. A tree branch ripped the sleeve from his jacket. A thorn drew blood from his arm. Hurdling the fence, he cried out in happiness to see his car.

Inside, safe, the doors locked, the music going, he tried to stop his body from trembling. But his limbs would not obey. Then he remembered the piece of aluminum foil in his pocket. Quickly he ate the four Seconals.

When he turned onto the Long Island Expressway for the drive back to East Meadow, the lights from other cars were growing blurry. The highway surface felt like a downy mattress. Fritz was sleepy, drifting out, but he blessed the downs. They would make everything all right. They always did.